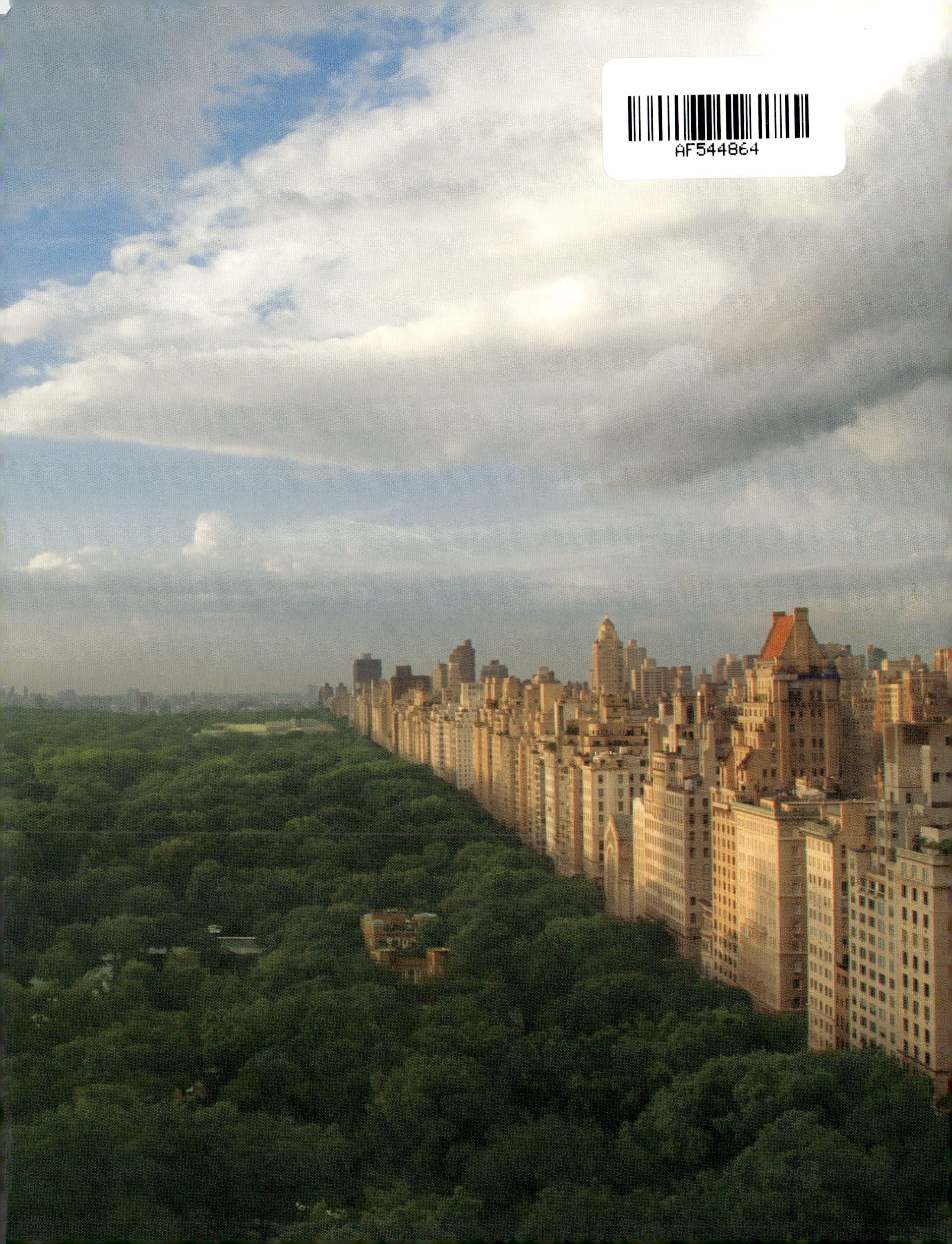

NEW YORK
SNAPSHOTS

CARTER BERG

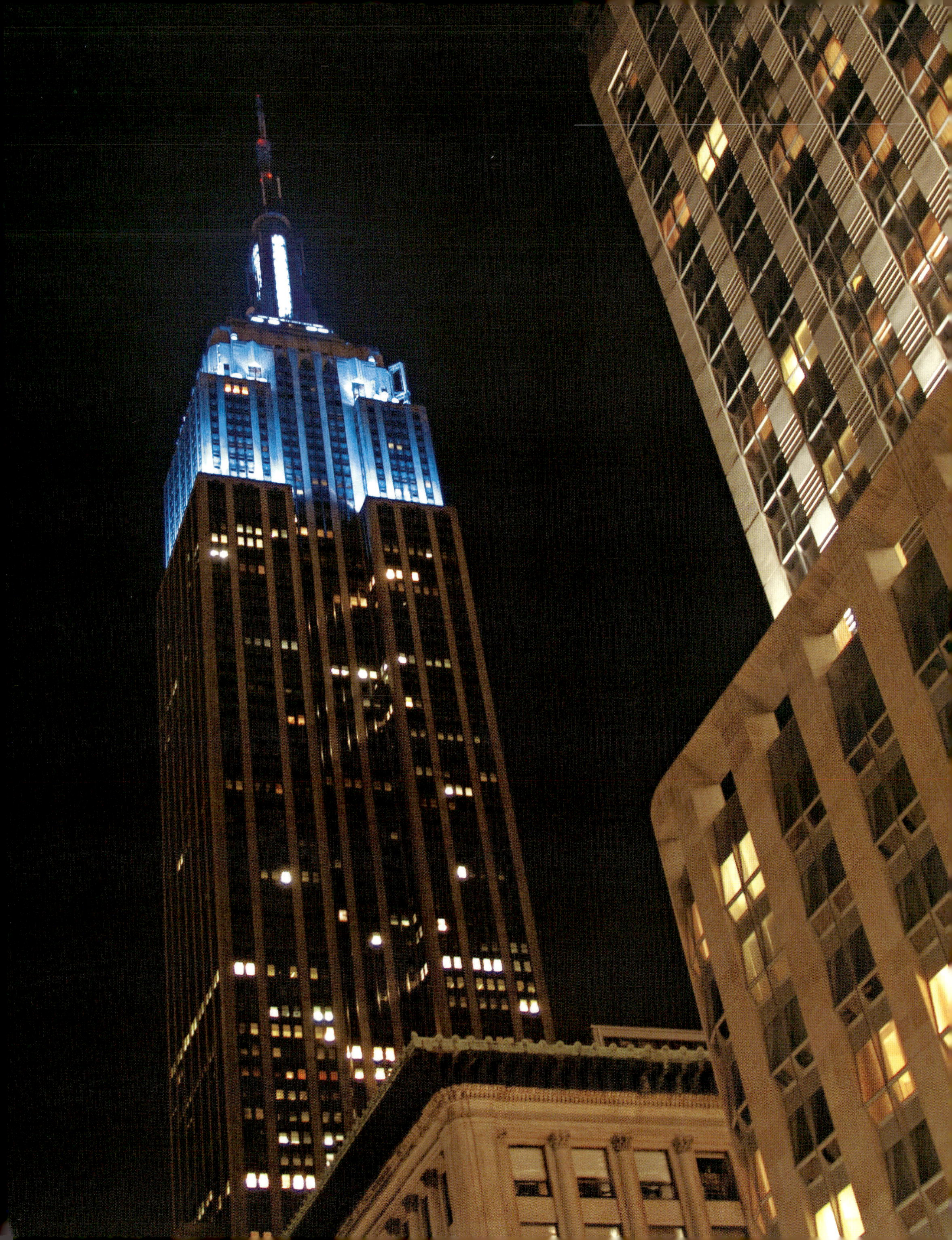

NEW YORK
SNAPSHOTS

CARTER BERG

teNeues

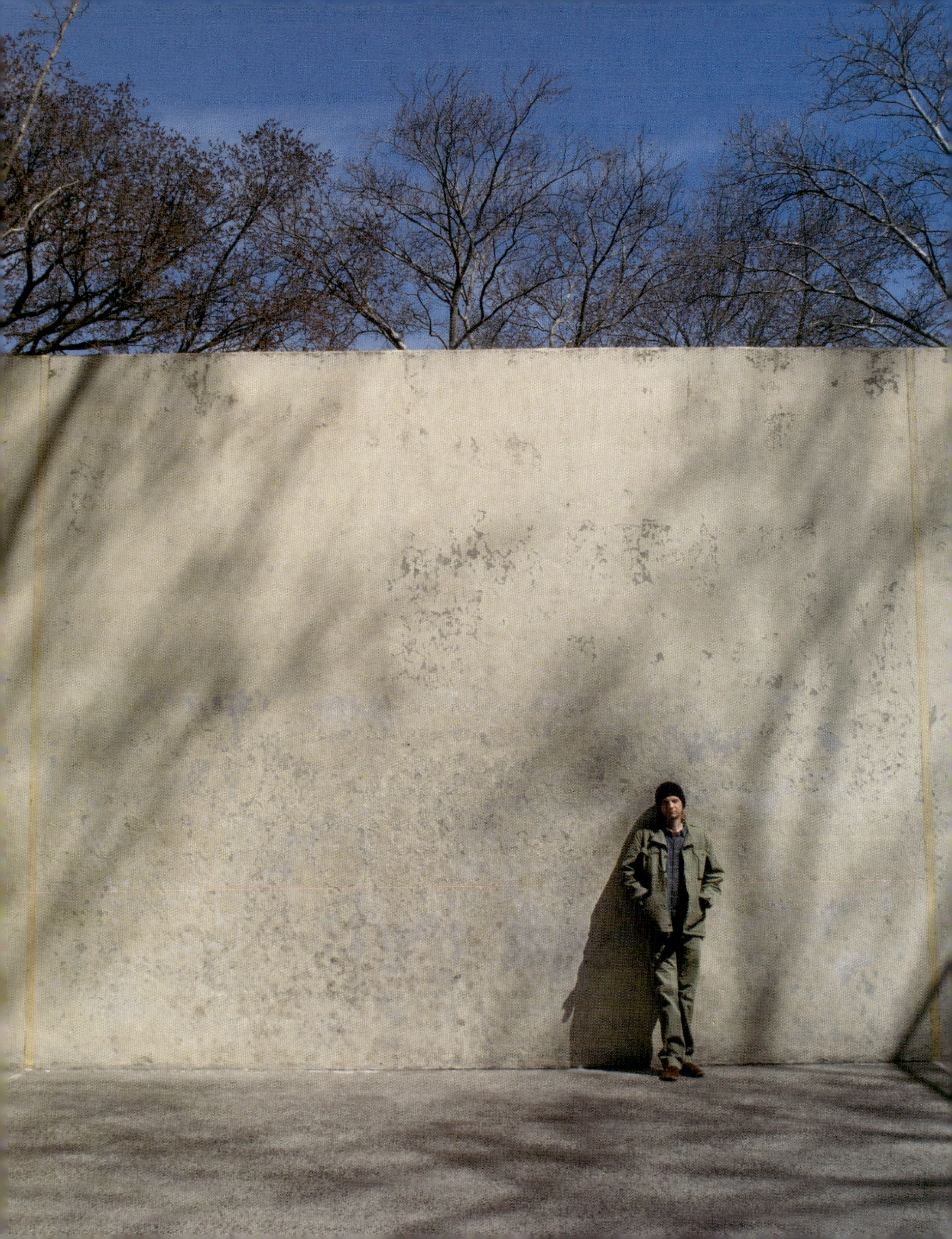

INTRODUCTION

THIS BOOK IS MY VISION of the place where I grew up and still live. Shot throughout the seasons over a number of years, these photographs were mostly taken while I was running errands or on my way to assignments—always with my camera in hand. I read on a T-shirt once that there are two types of pain—the pain of discipline and the pain of regret. For me the regret comes when you go to buy a carton of milk and you walk past your camera sitting idly on your desk. You think that there couldn't possibly be a picture worth taking in the ten minutes it takes to go to the corner deli. So, you decide to leave your trusty old SLR at home. Then right outside your door while you're stepping over a puddle, you see a dramatic reflection of the clouds shrouding the skyscrapers. You may never find another image just like this one. By the time you return with your camera three minutes later the moment is gone; the clouds are a different shape or the light has changed. I guess you can only hope that sometime soon you'll discover another image that is as interesting or beautiful—just not that particular one. Finding great photographs is like a treasure hunt—you might have to search high and low. Or you never know—the most interesting picture you shoot all year could even be of the dry cleaners right across the street from your apartment.

The selection of photographs I've presented here mix the elegance of elaborate architectural details and striking skylines with the unusual shapes and rough random details on everyday surfaces like sidewalks, doorways, and lampposts. I deliberately combined funky, out-of-the way corners with well-known landmarks. It's the contrast of high-and-mighty and down-and-dirty that make New York so full of life for me. Hopefully, *New York Snapshots* will offer both New Yorkers and visitors a new way of seeing and appreciating a place that's unlike any other. I'll be the first to admit that New York's beauty isn't always obvious. Even for those really crazy about this great place, it can sometimes get so chaotic or be a bit too heavy on the grit and grime. Still, even if you fall temporarily out of love with this town, don't give up hope. If you give it time, you'll start to appreciate the city all over again. Tomorrow you might glance up the side of a random building and see a 10-foot dragon carved out of stone—looking right down at you! Or, while you're impatiently waiting for the lights to change, you could notice the way the sunlight casts shadows on a beat-up street sign. Either way, you'll feel a little rush—and maybe even crack a smile. That's how it happens. New York has hooked you once again, and you're caught up in the magic of the city as if you've never seen it before.

CARTER BERG

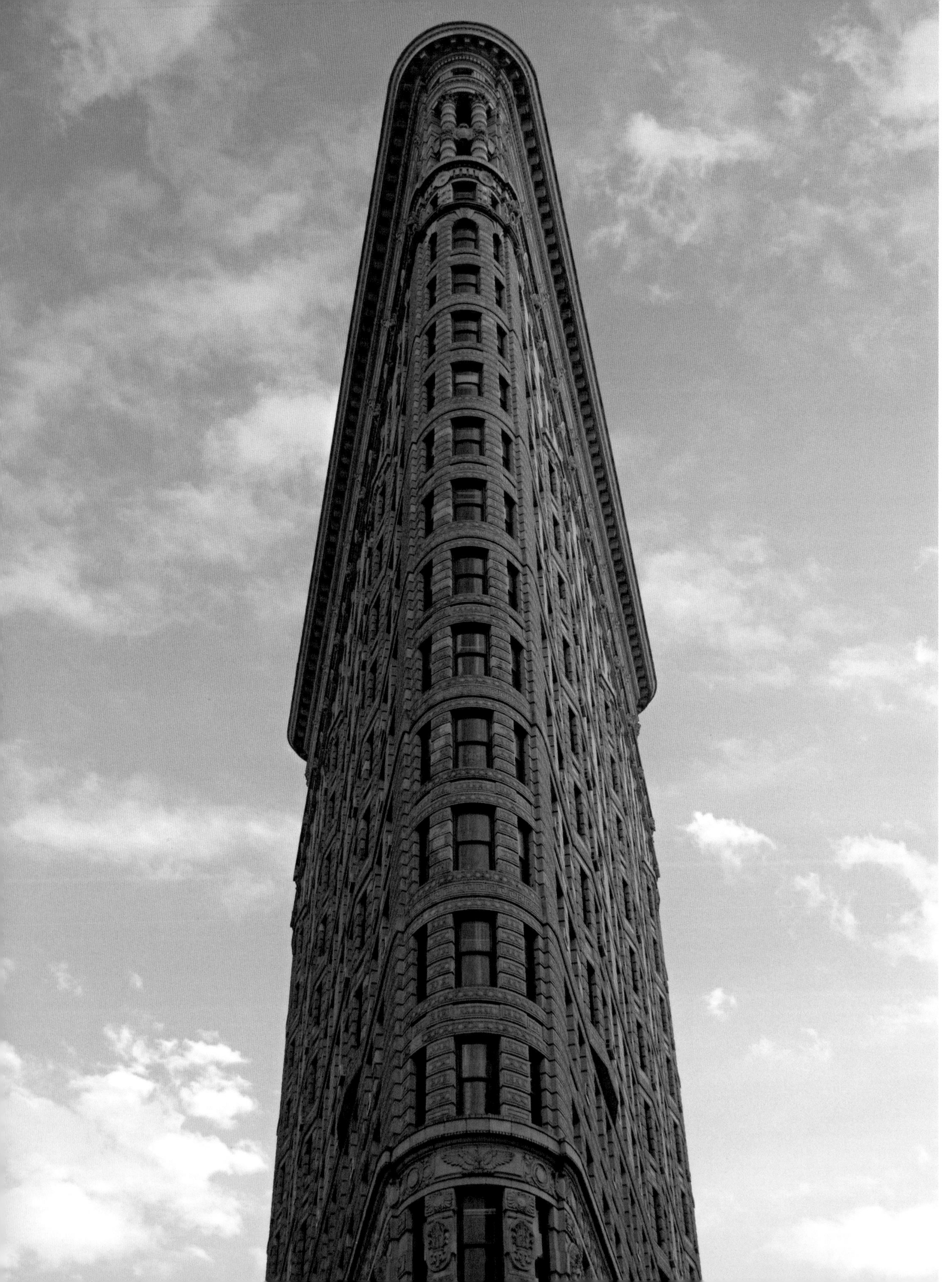

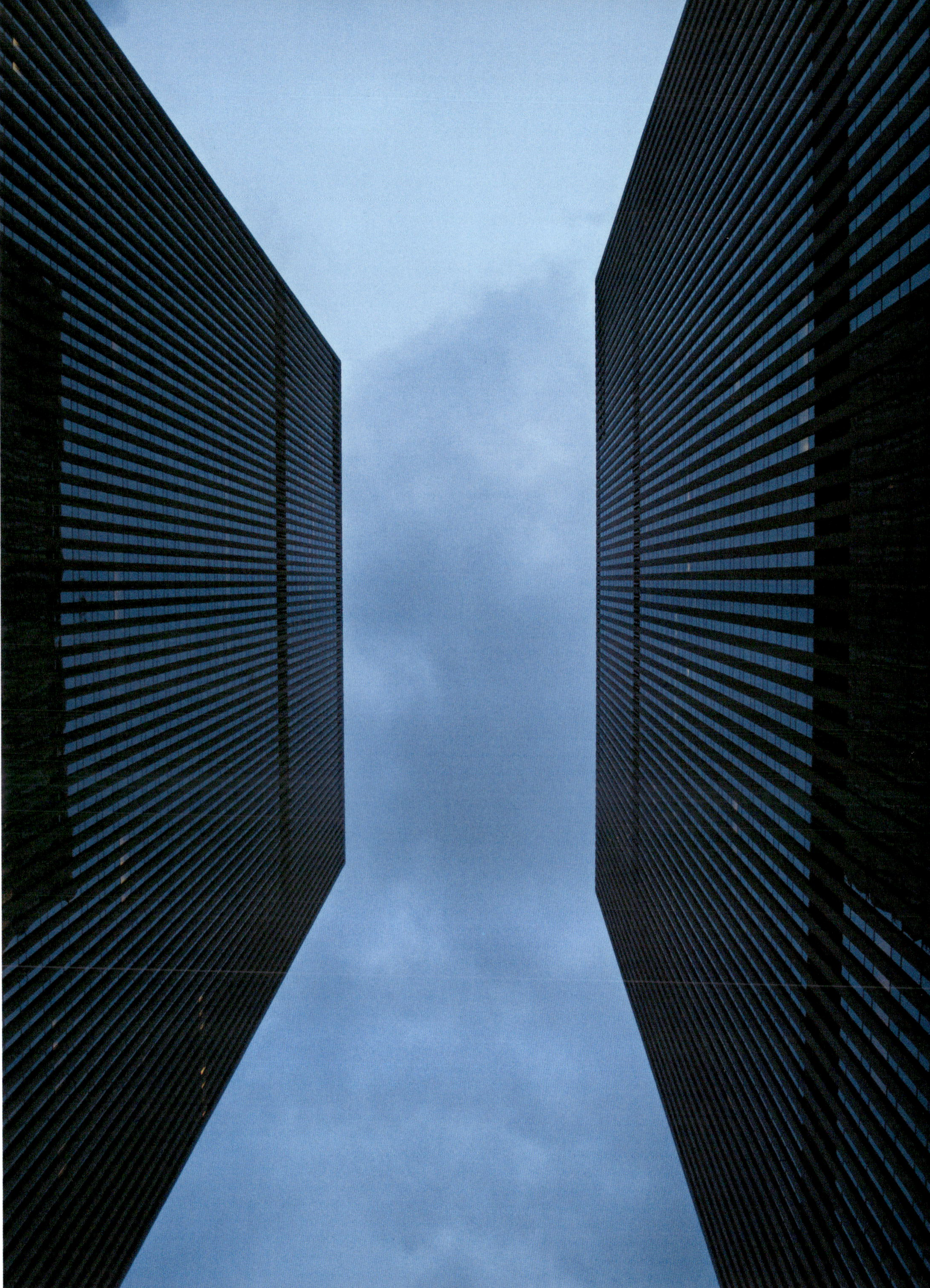

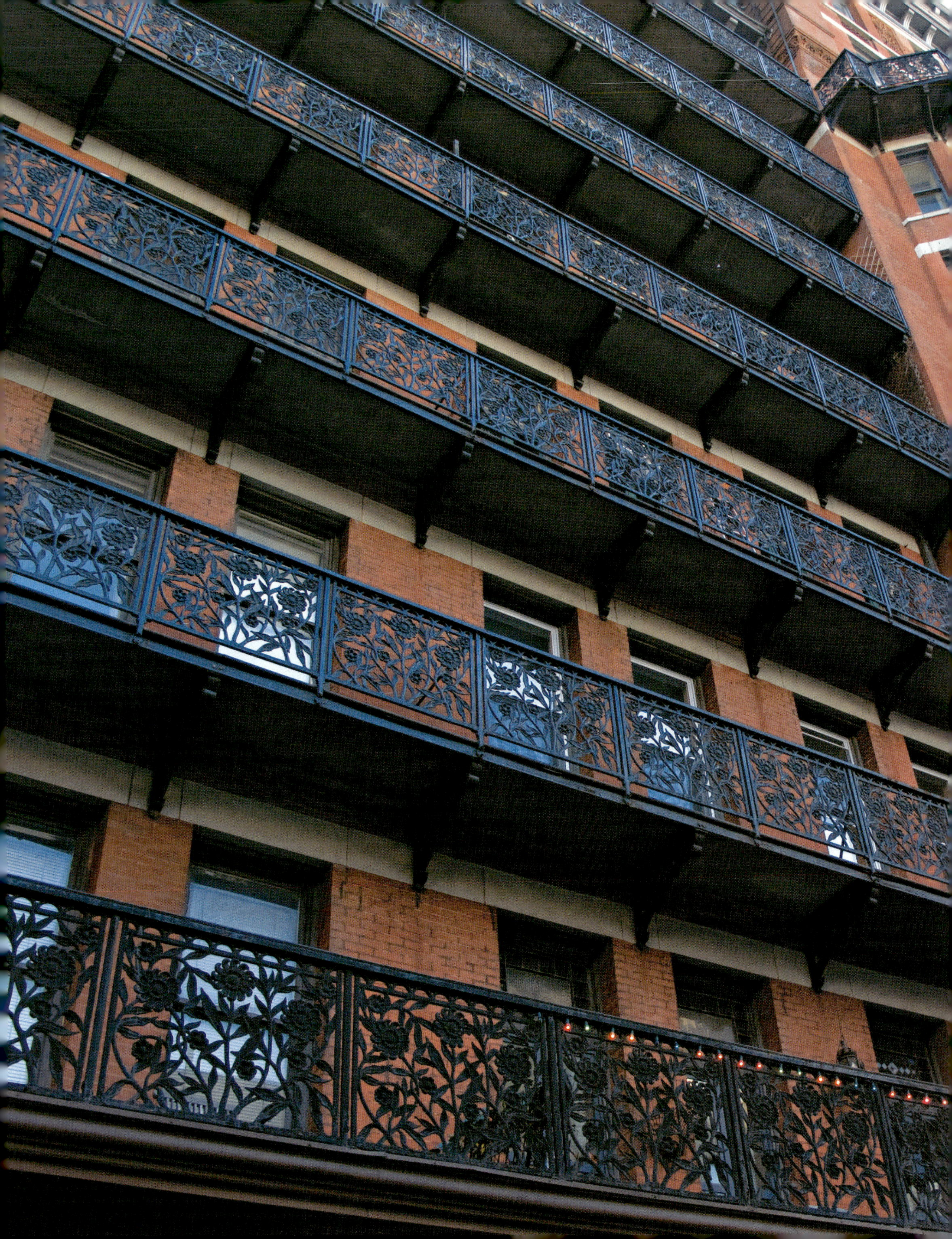

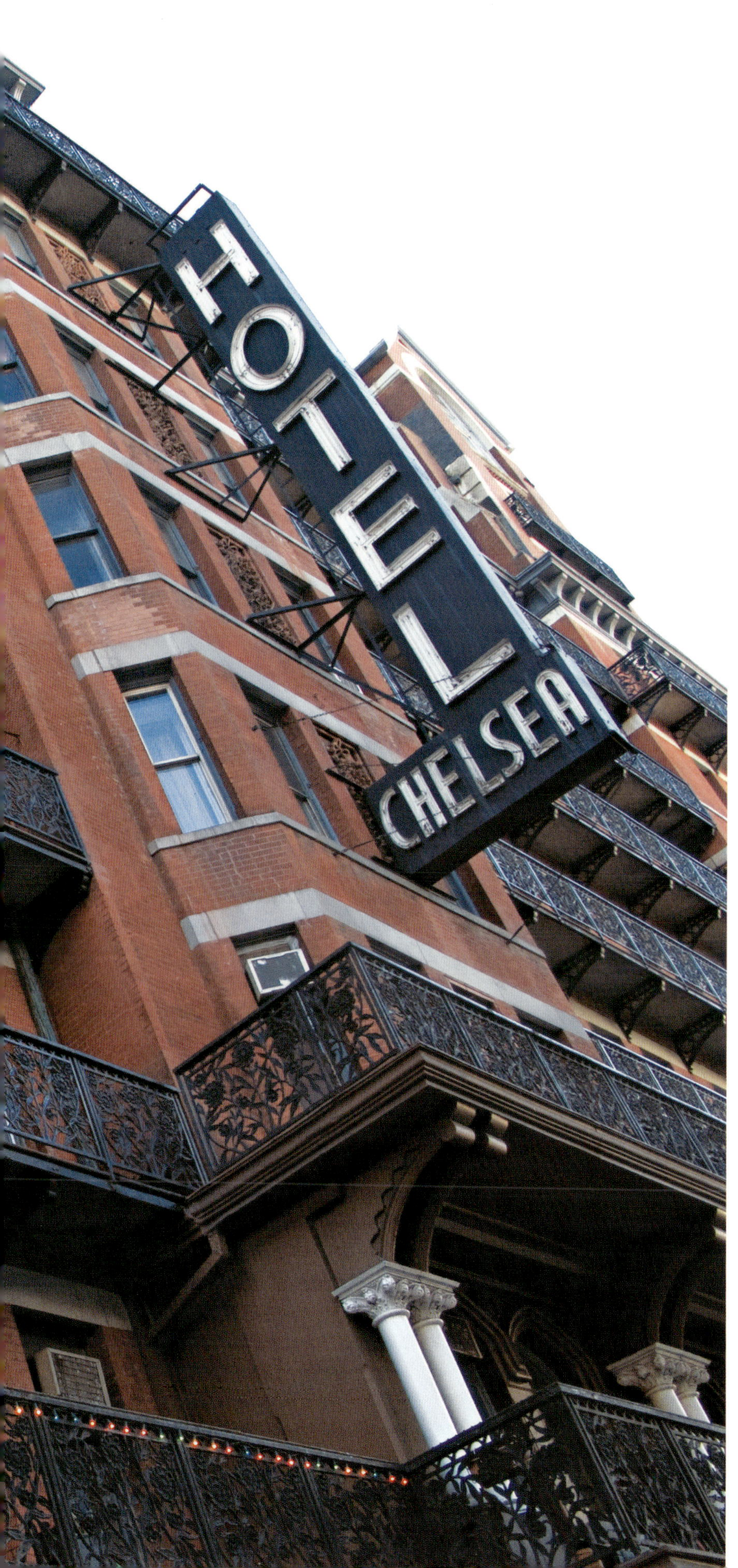
HOTEL
CHELSEA

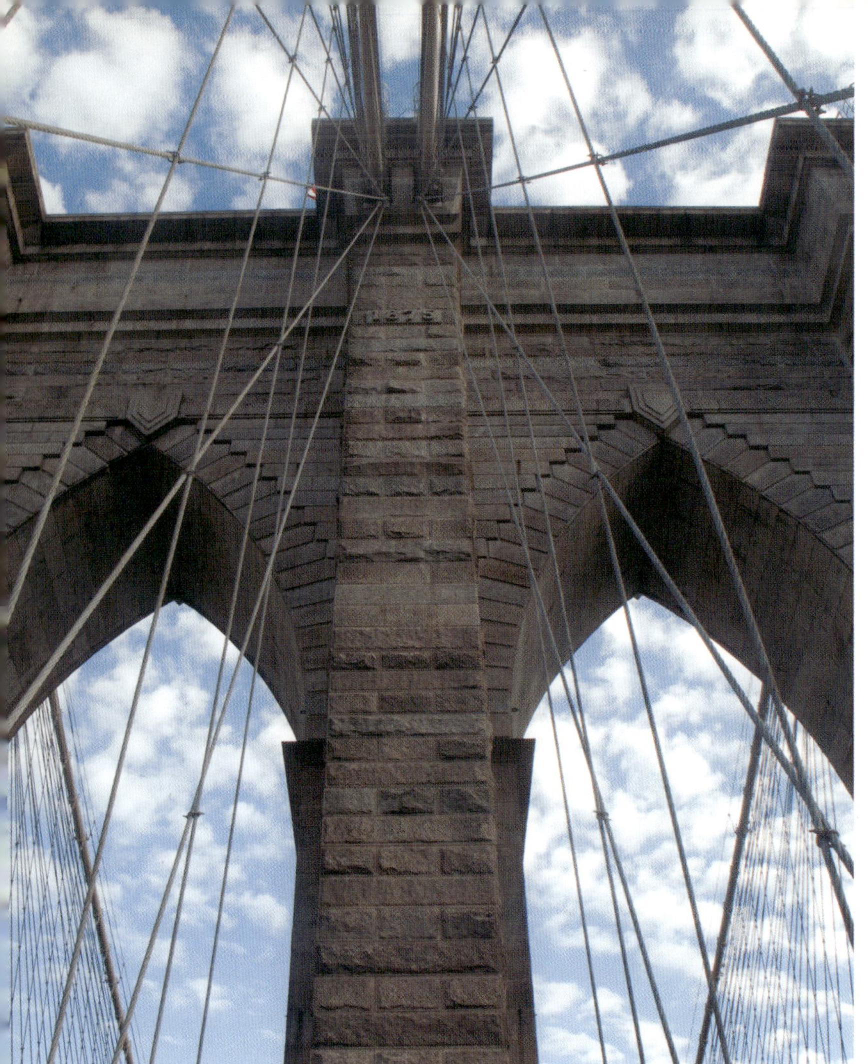

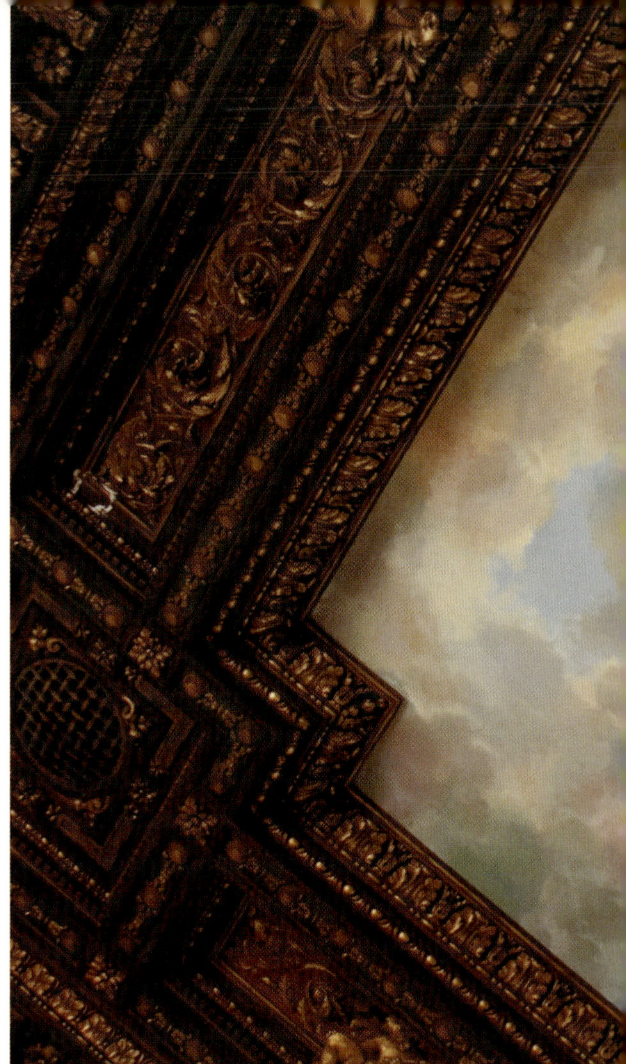

PARENTS AND TEACHERS SOMETIMES GIVE US A HARD TIME for not looking where we're going. We're taught to gaze straight ahead—pretty sensible advice in a city full of crowded sidewalks and fast-moving traffic. Yet if we take a moment now and then to look up instead, what an amazing selection of shapes and colors are to be found just above our heads. So, even if you're really busy, just once or twice a day step out of the way of the rushing crowds and look up. You might be glad that you did. It only takes a minute.

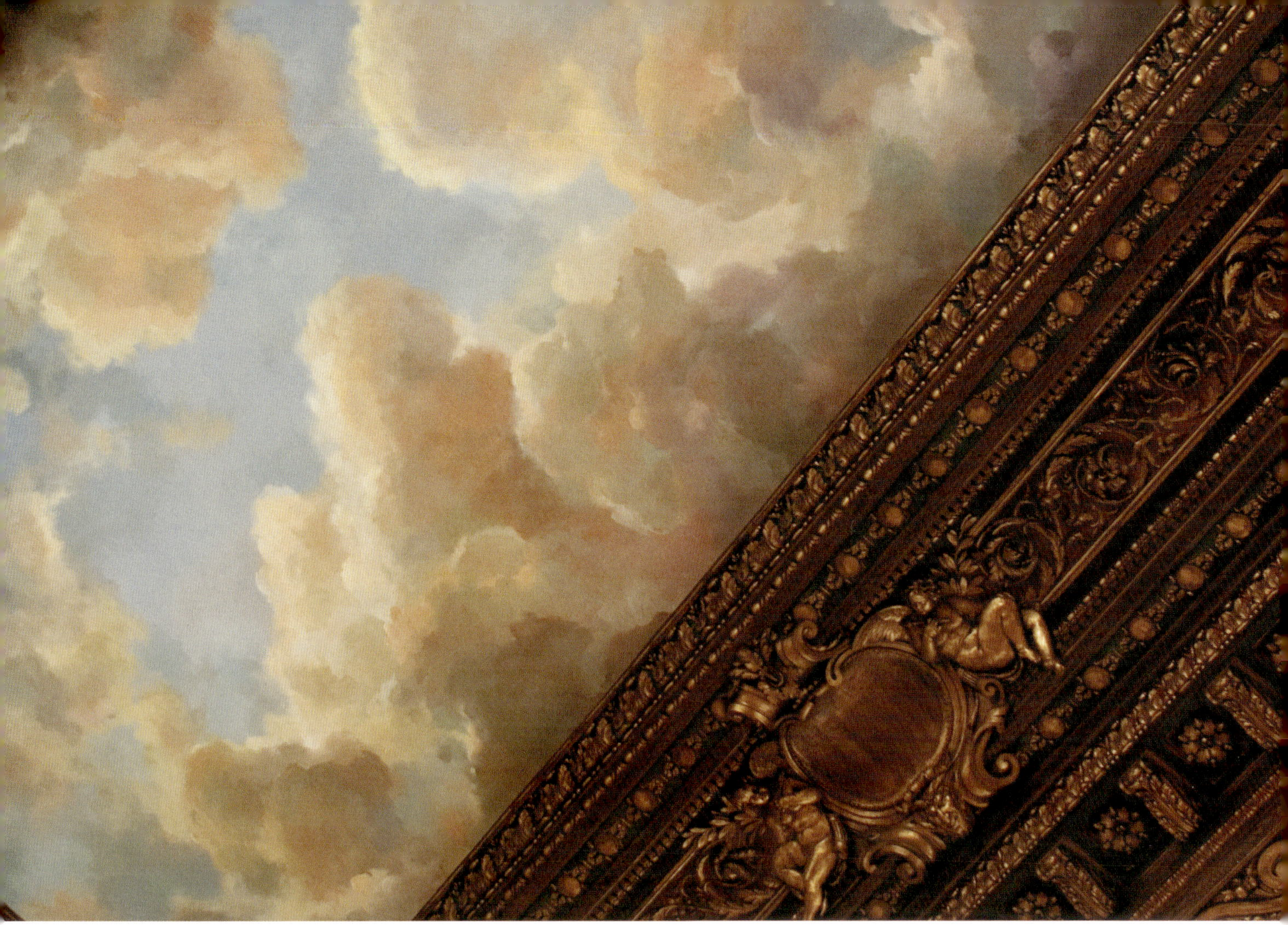

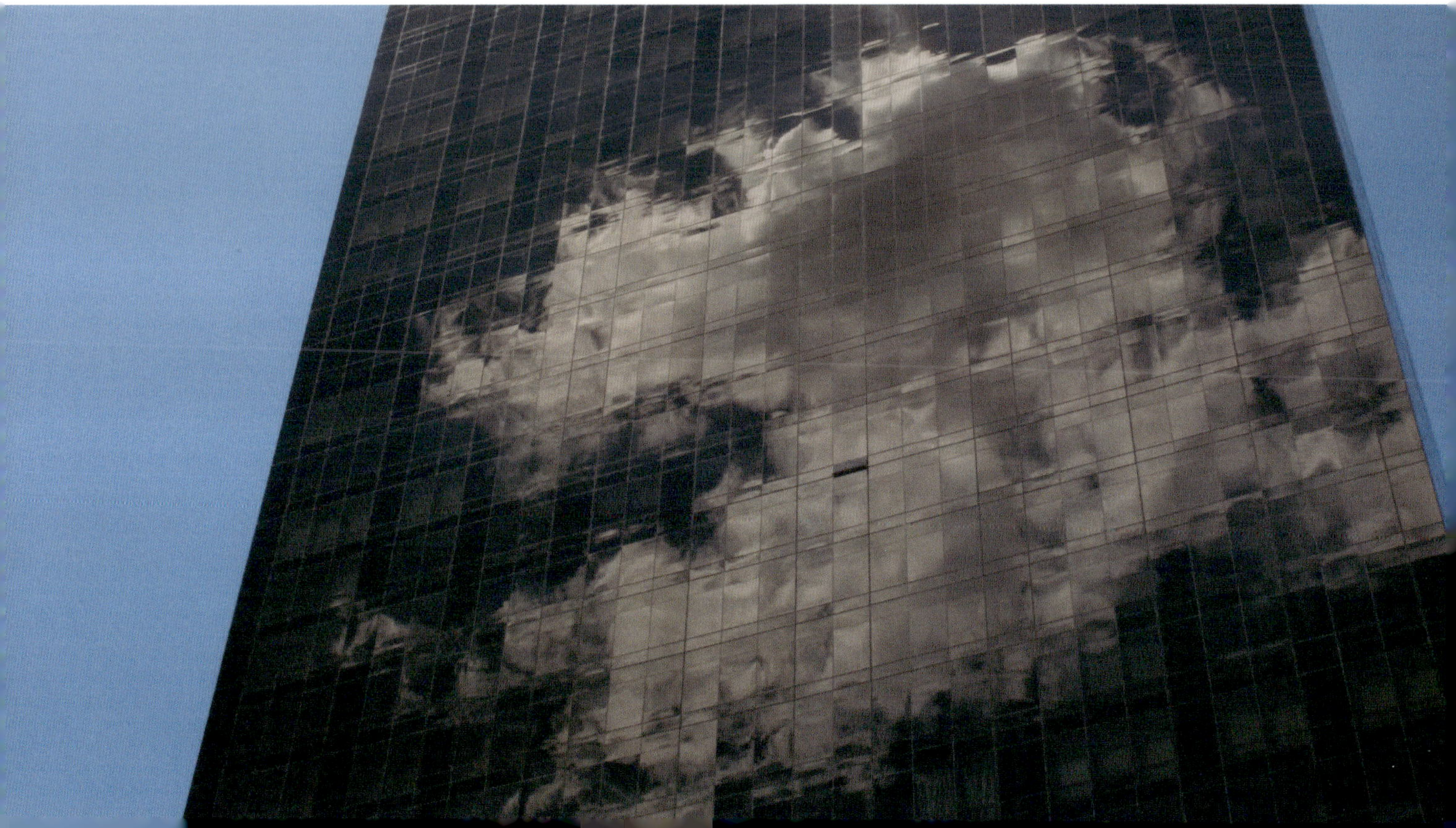

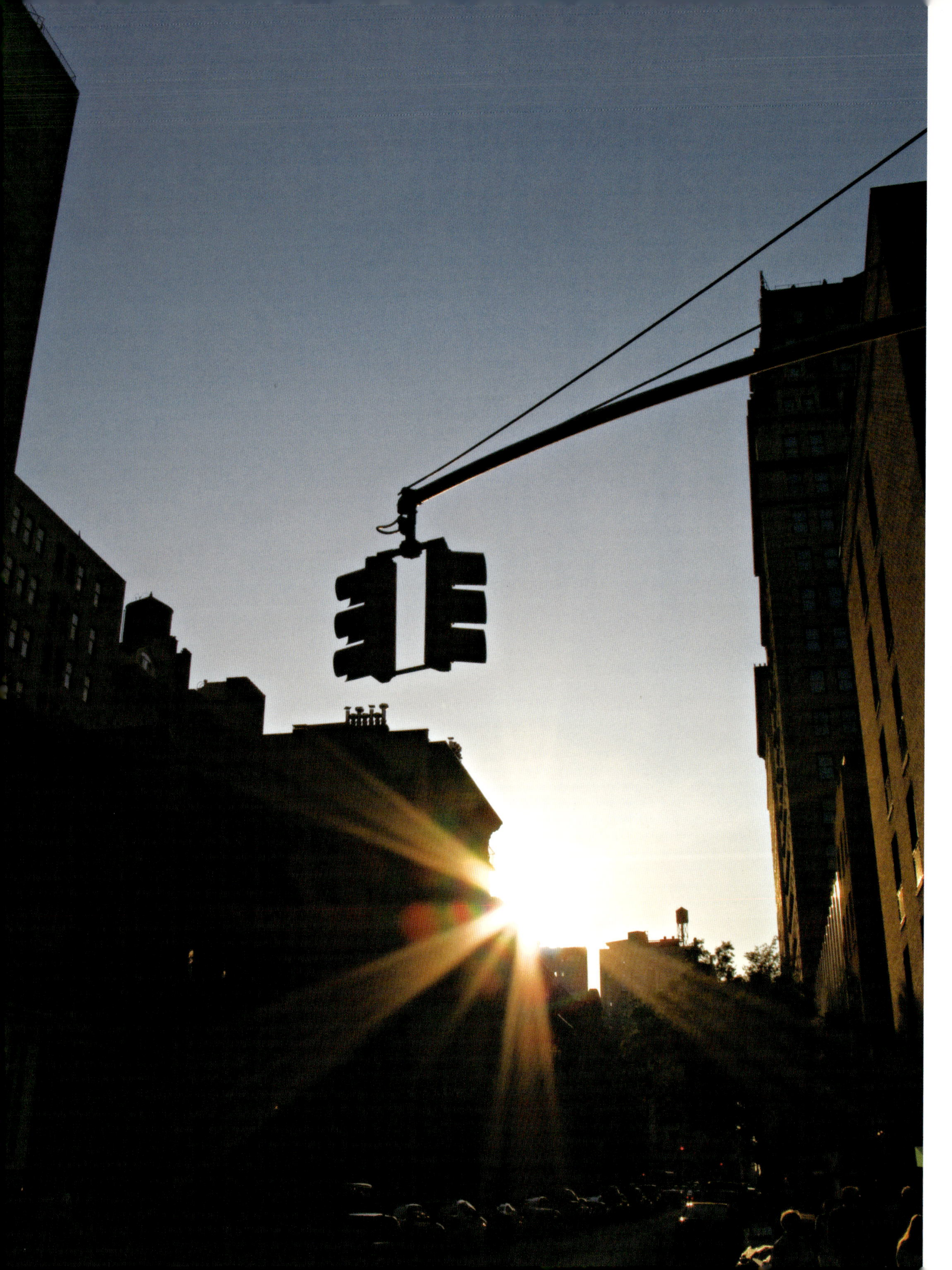

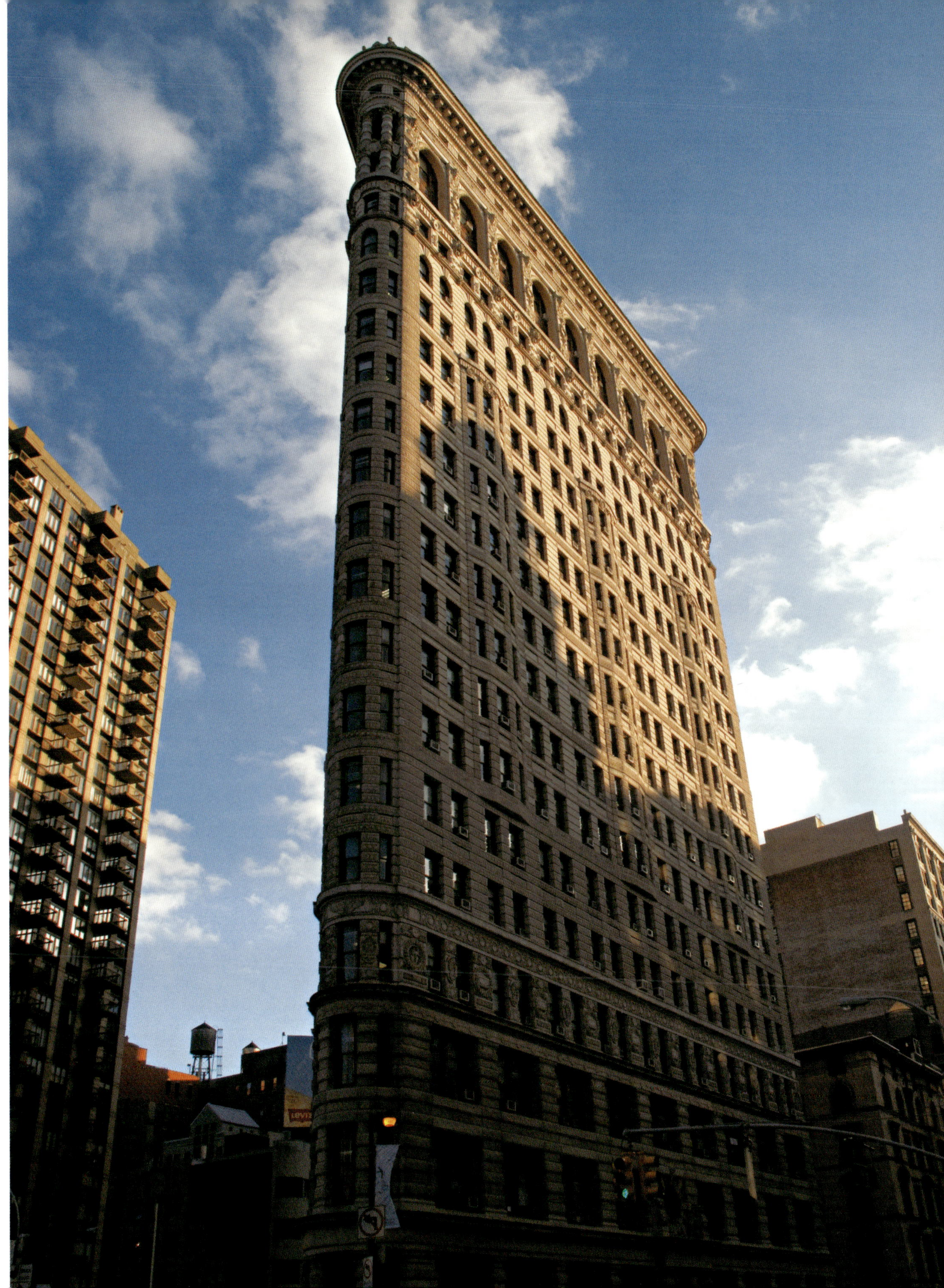

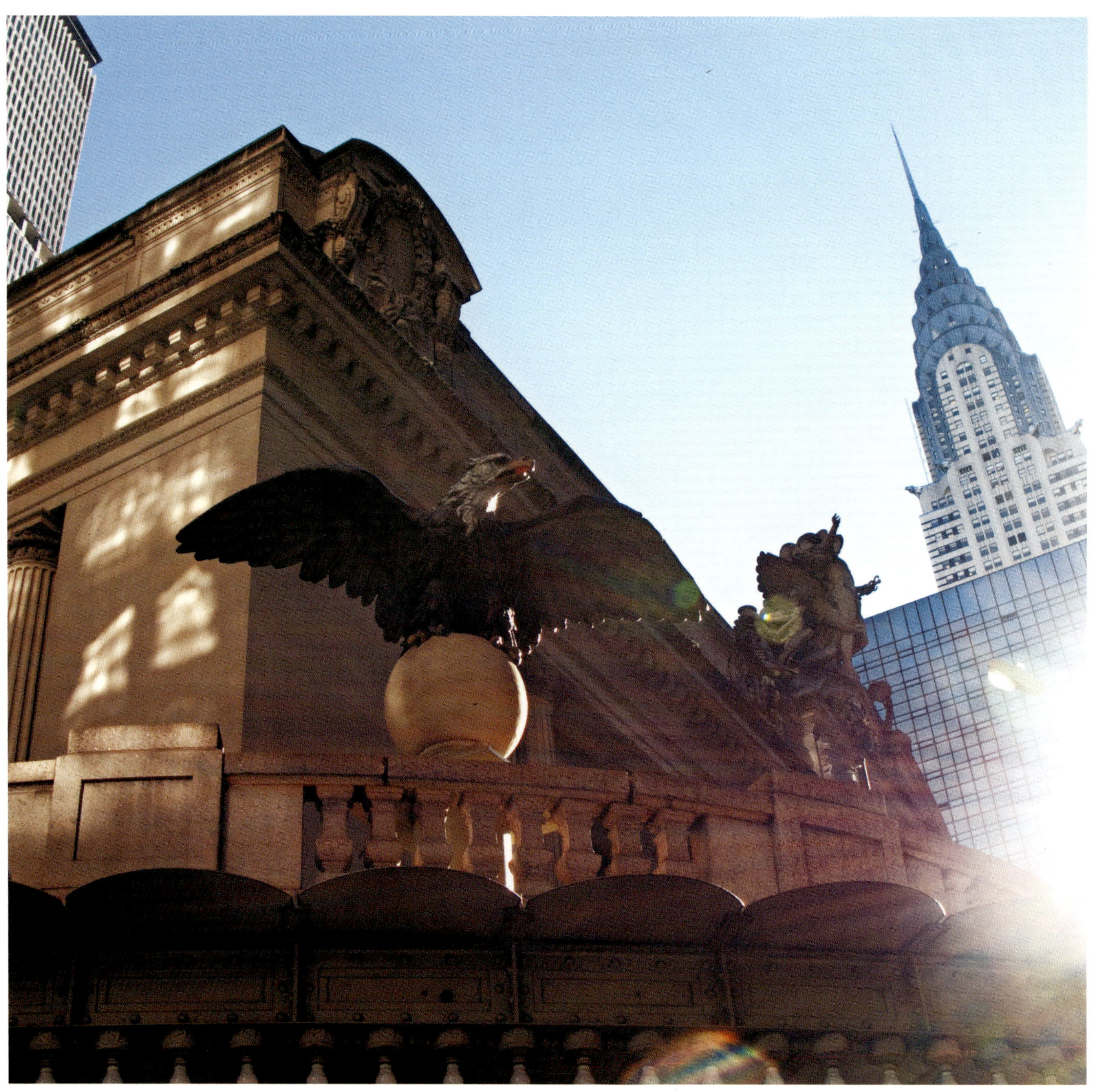

VISITORS TO NEW YORK are sometimes surprised to see how many details are on the facades. The whole of the city is like one big sculpture garden. The carvings range from tributes to ancient architecture as well as powerful creatures from the wild—or the artists' imaginations.

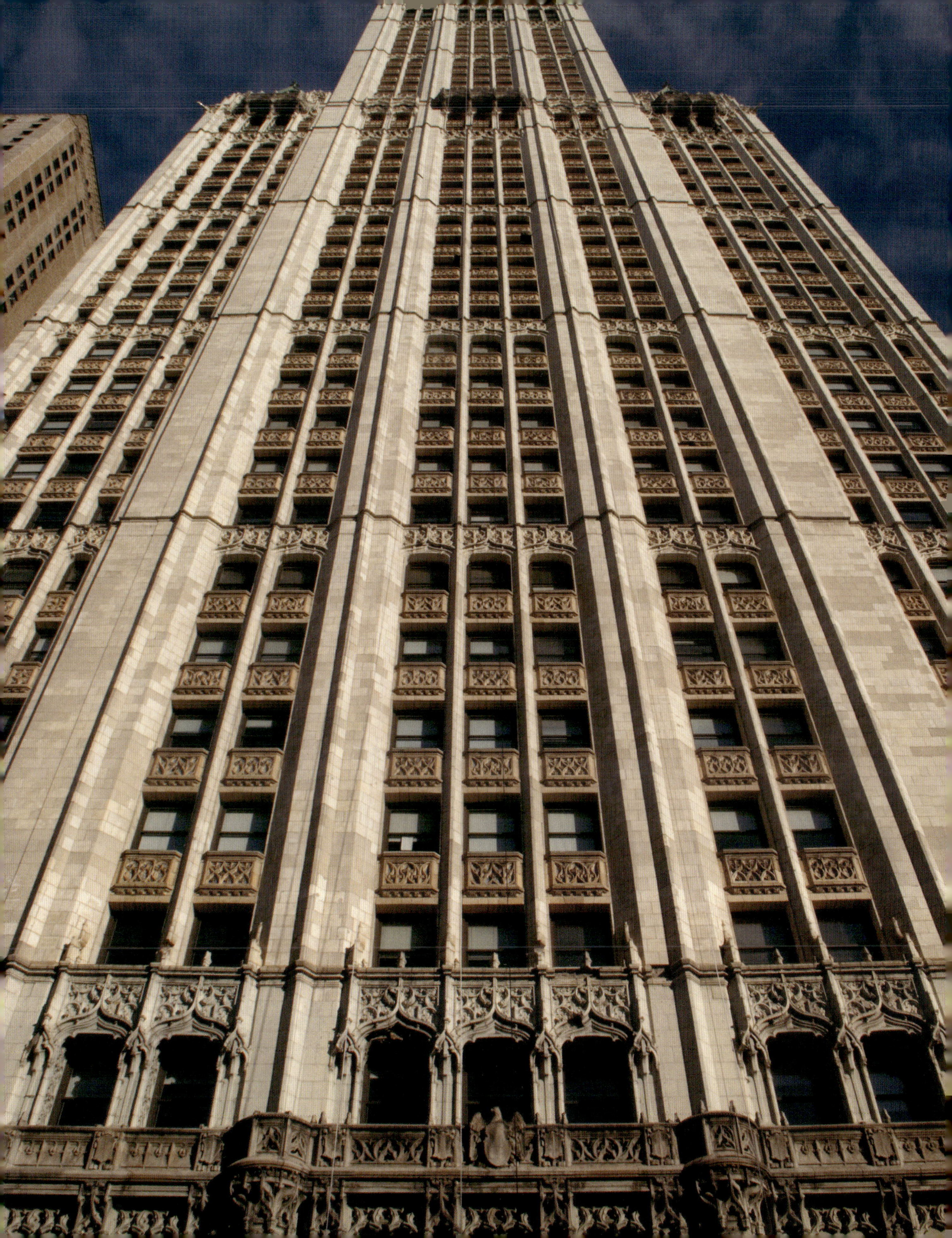

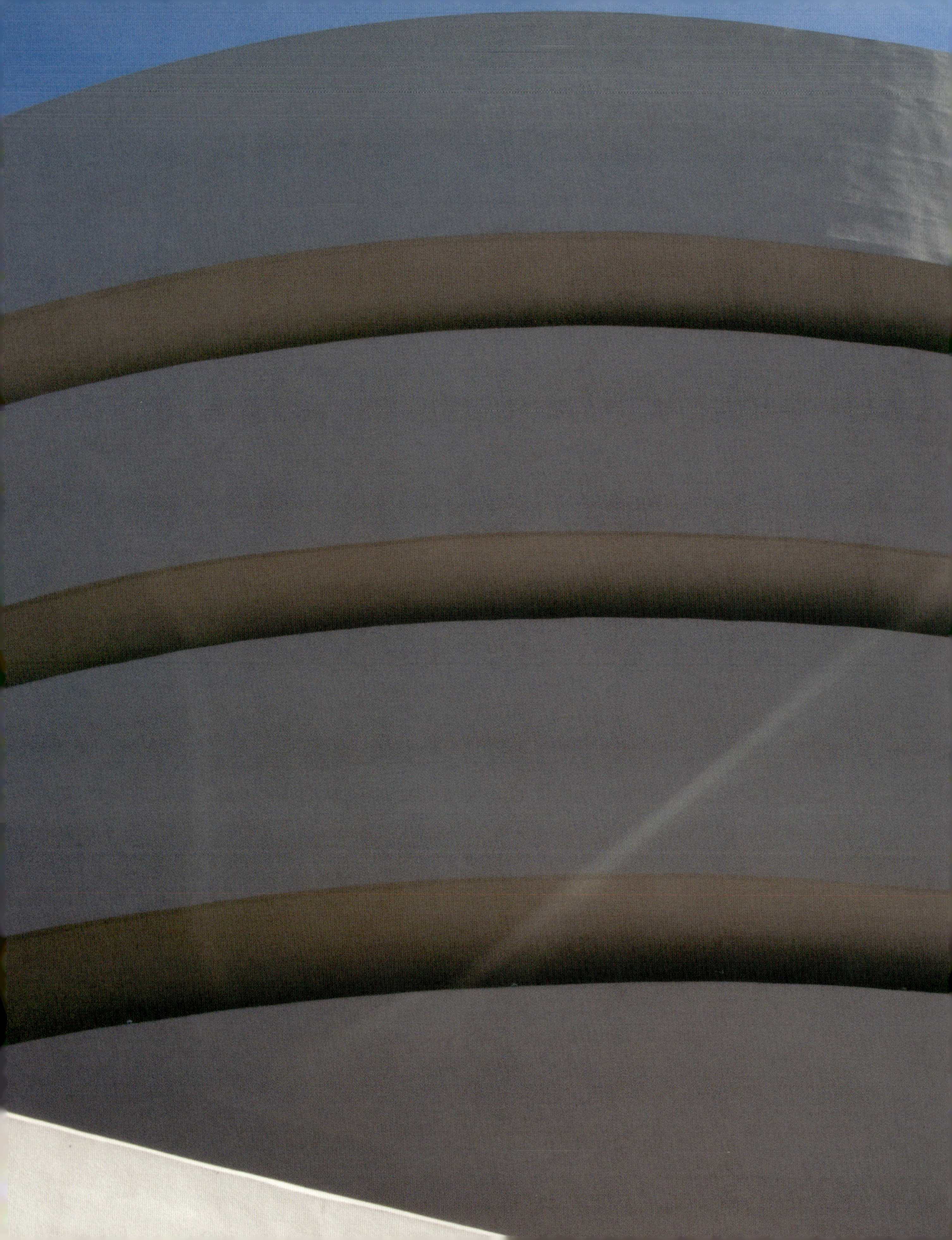

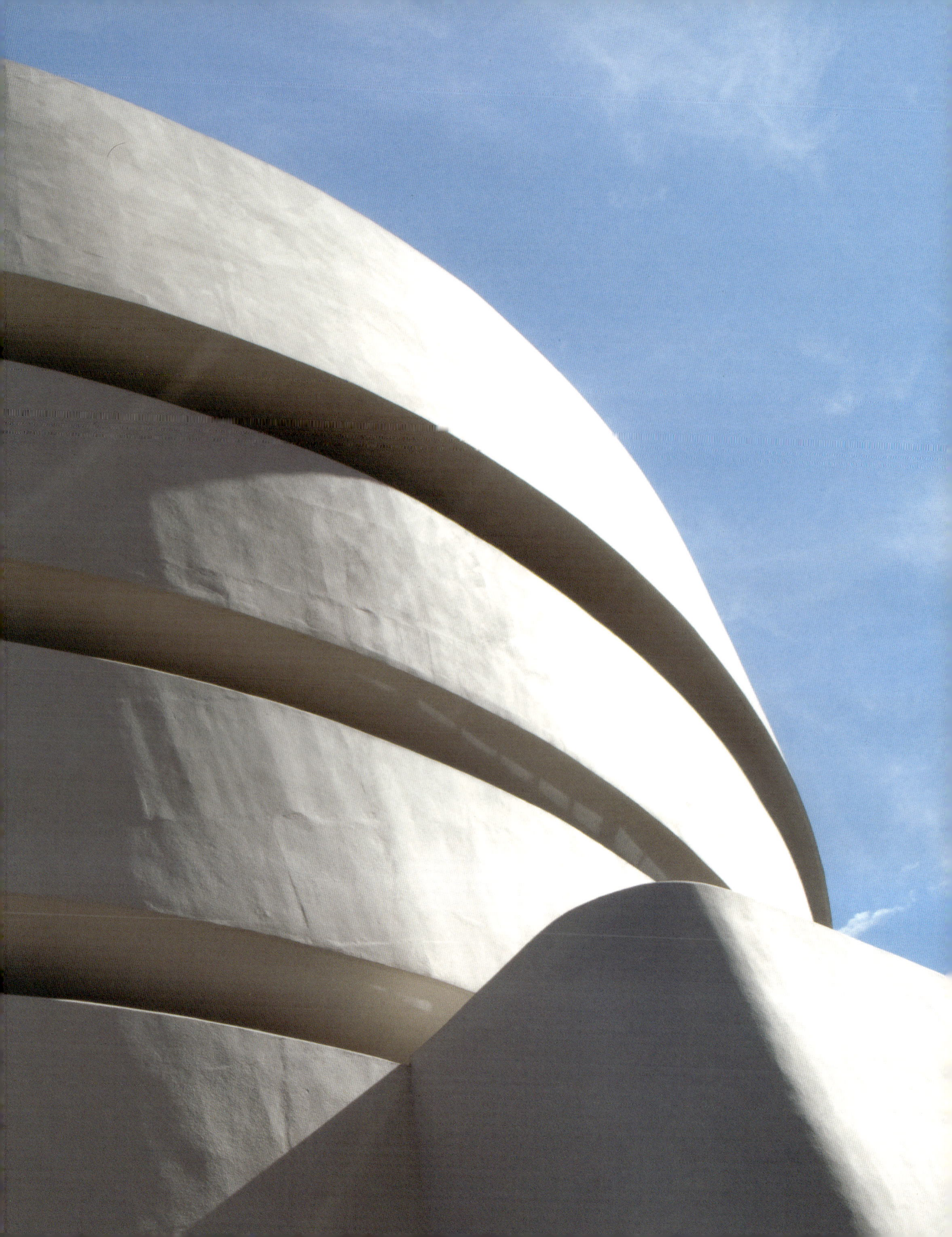

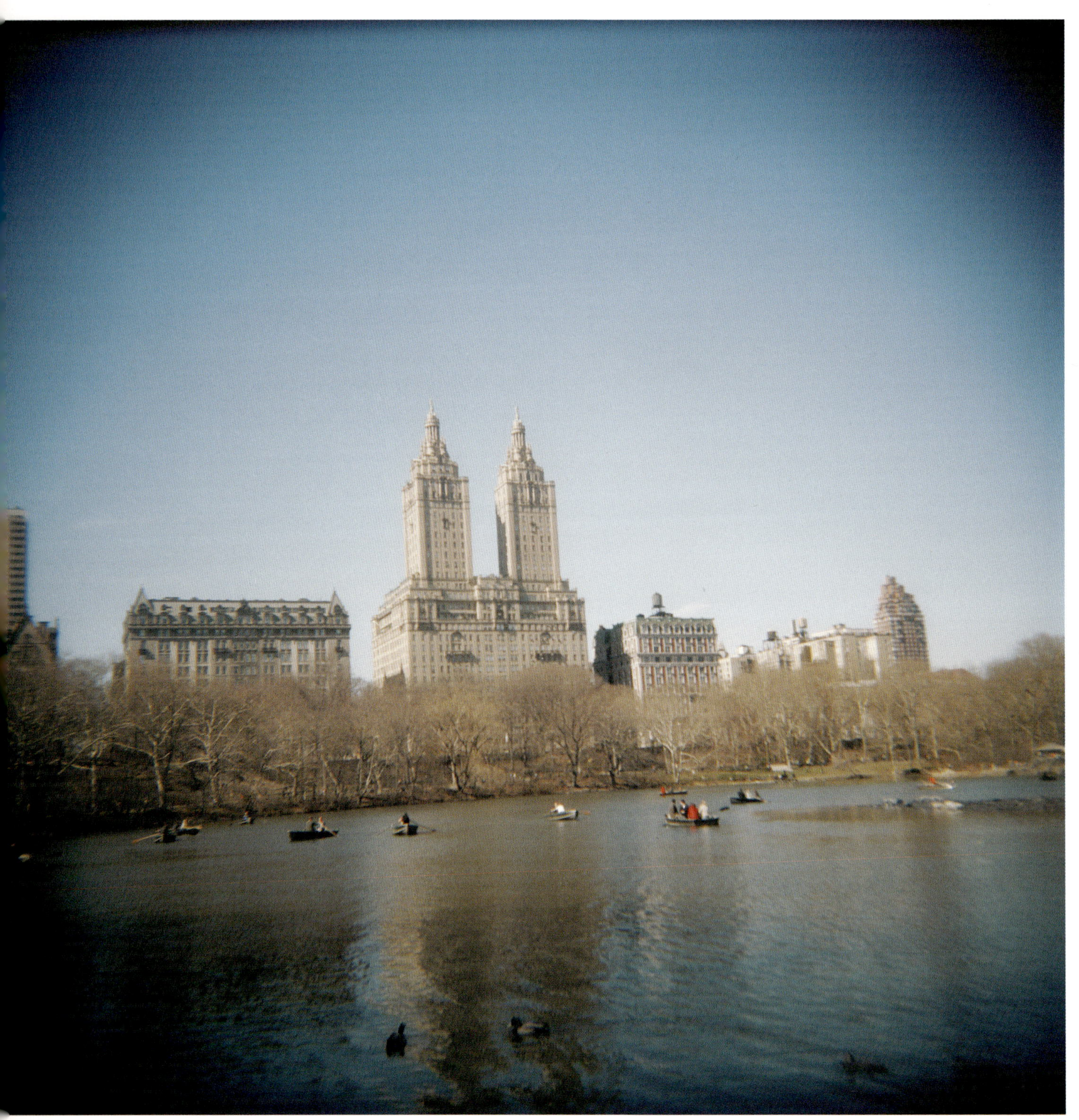

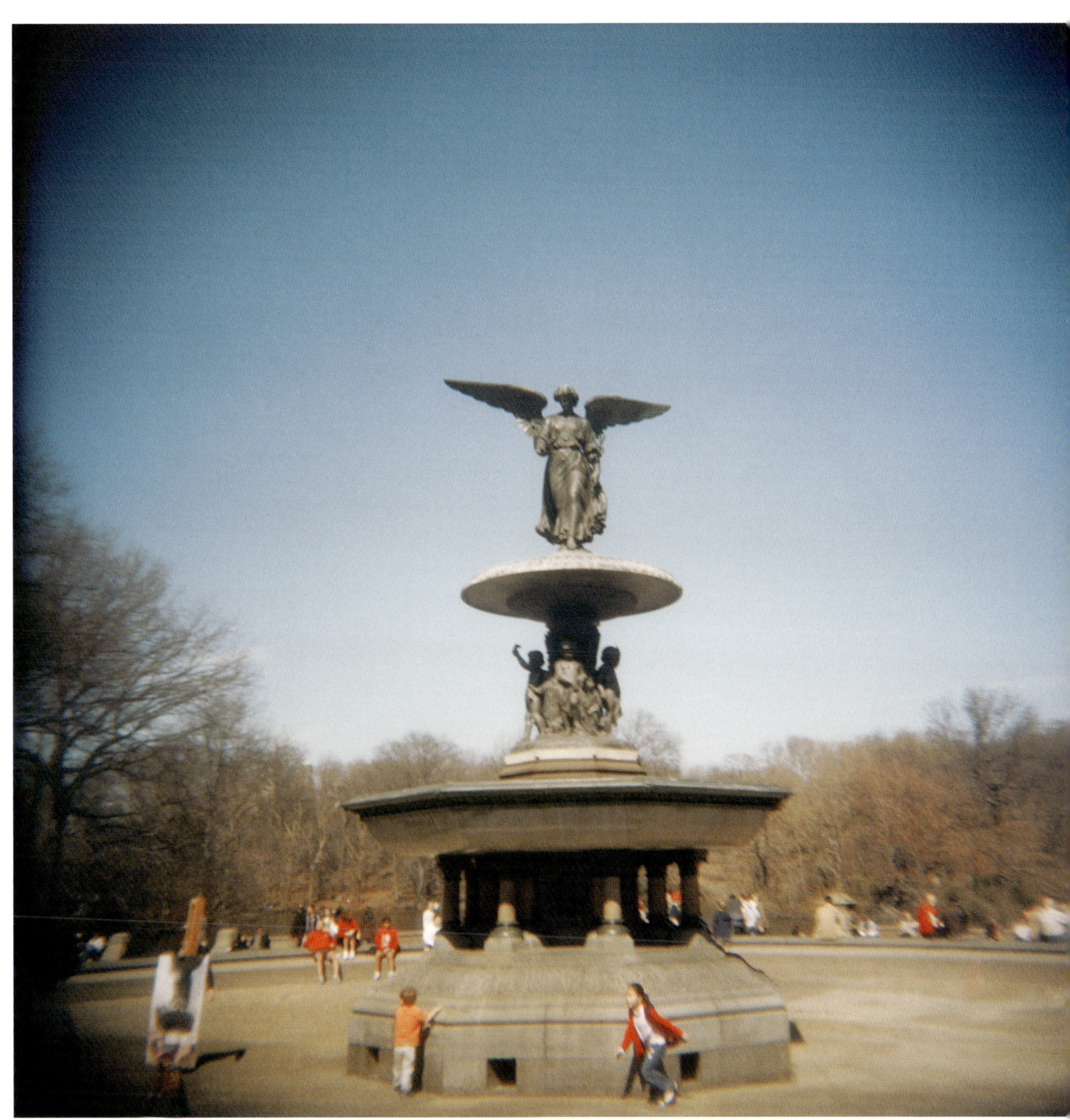

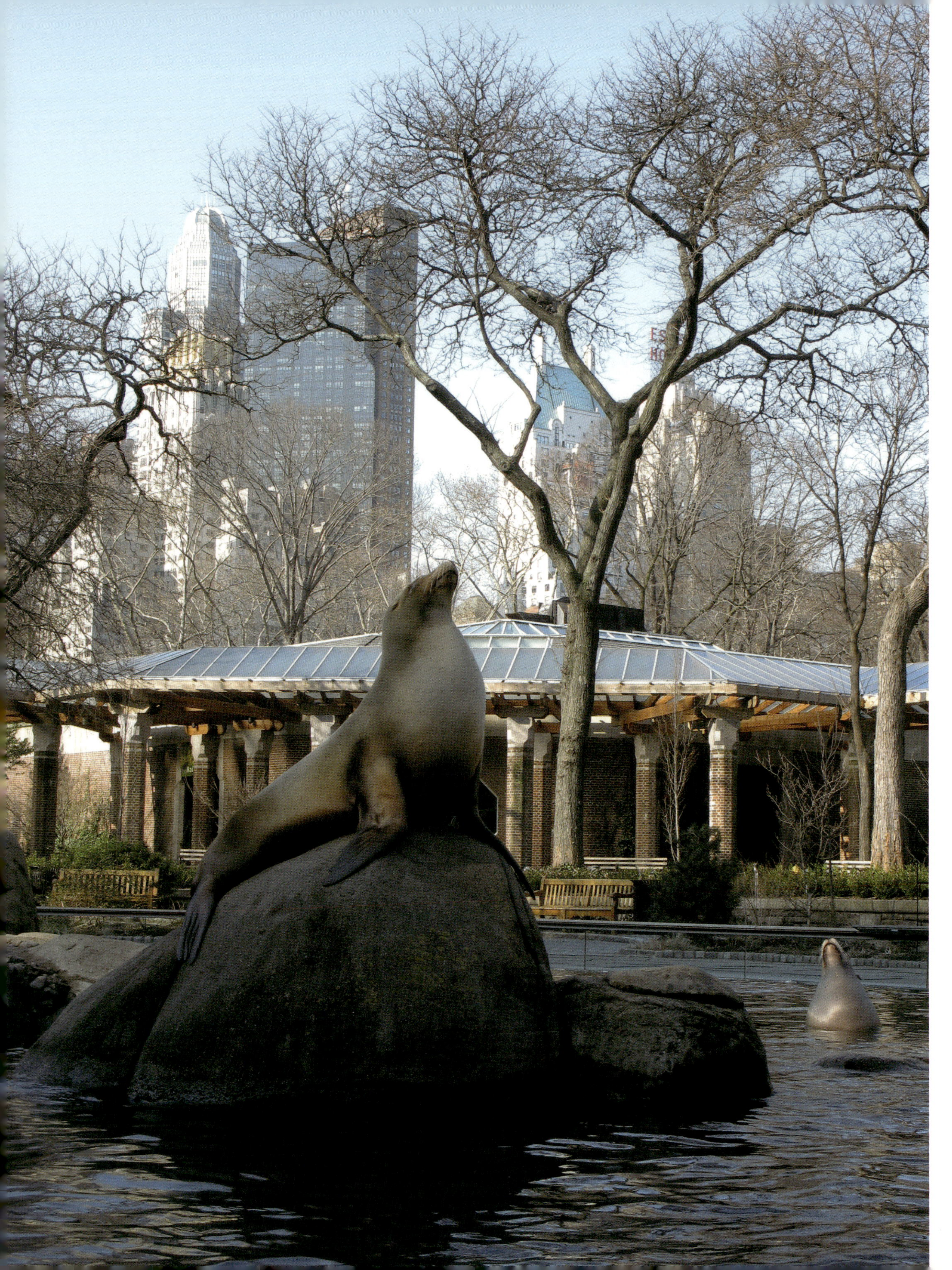

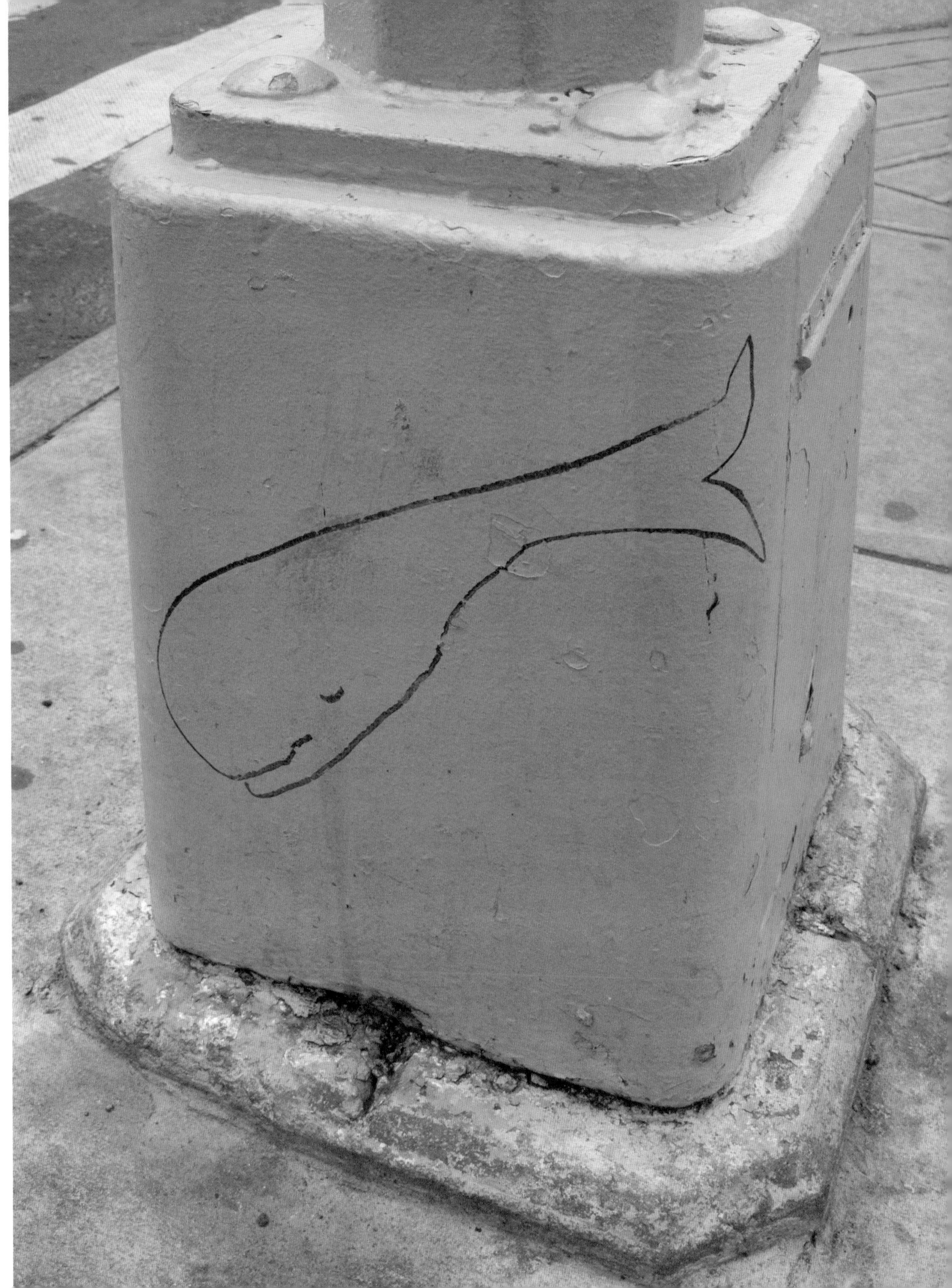

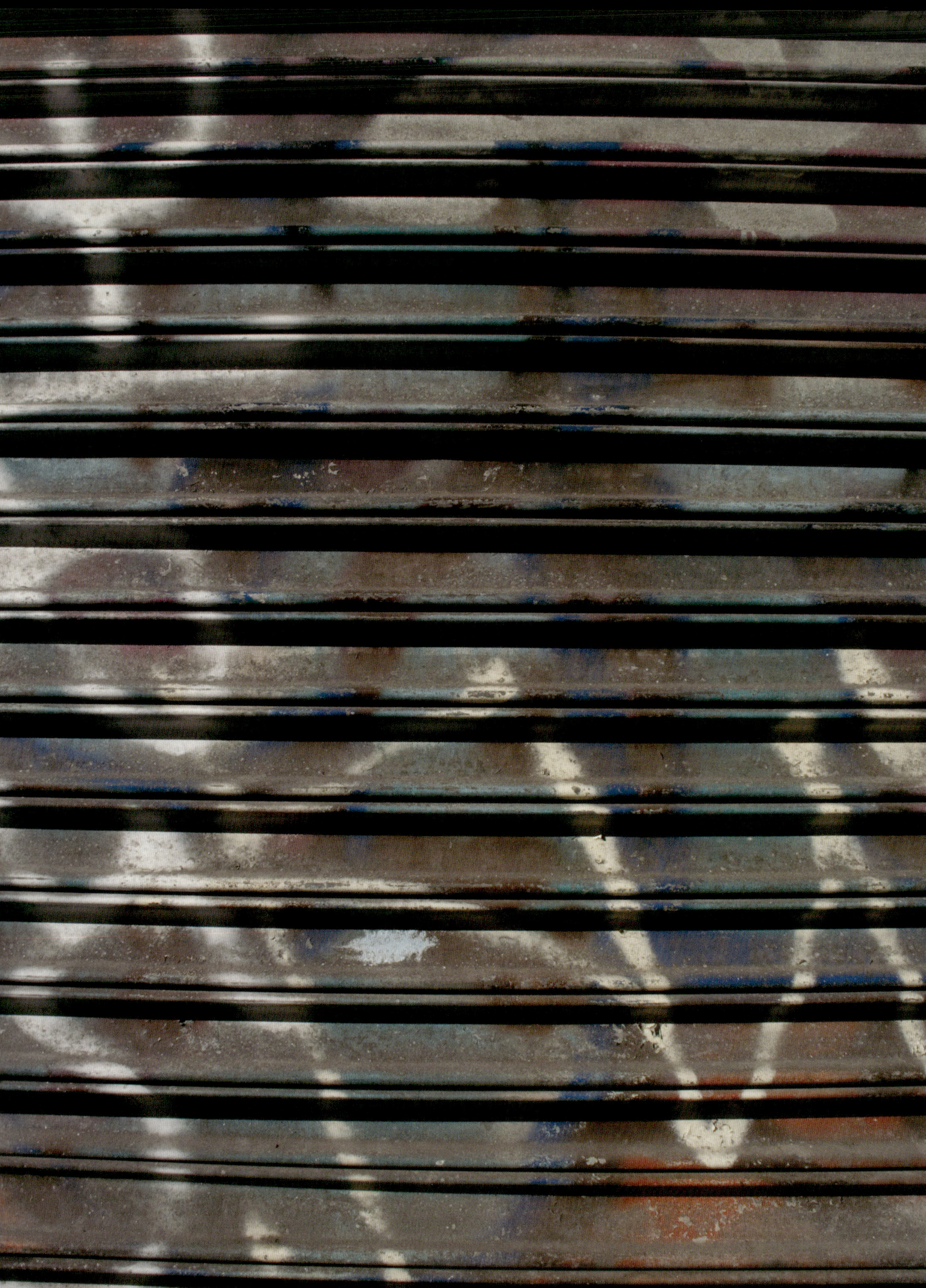

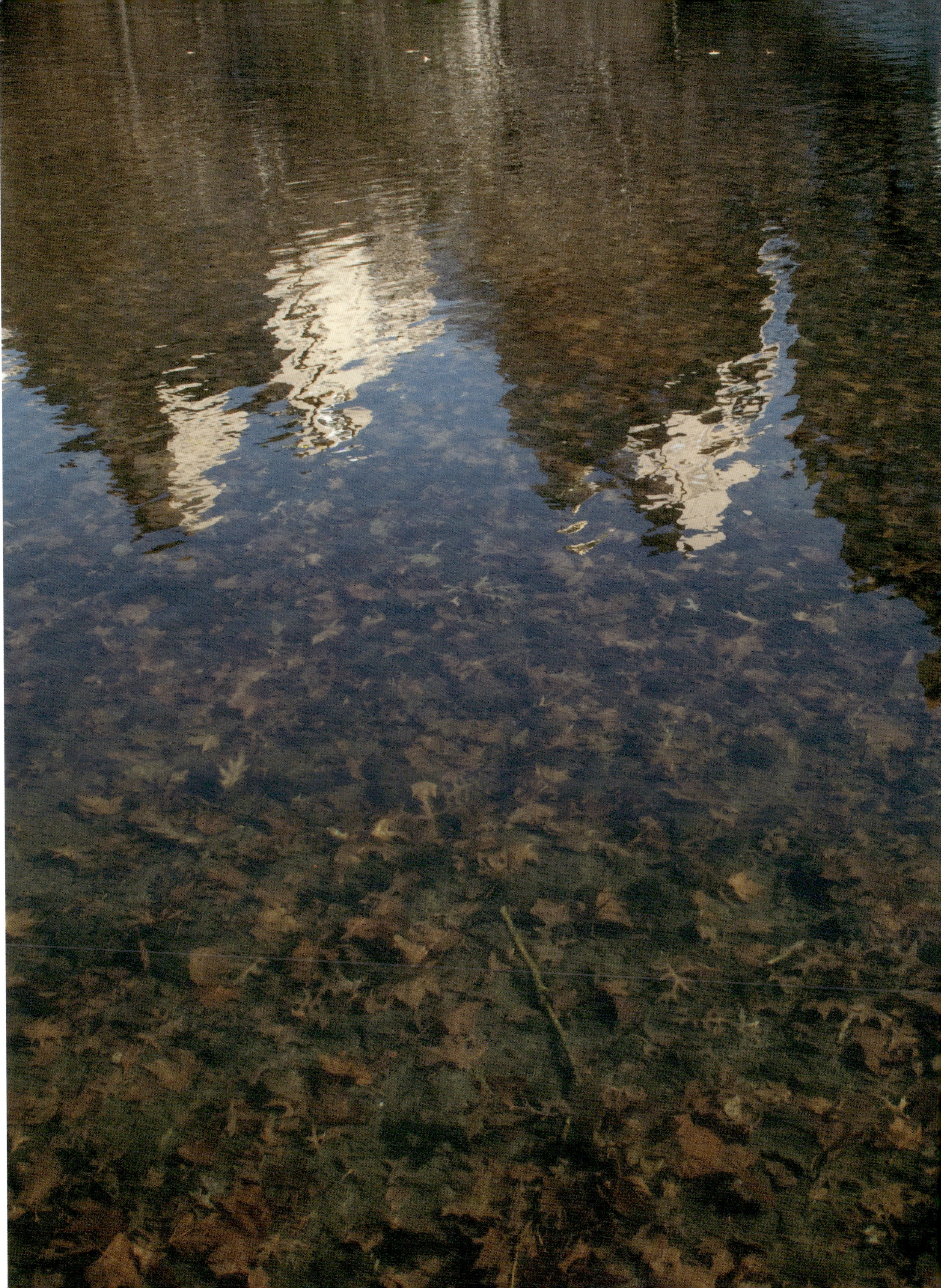

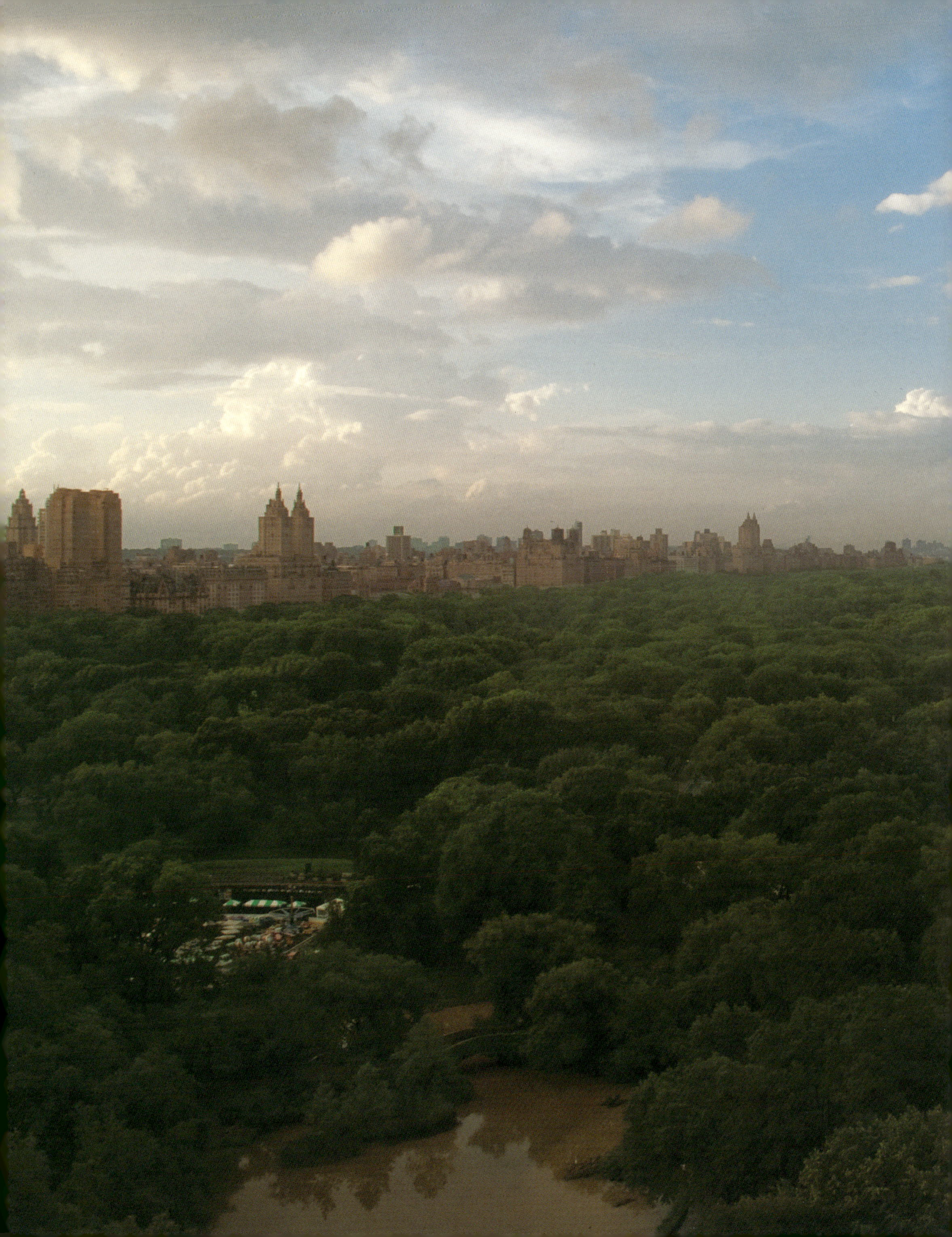

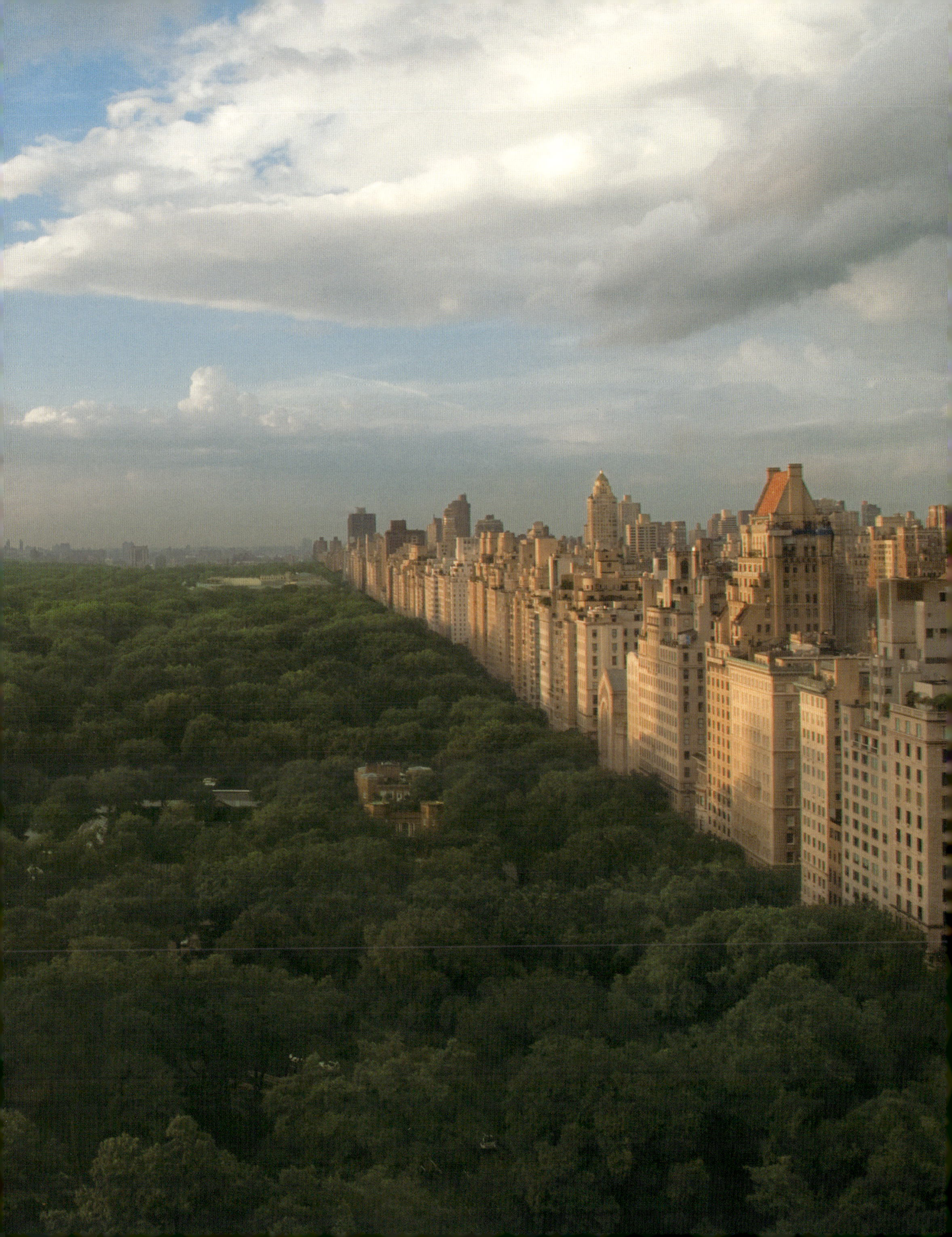

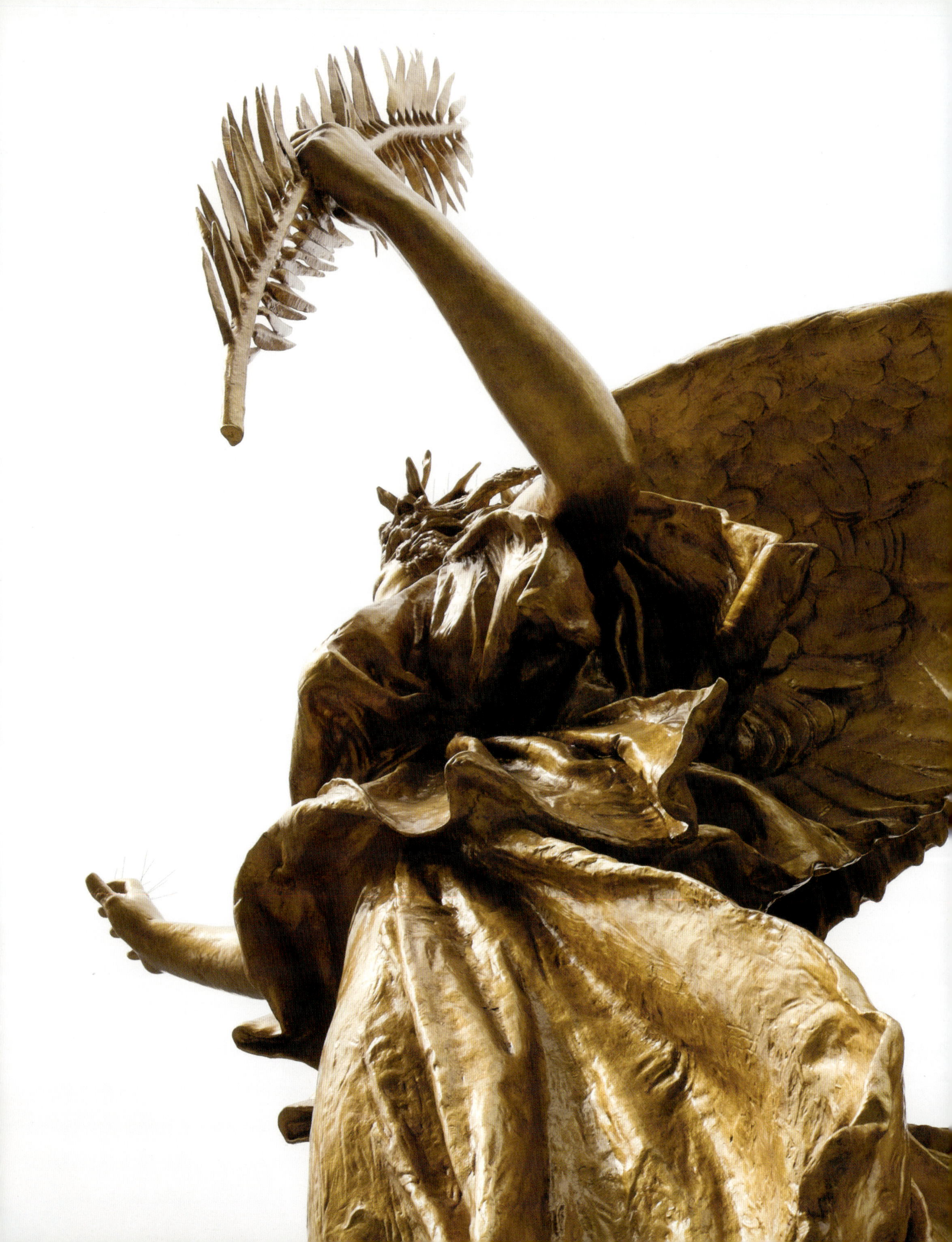

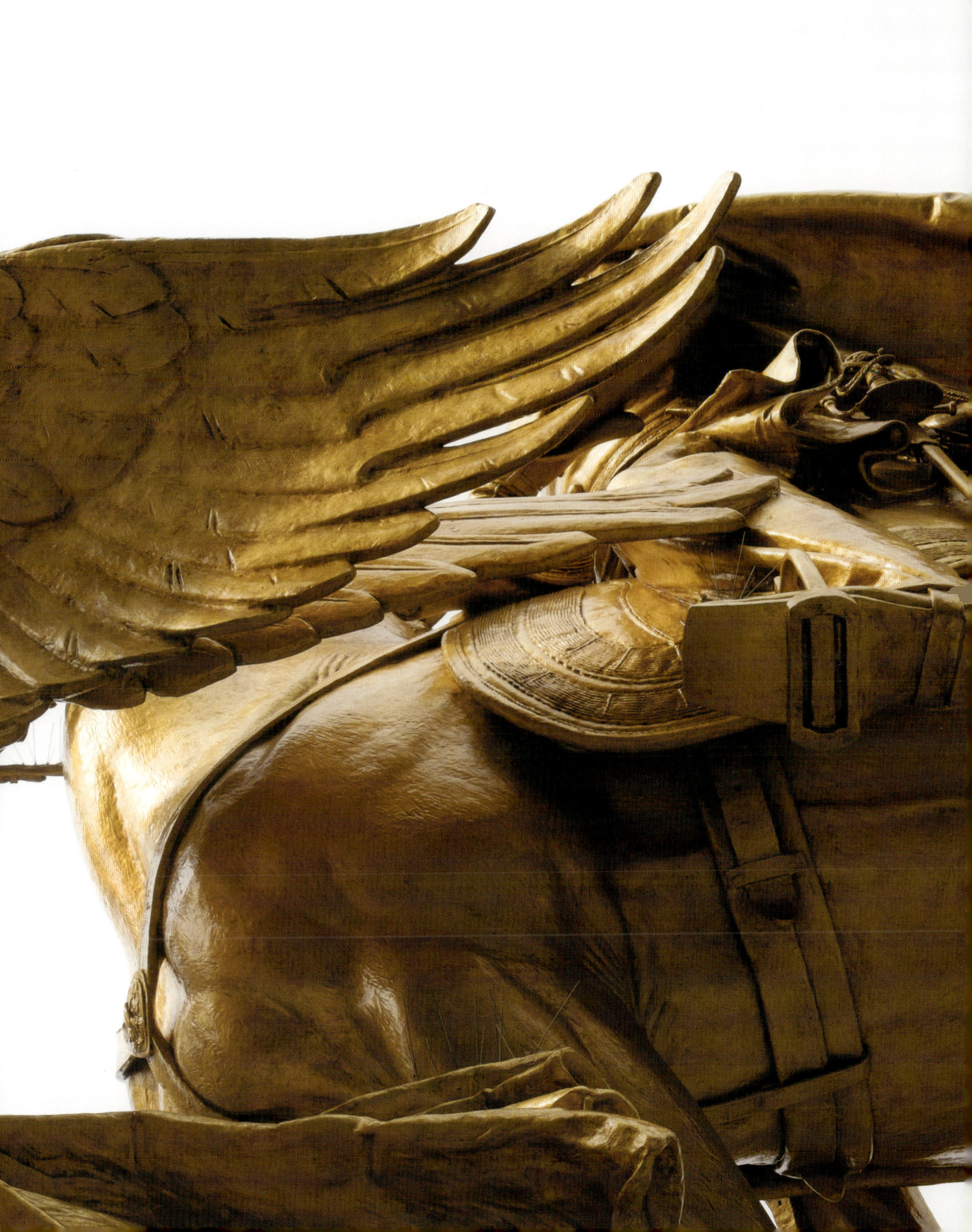

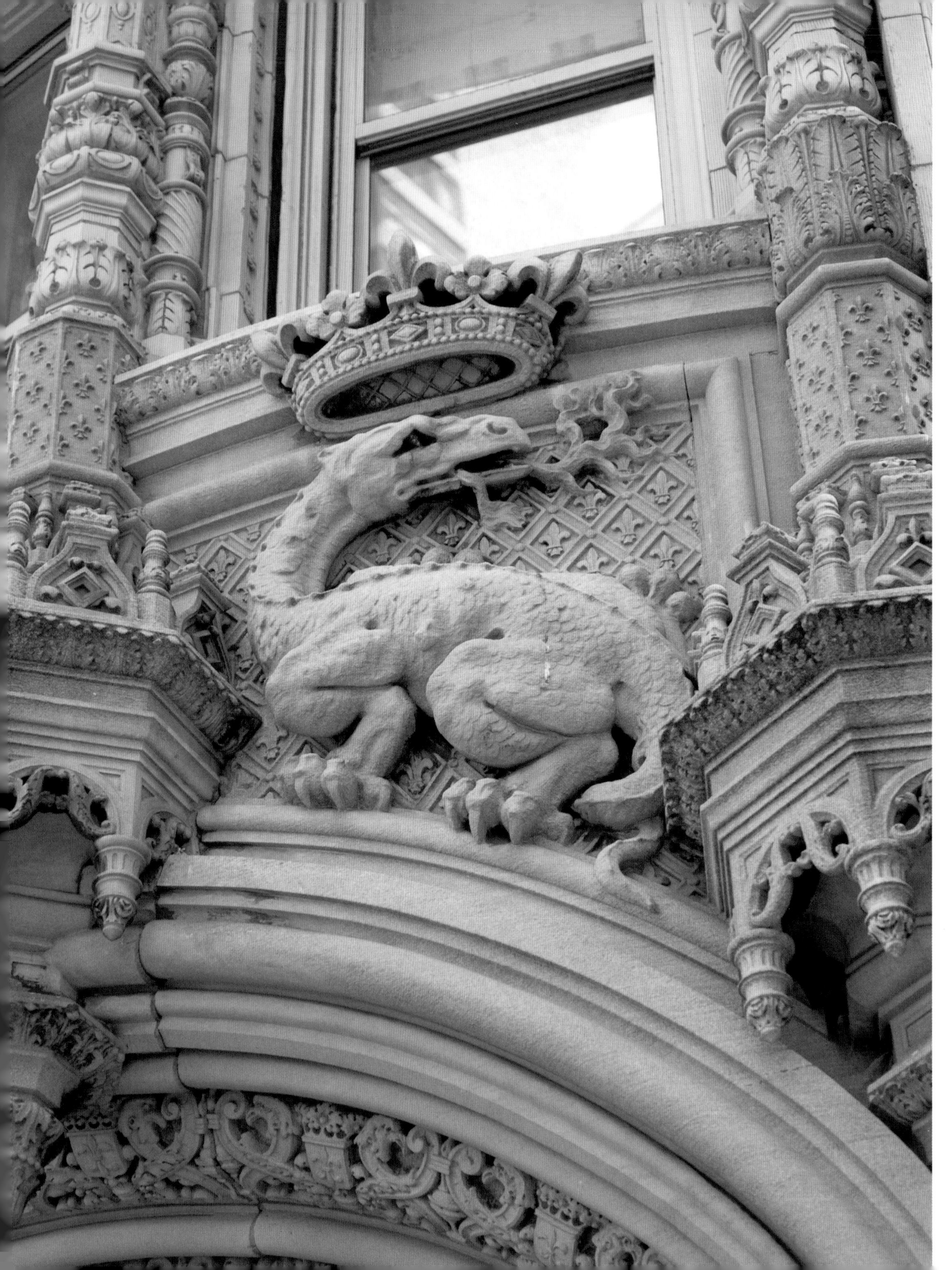

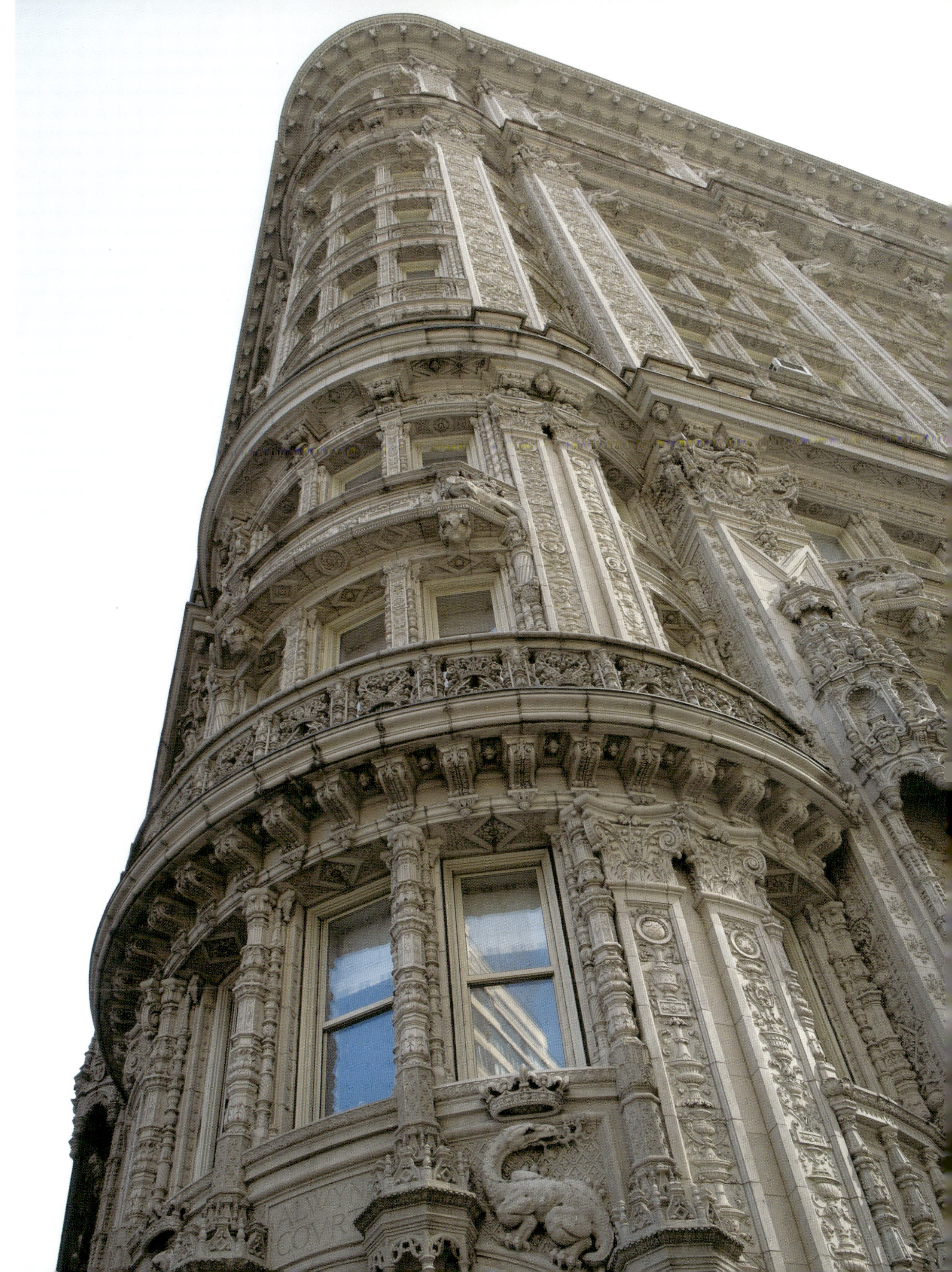
ALWYN
COVR

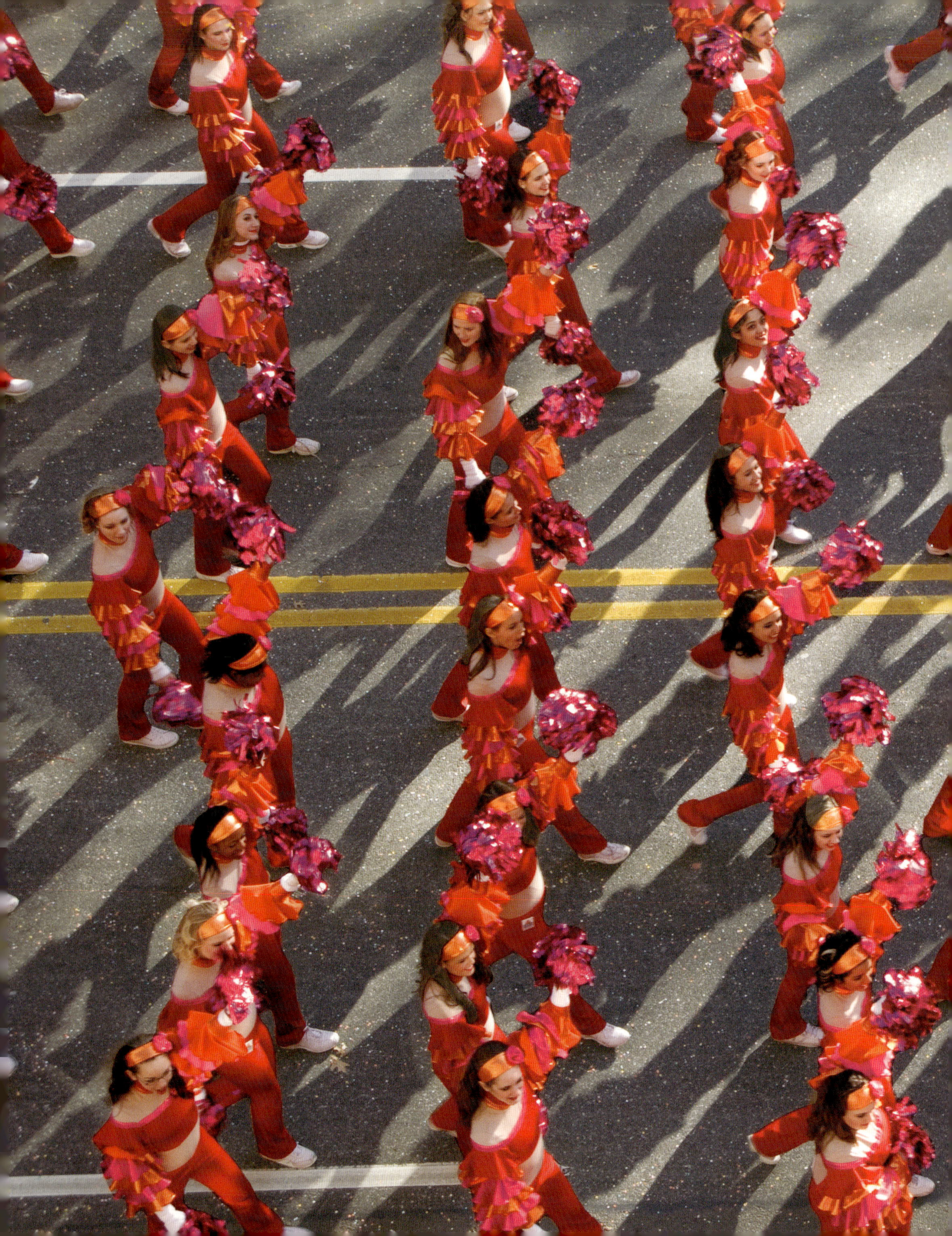

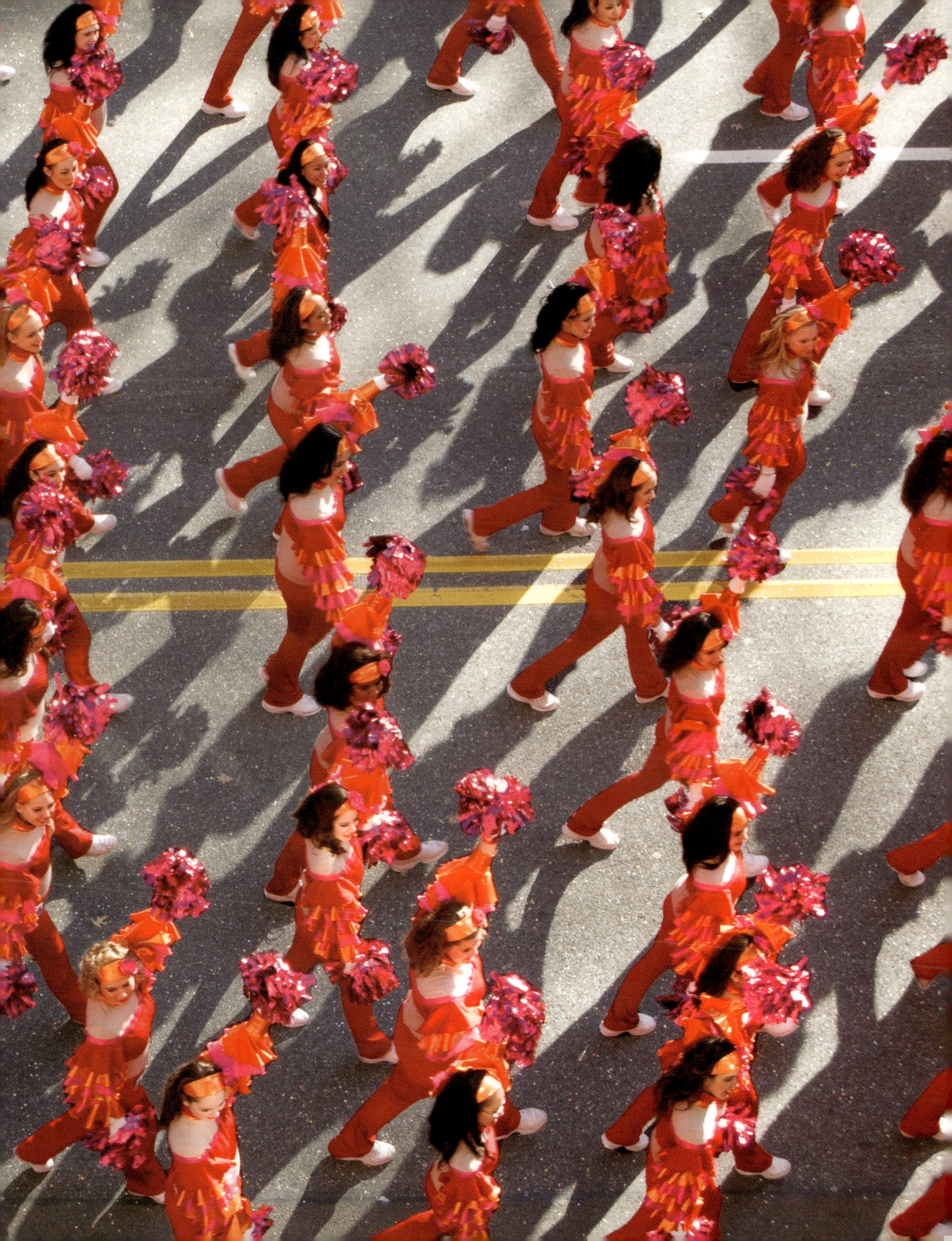

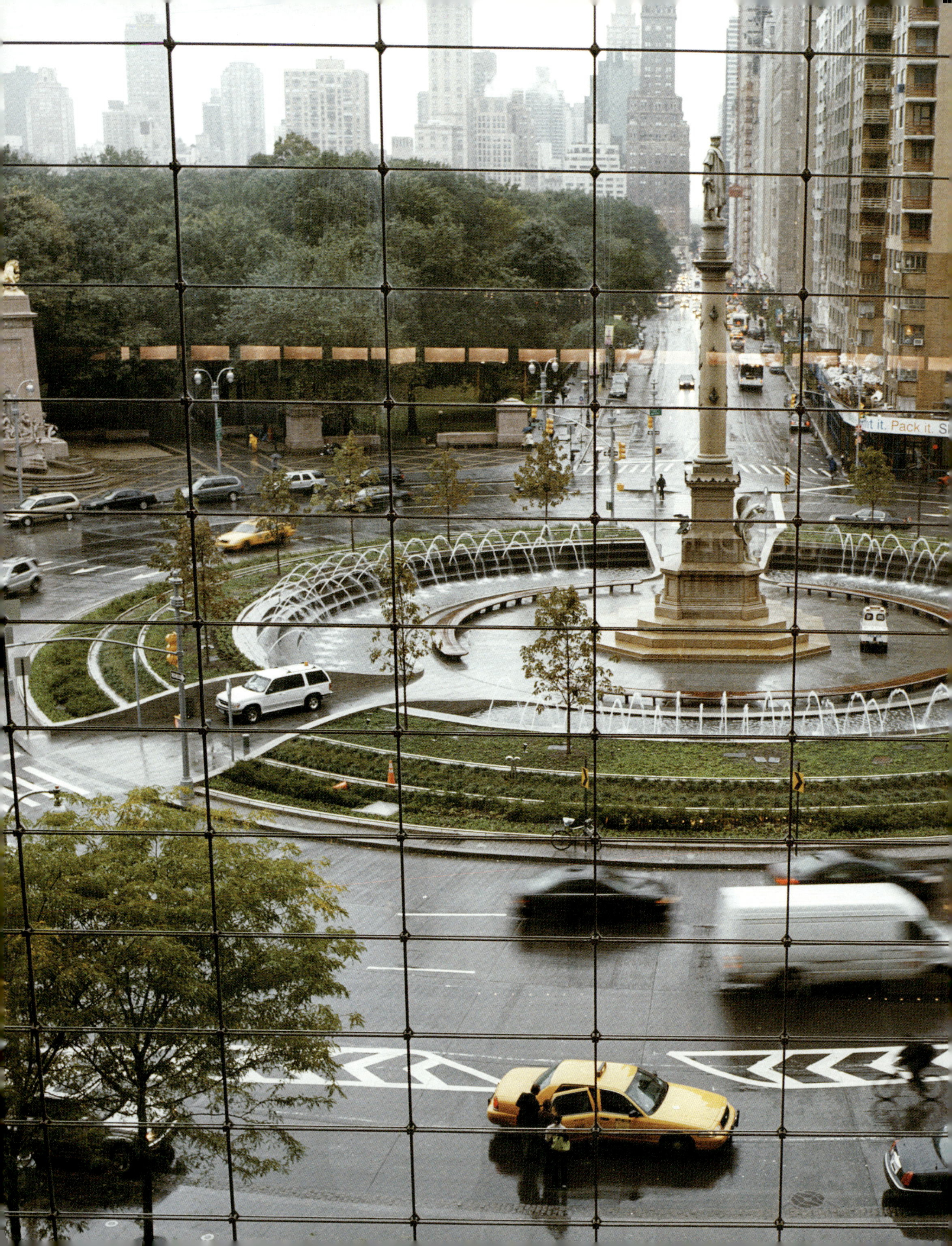
it. Pack it.

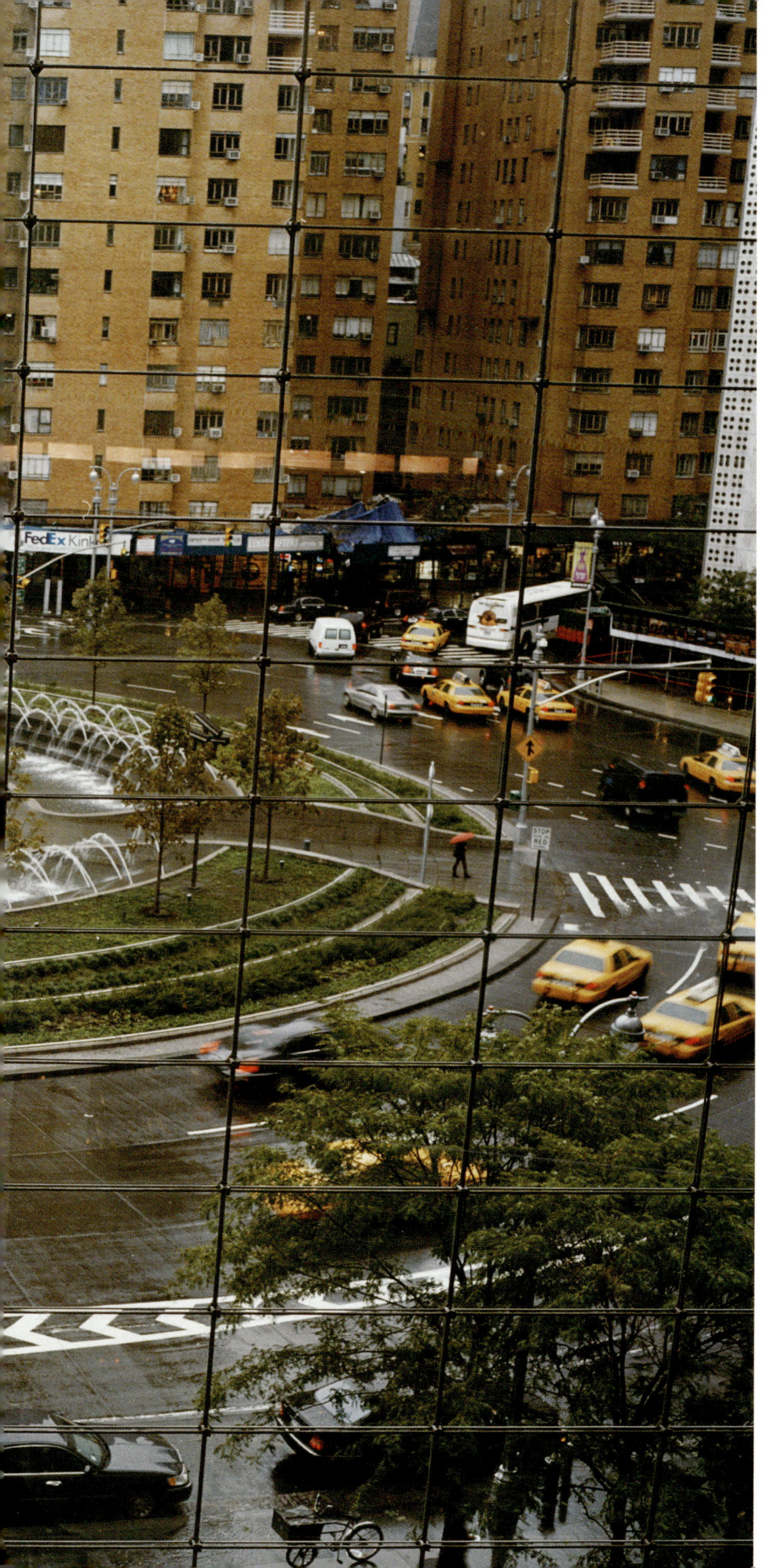
FedEx

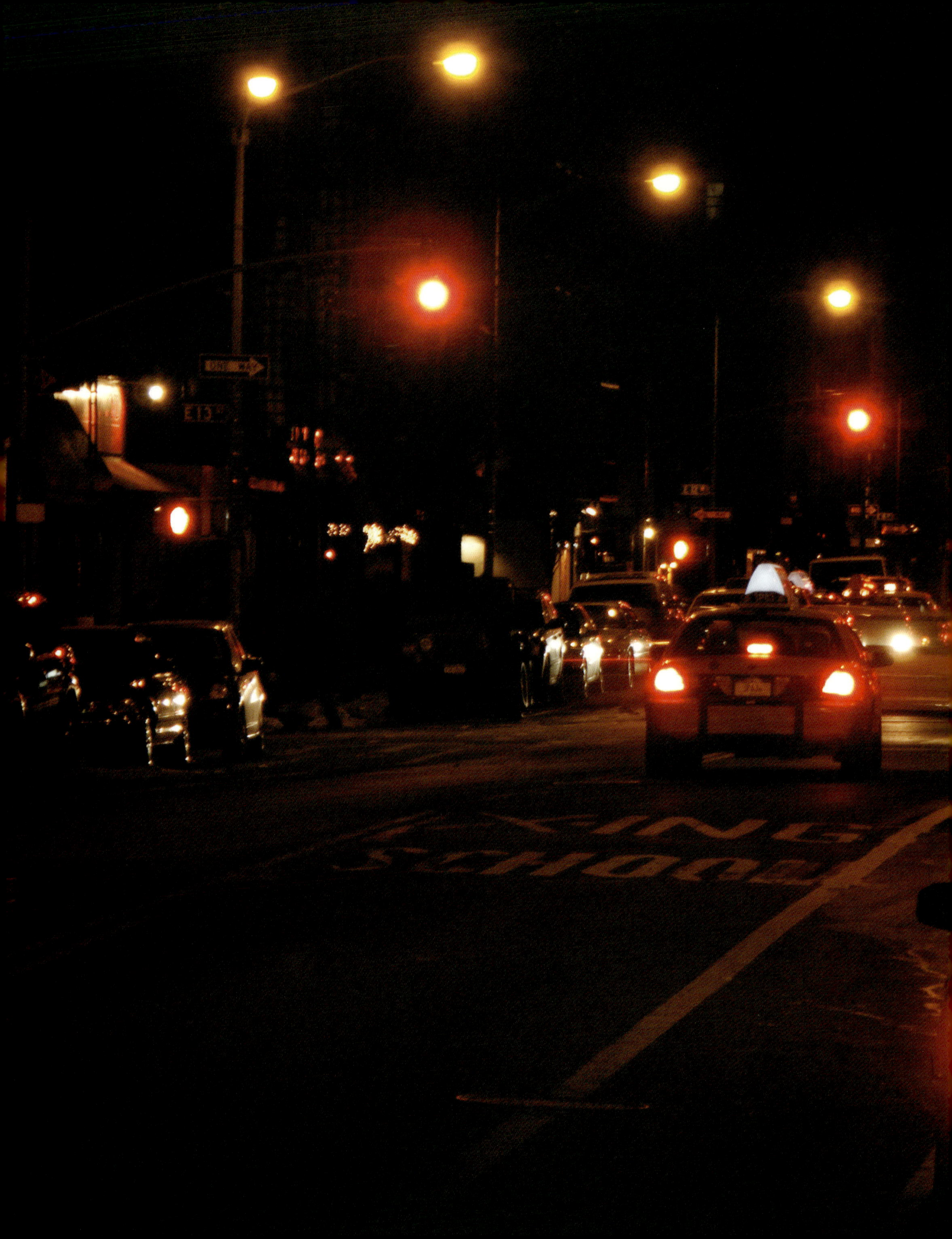

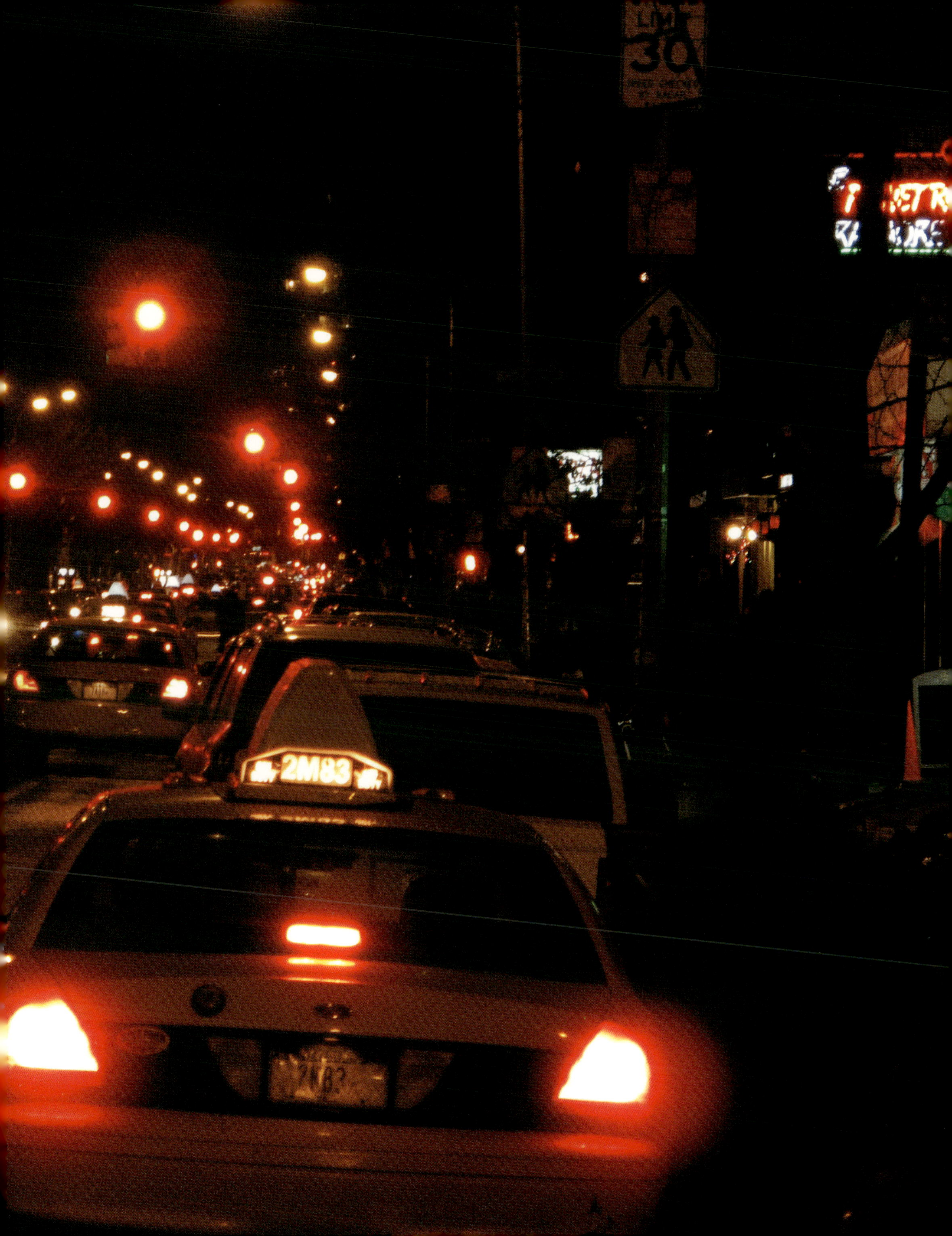
30
2M83

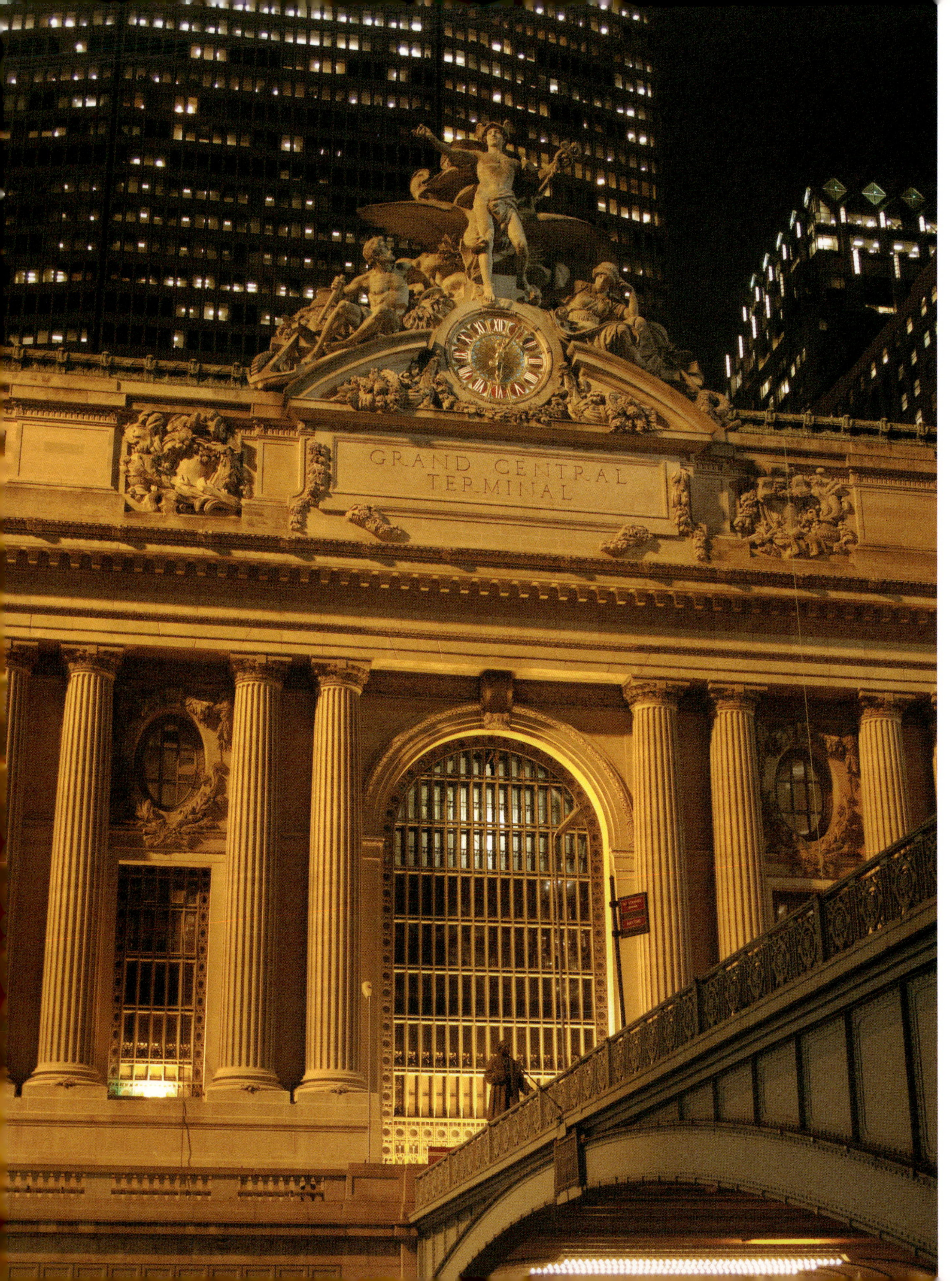
GRAND CENTRAL
TERMINAL

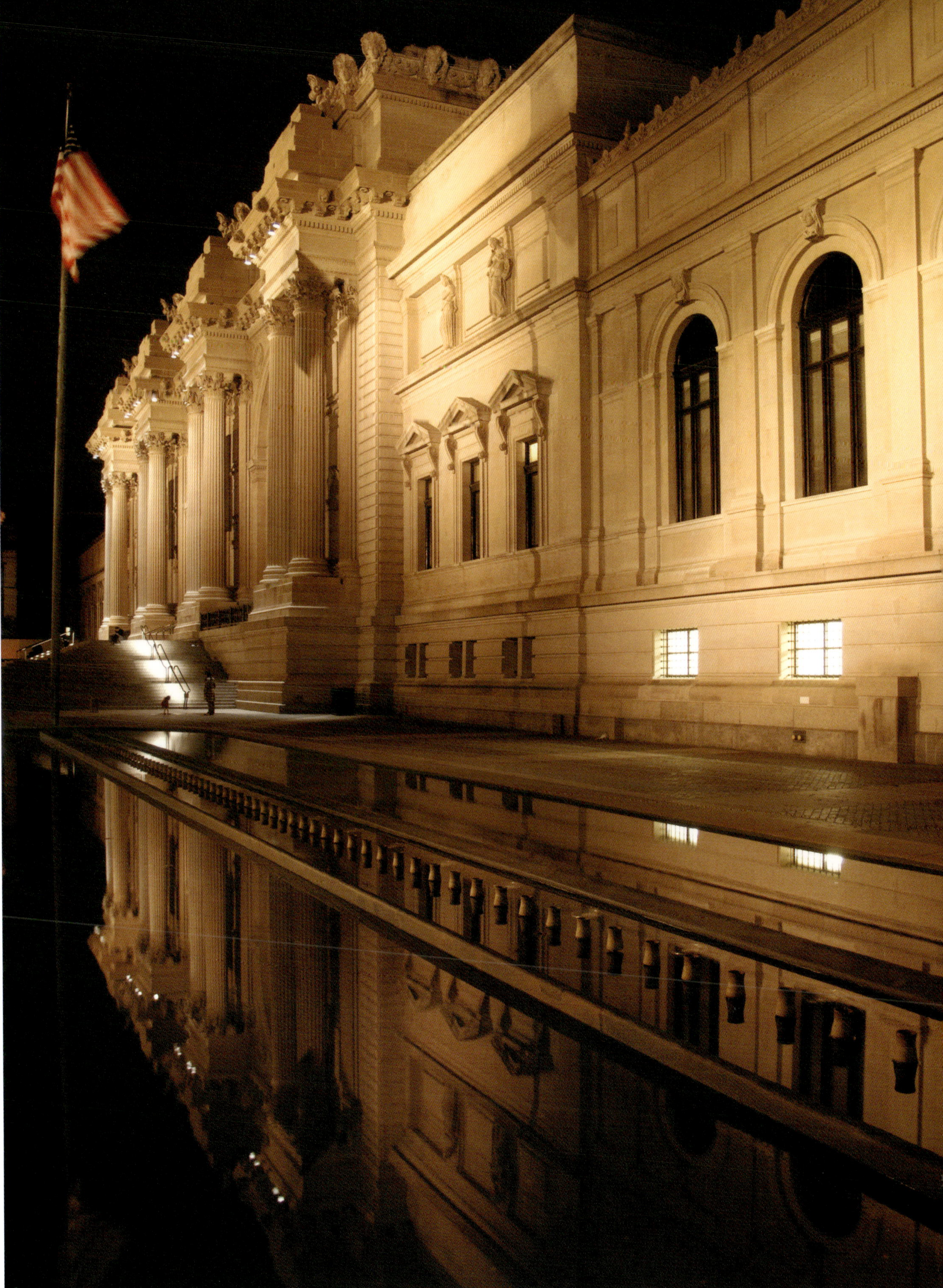

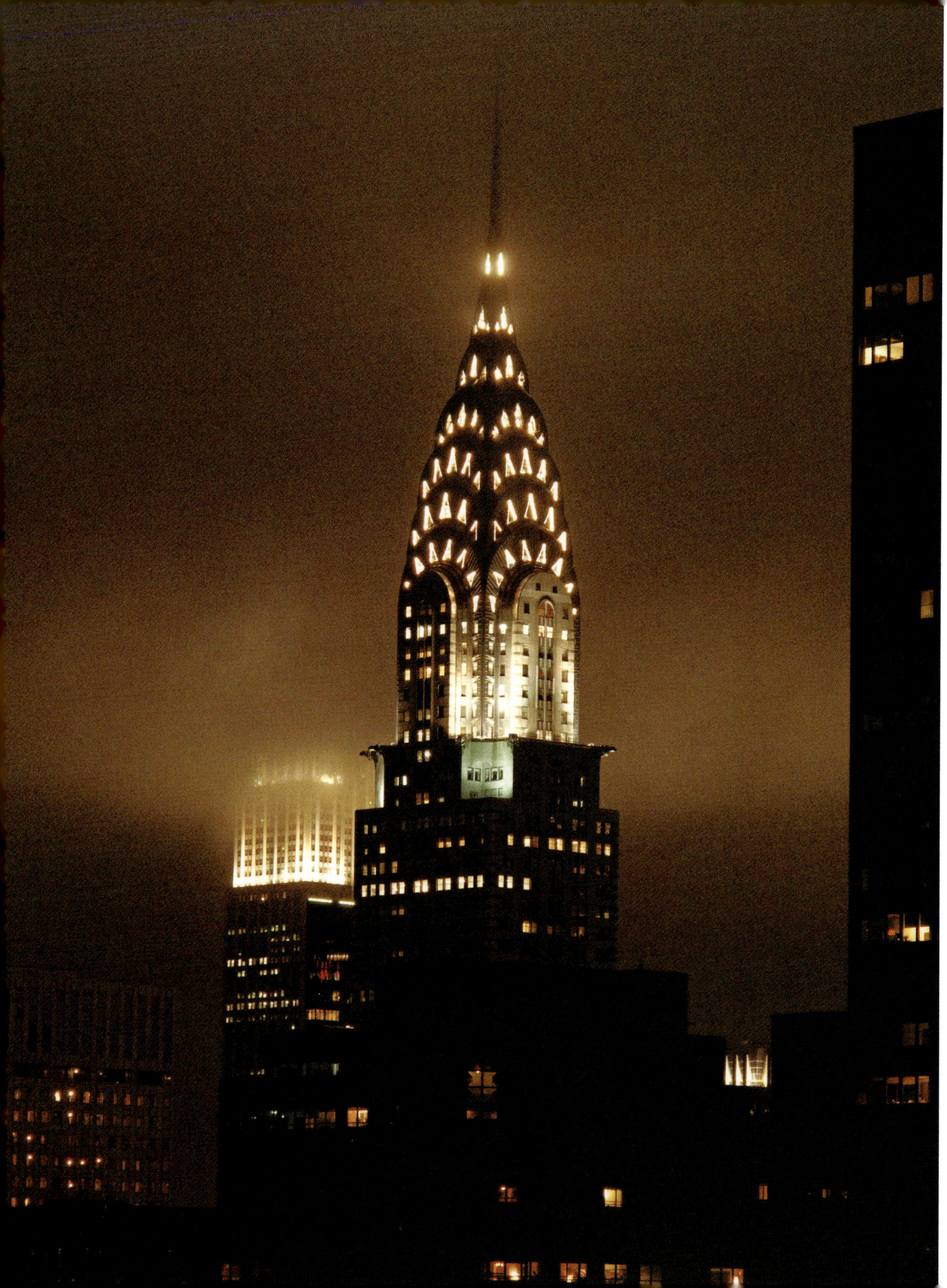

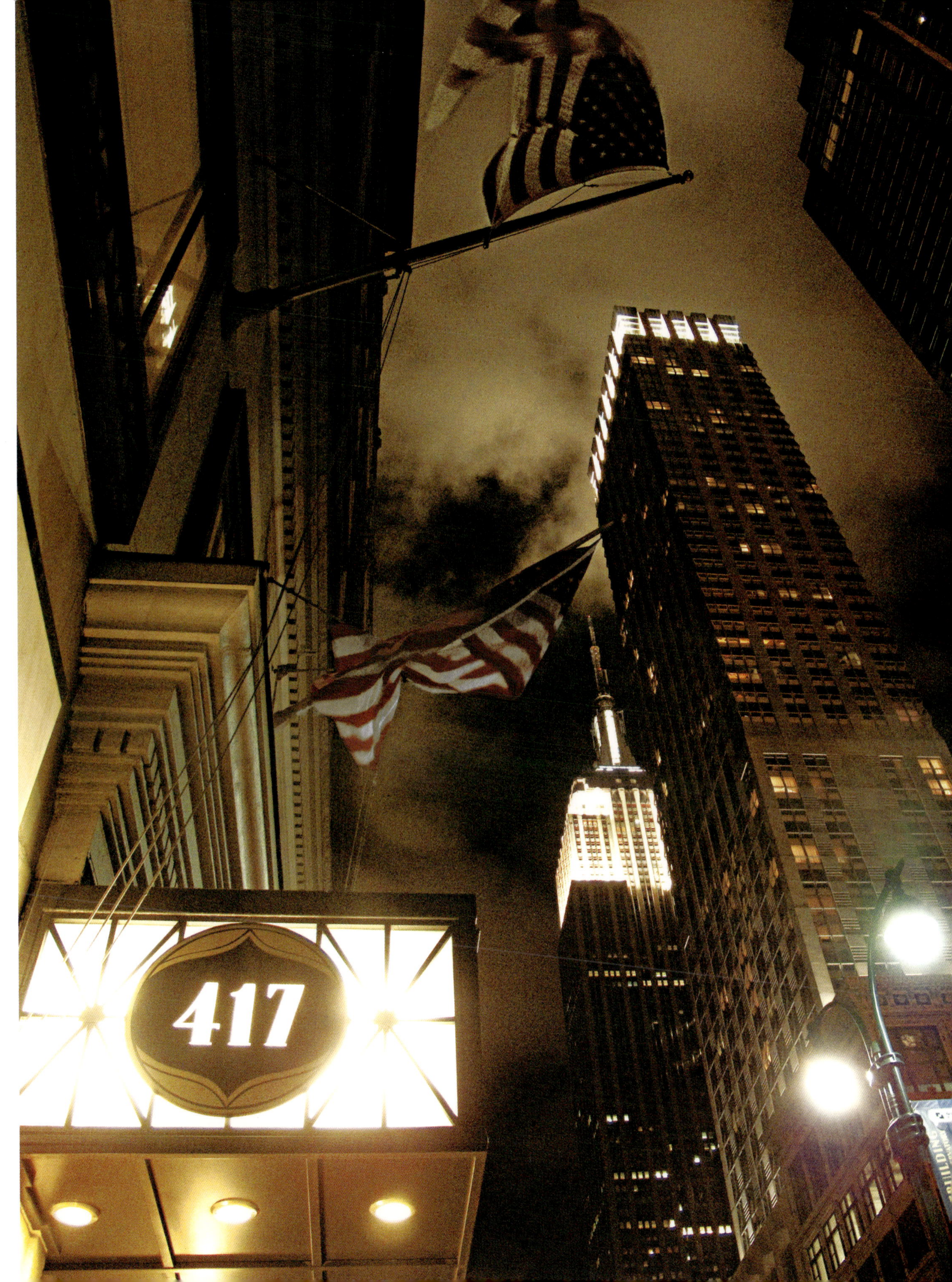
417

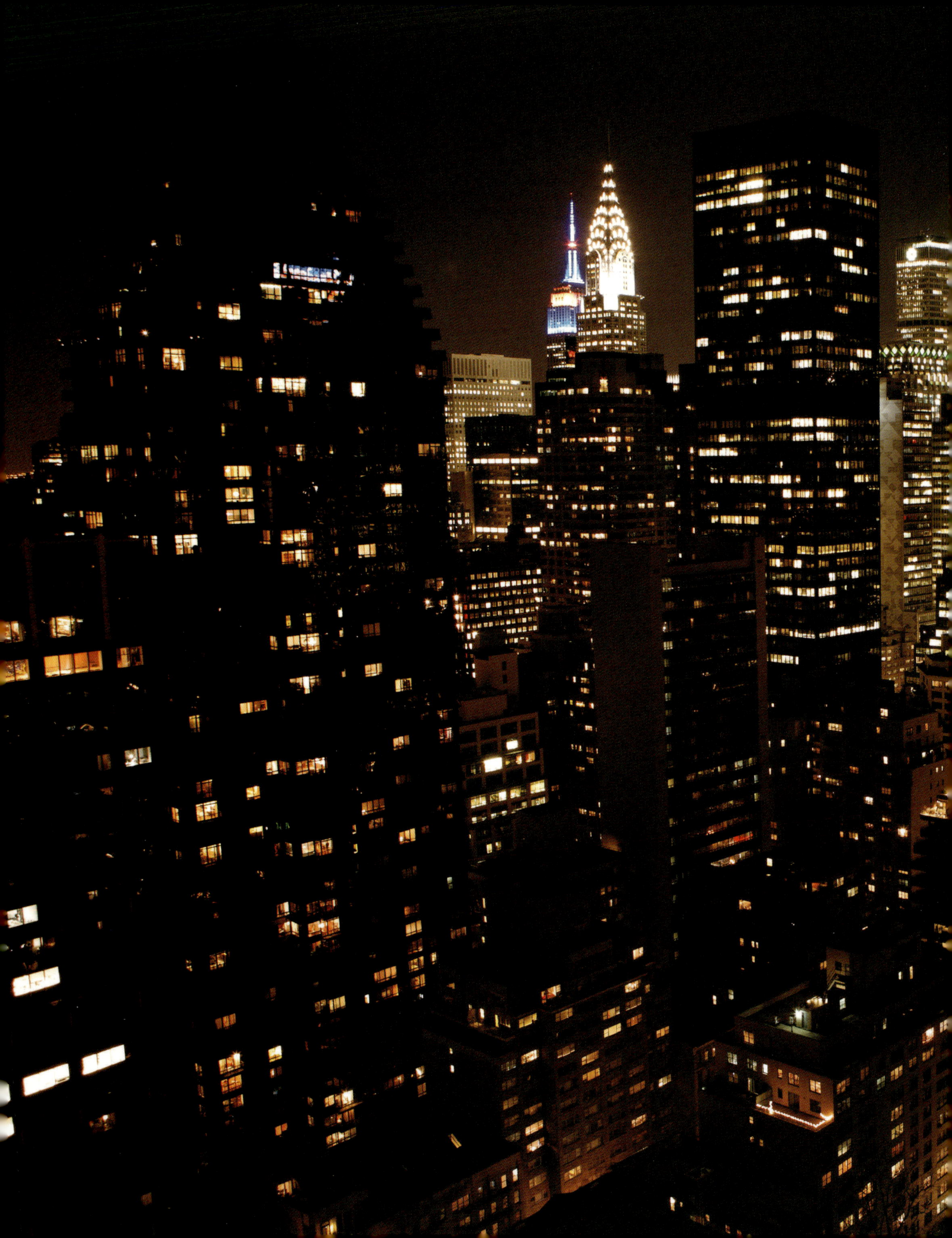

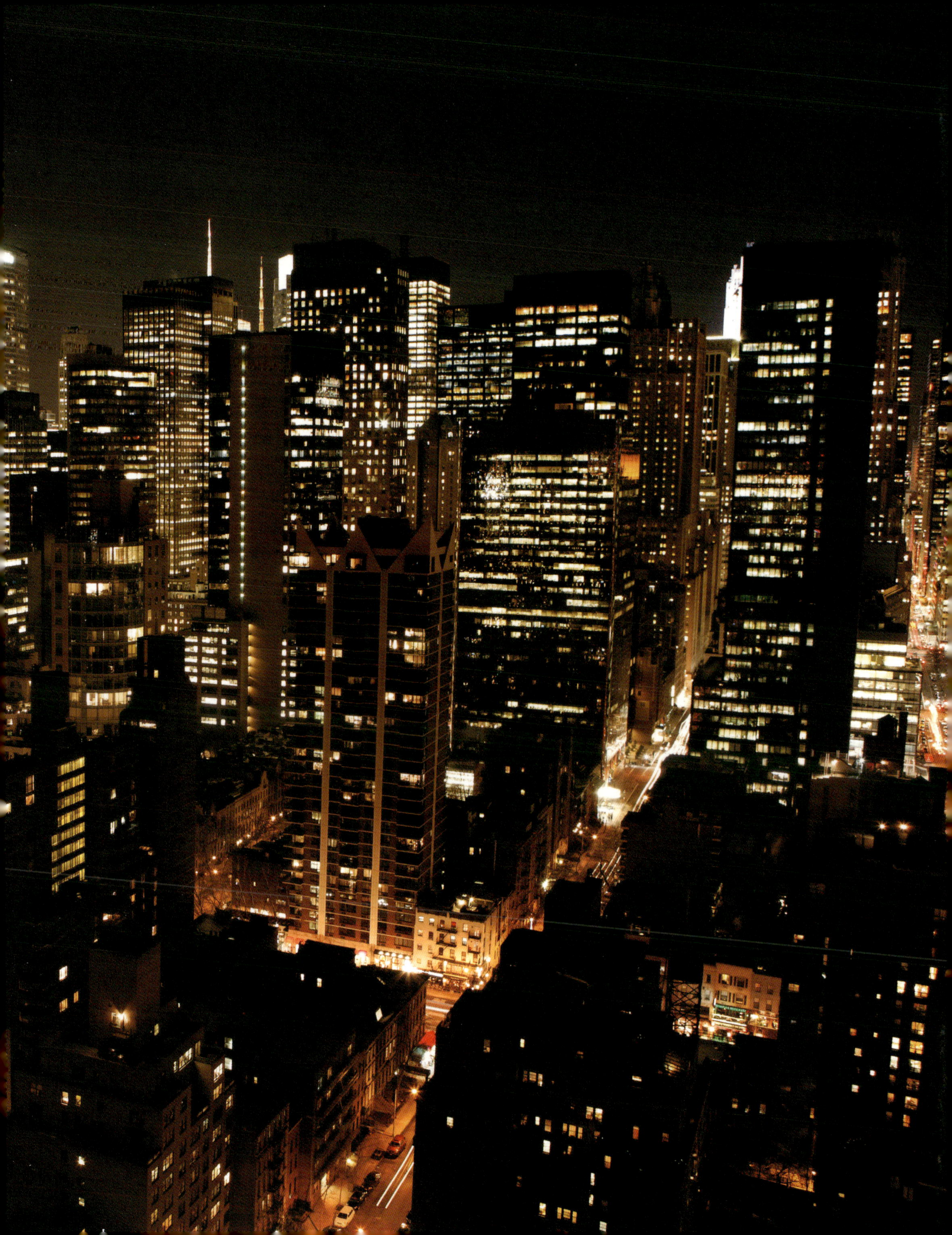

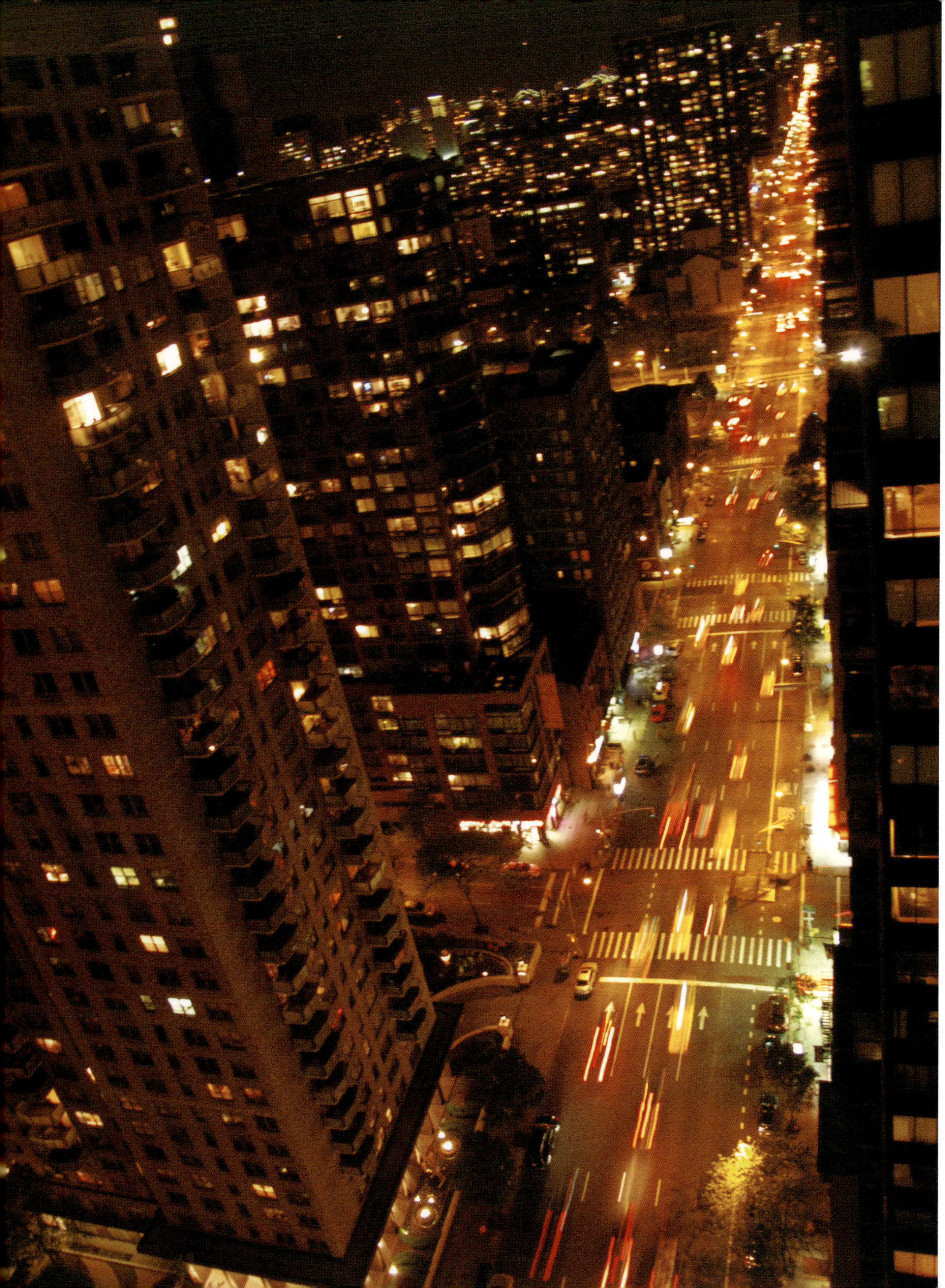

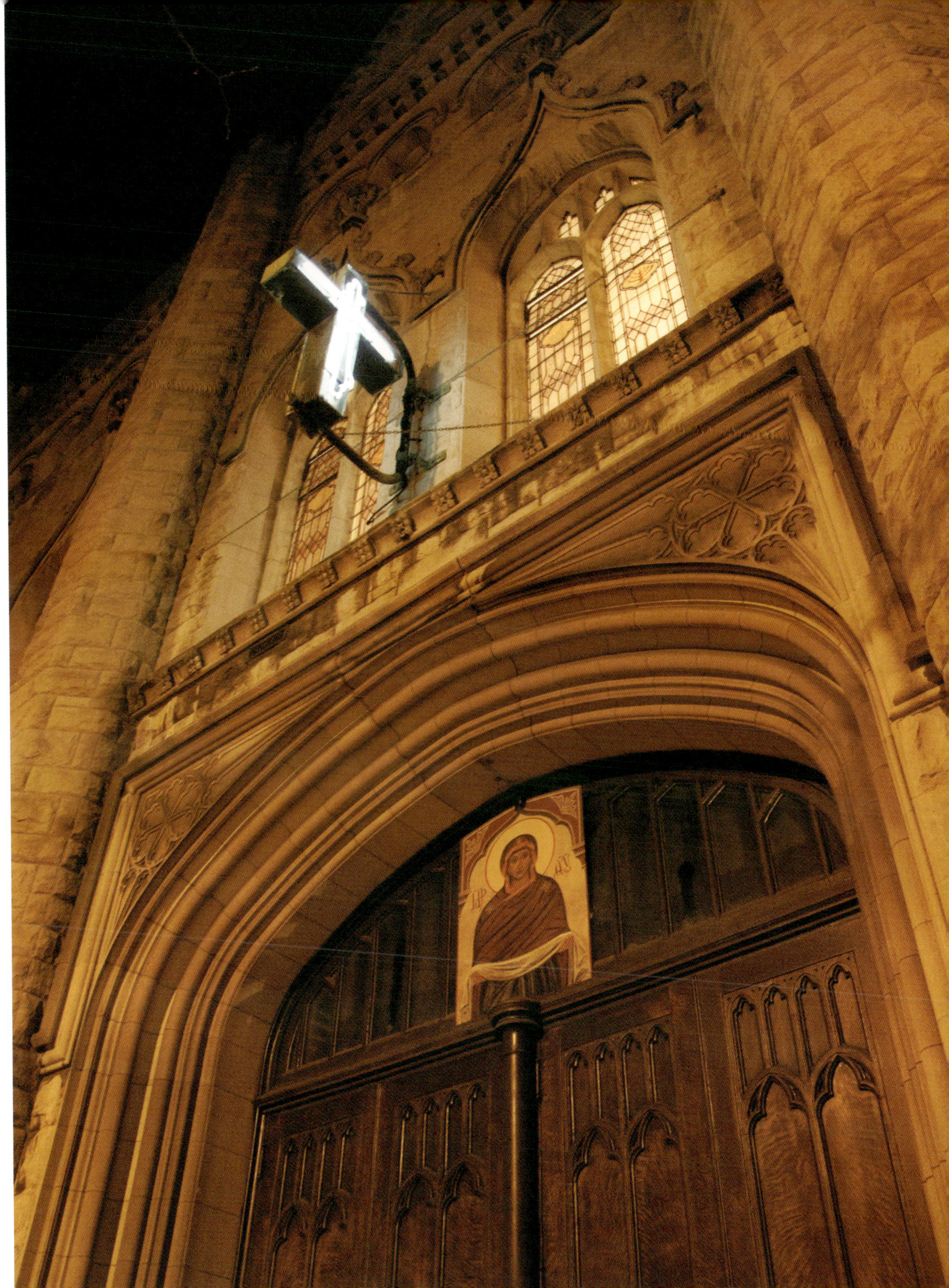

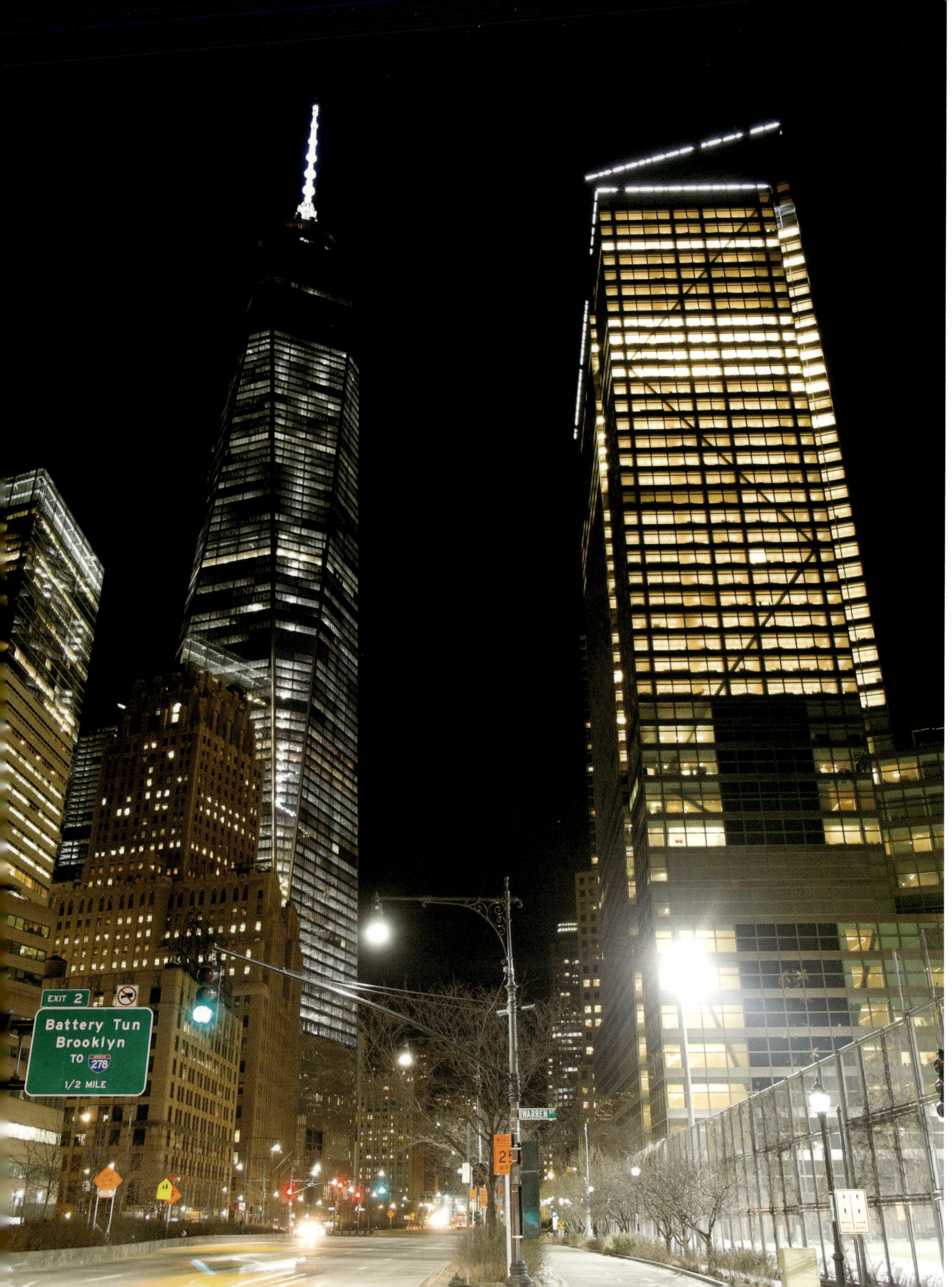
EXIT 2
Battery Tun
Brooklyn
TO 278
1/2 MILE
WARREN ST

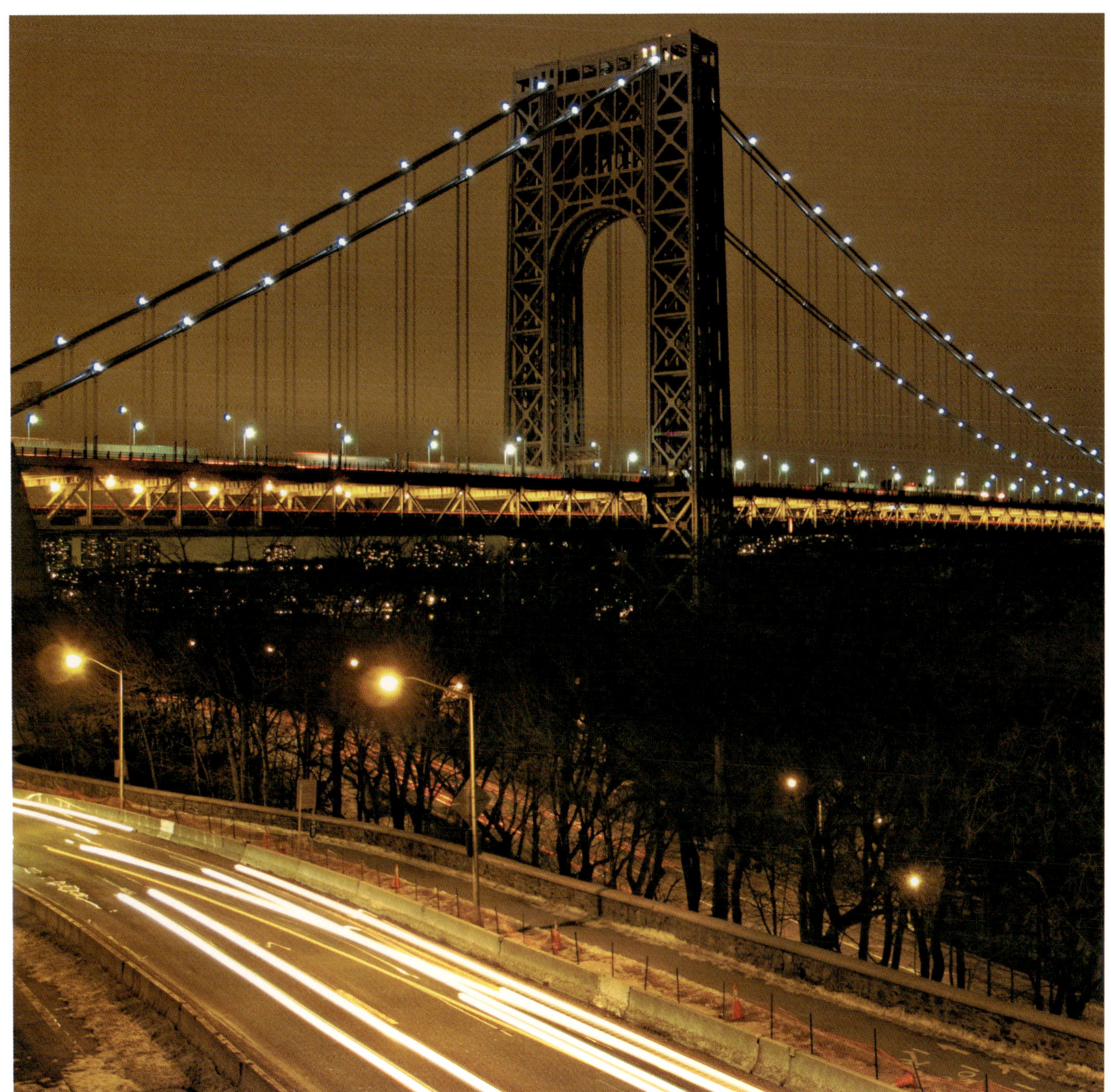

I'M VERY IMPRESSED by the new Freedom Tower. This building manages to be both dignified and powerful. I think it's a central part of the New York spirit that people do remember the past, but also move towards the future with a sense of hope.

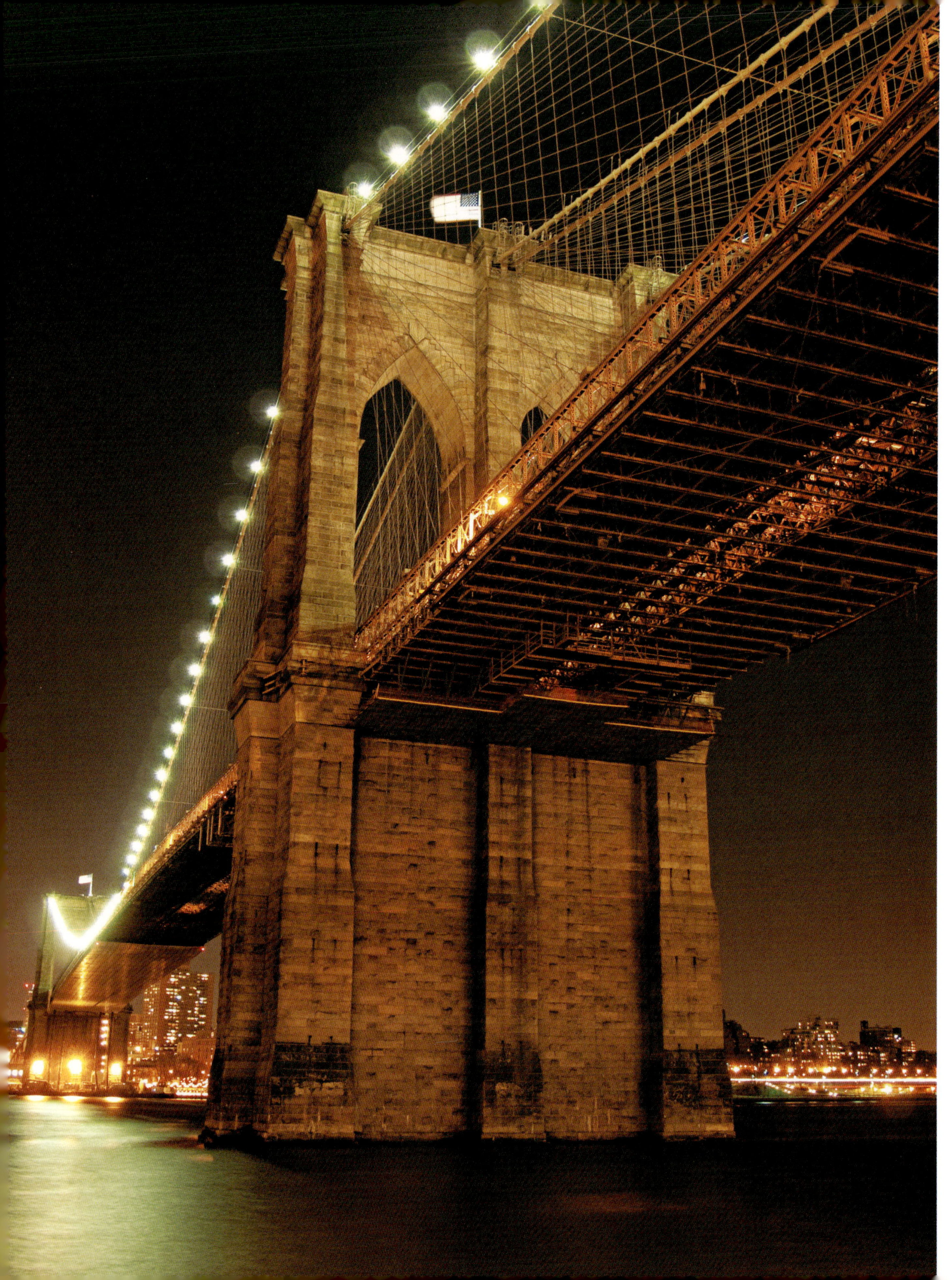

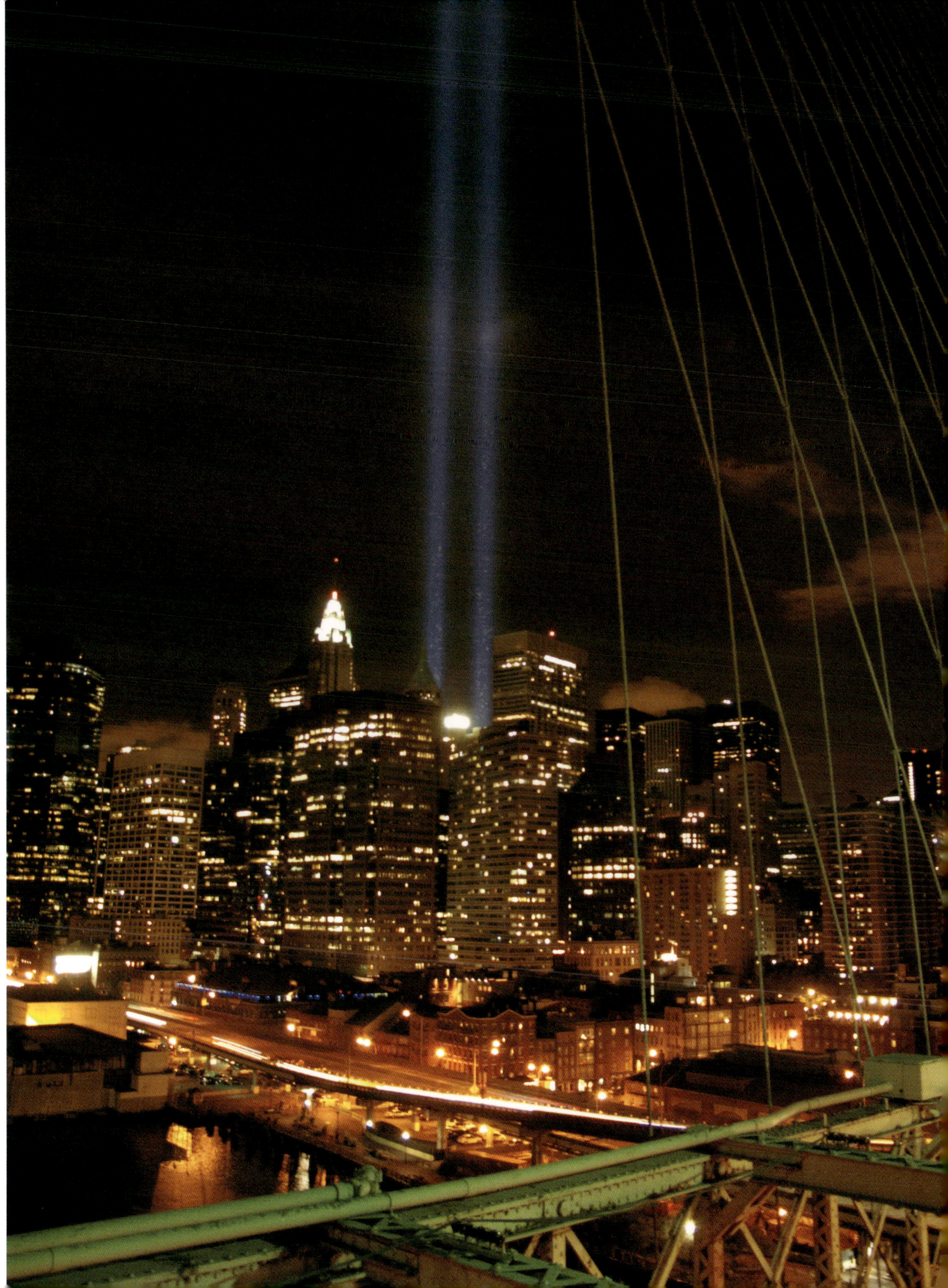

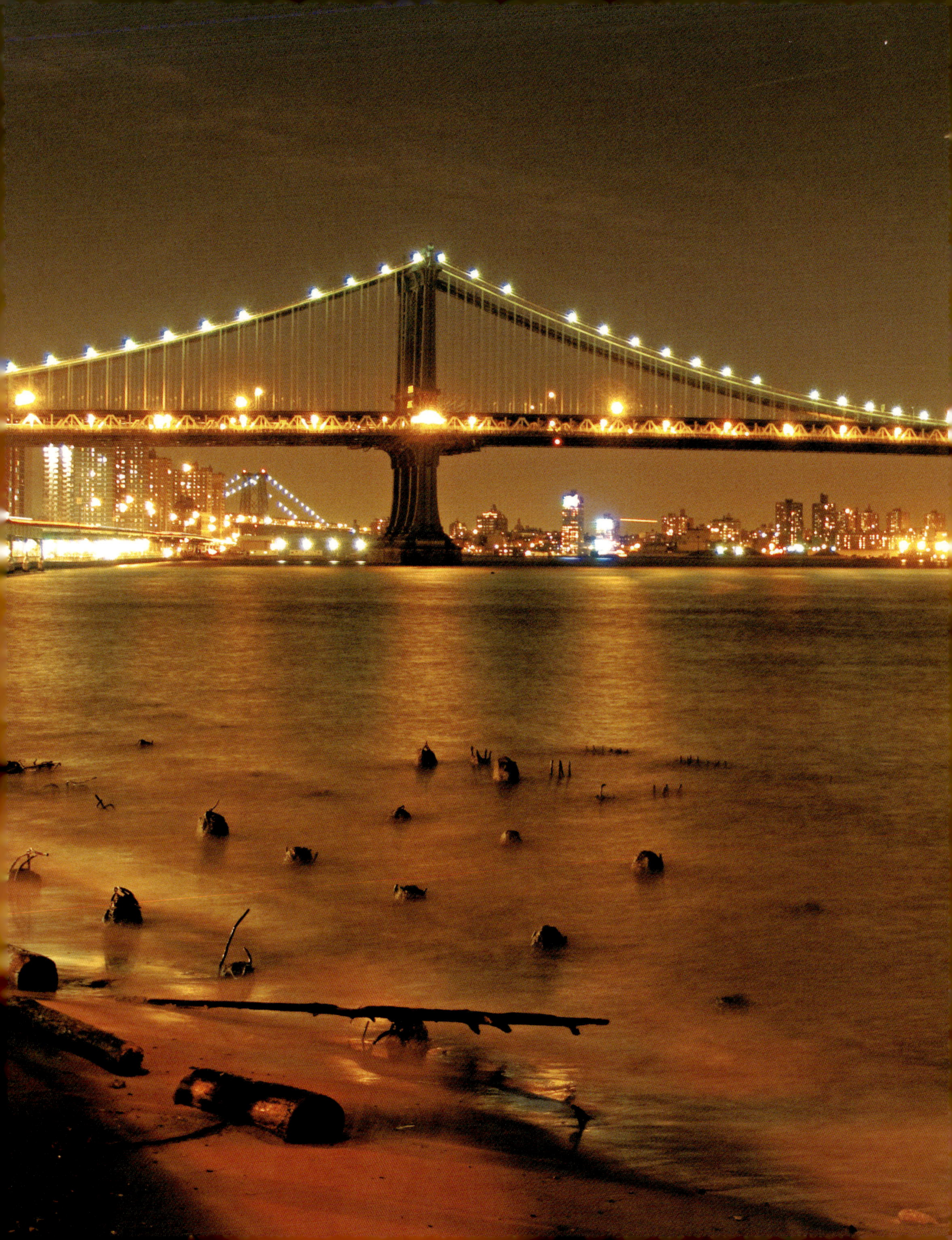

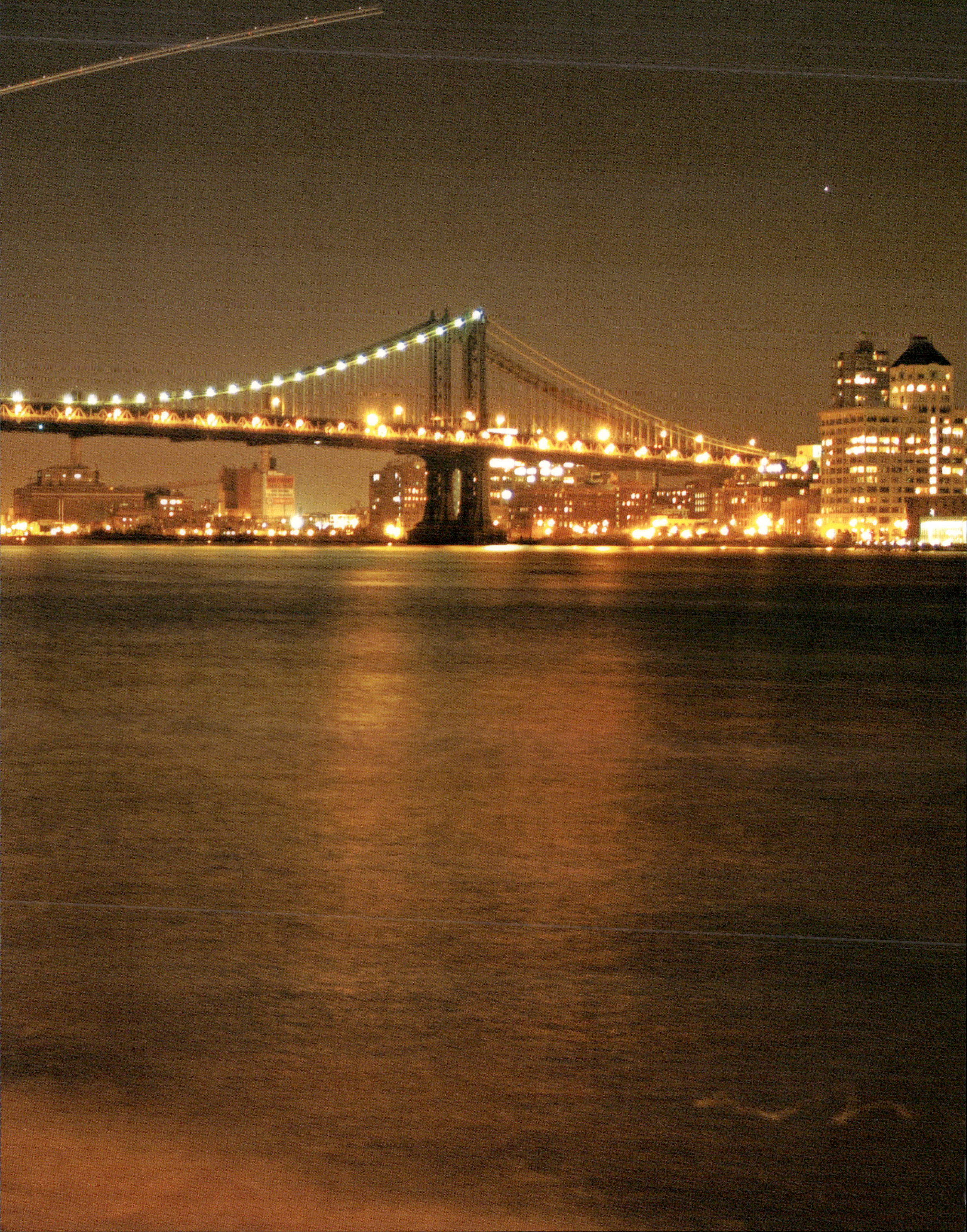

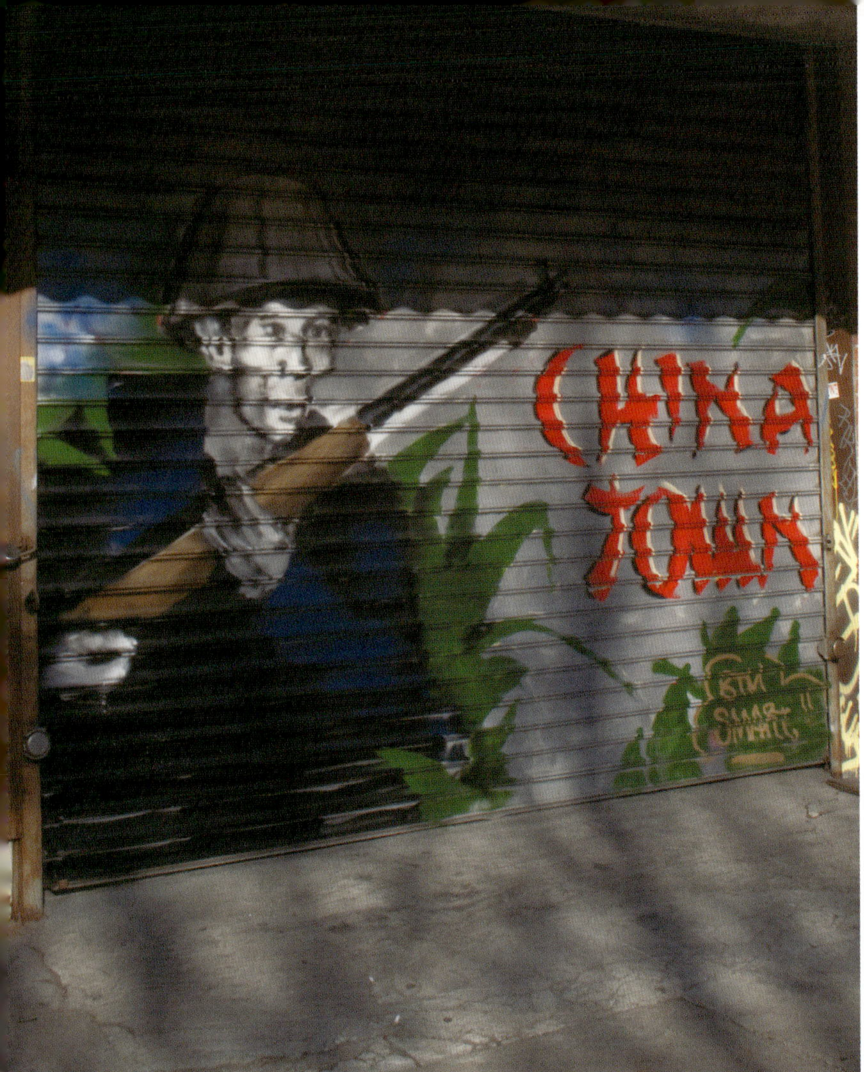

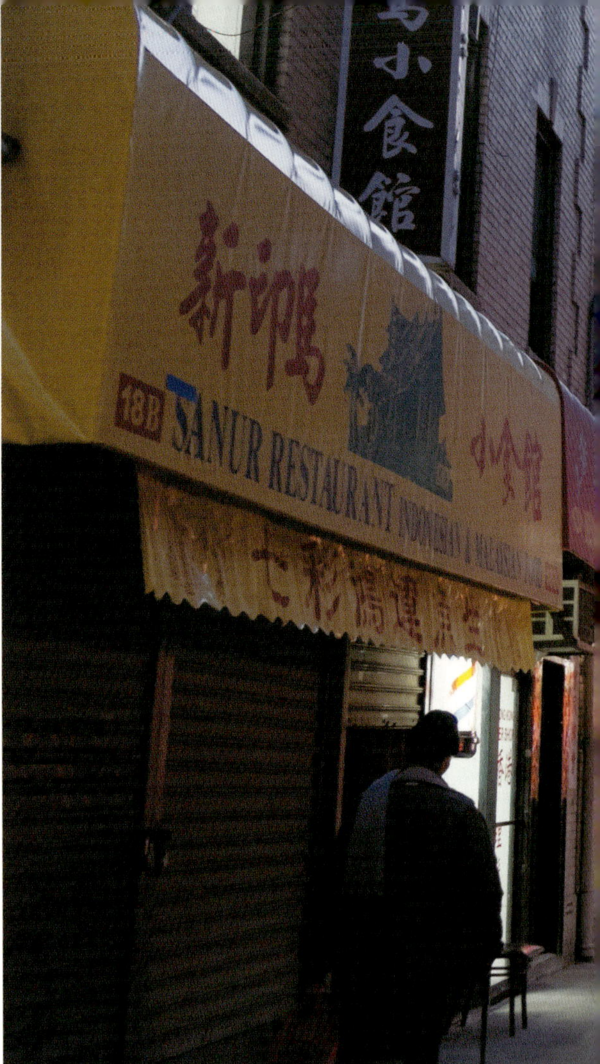

I WAS PRETTY PROUD OF MY CHINATOWN PAD. Although it was a bit rough around the edges, it was all mine. True, the stairs were creaking and the floorboards worn out, but it represented an exciting time when I was establishing myself as a professional photographer. It didn't have every amenity—far from it. The clapped-out fridge often kept me awake at night and there wasn't any air conditioning. In the summer nights, I'd prop a window open with a telephone book to catch a cool breeze. Well, one night one of the many stray cats that patrolled the back alleys behind Chinese restaurants took my jacked-up window as an open invitation. It crept into the room, only to be met by my feisty little Labrador mix. That's when these two tough little critters decided to settle their turf dispute right in the middle of my bed. I awoke with a violent start—and probably some cursing that woke most of my neighbors. I've never felt my heart beat so fast! The next day I treated myself to an air conditioner—keeping a safe (and cool) distance between me and New York's urban wildlife. I never saw that cat again, but every now and then I'd catch Charley looking at the window—anticipating a rematch, I suppose!

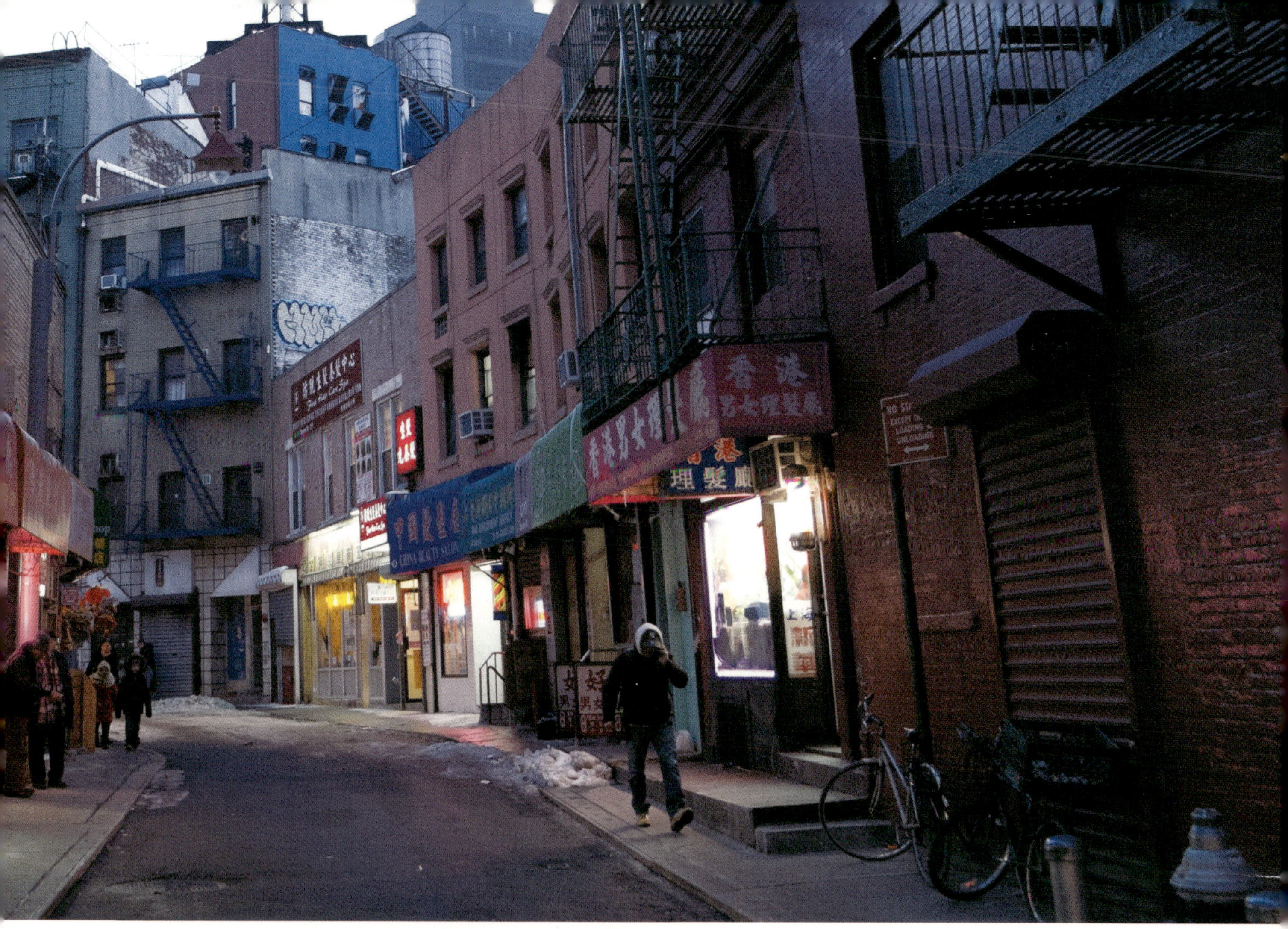
香港
男女理髮廠
理髮廠
CHINA BEAUTY SALON

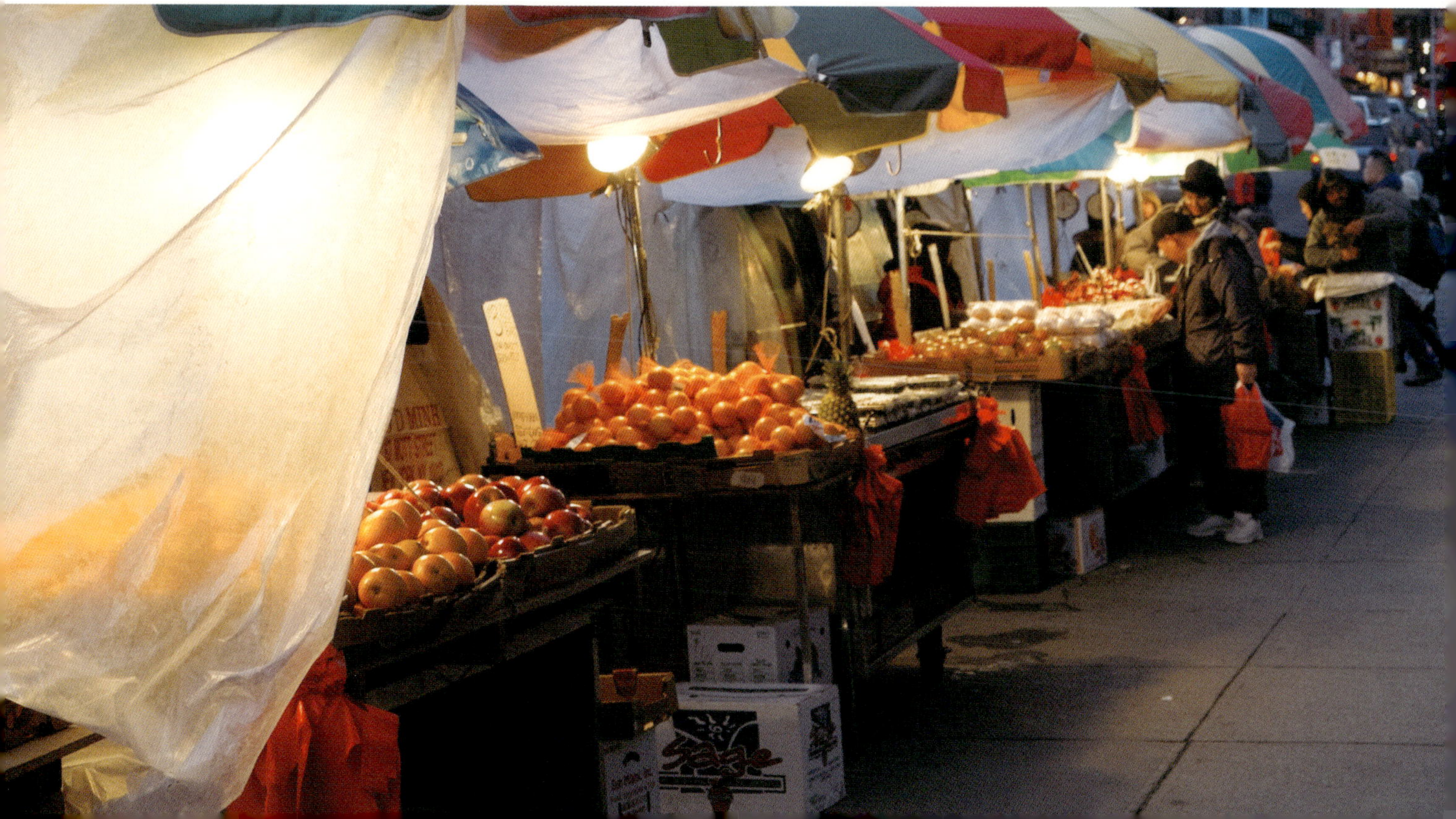

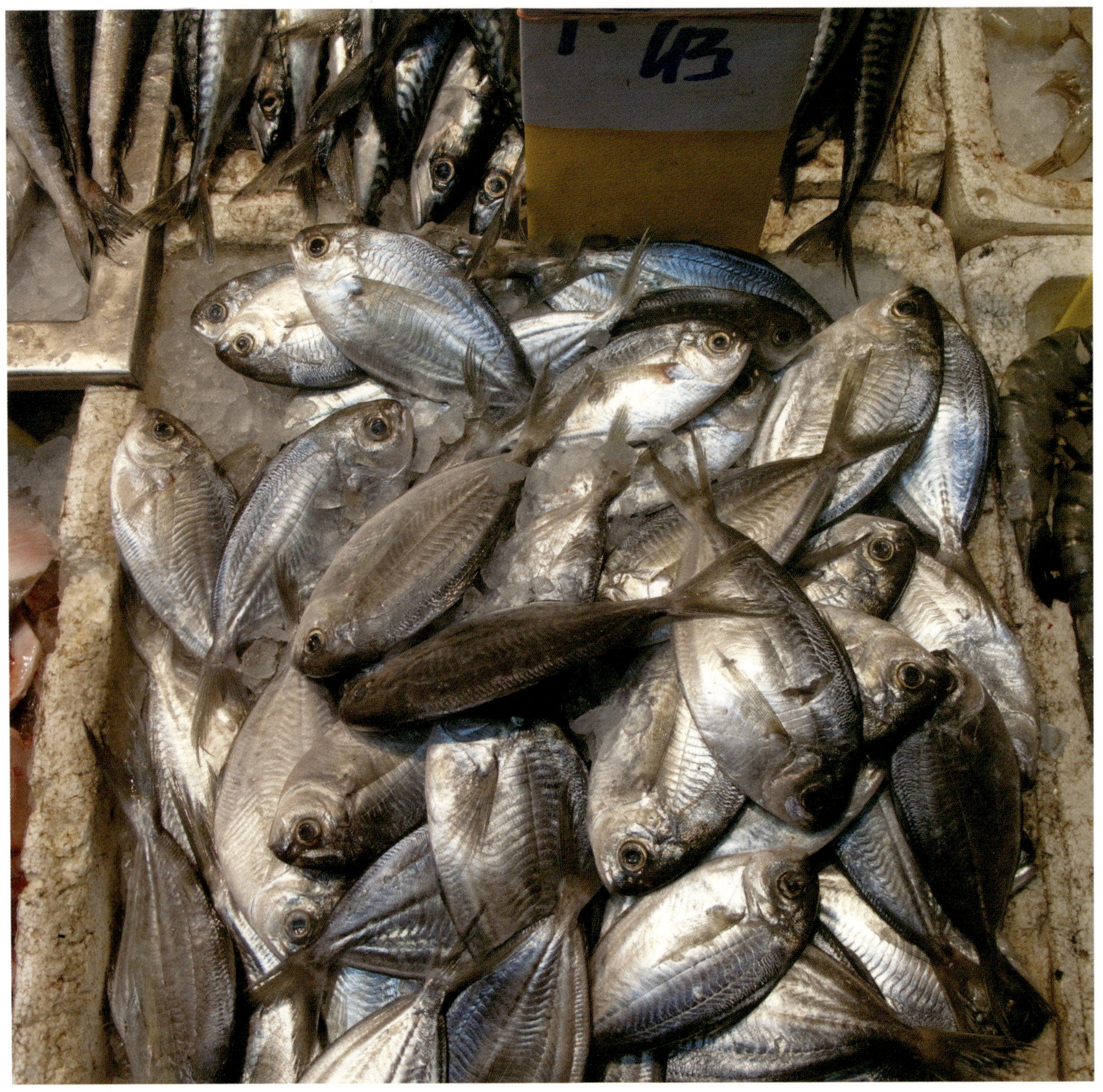

NEW YORK CONTAINS an amazing collection of ethnic markets, offering spices, condiments, and exotic fruits and vegetables for every kind of dish.

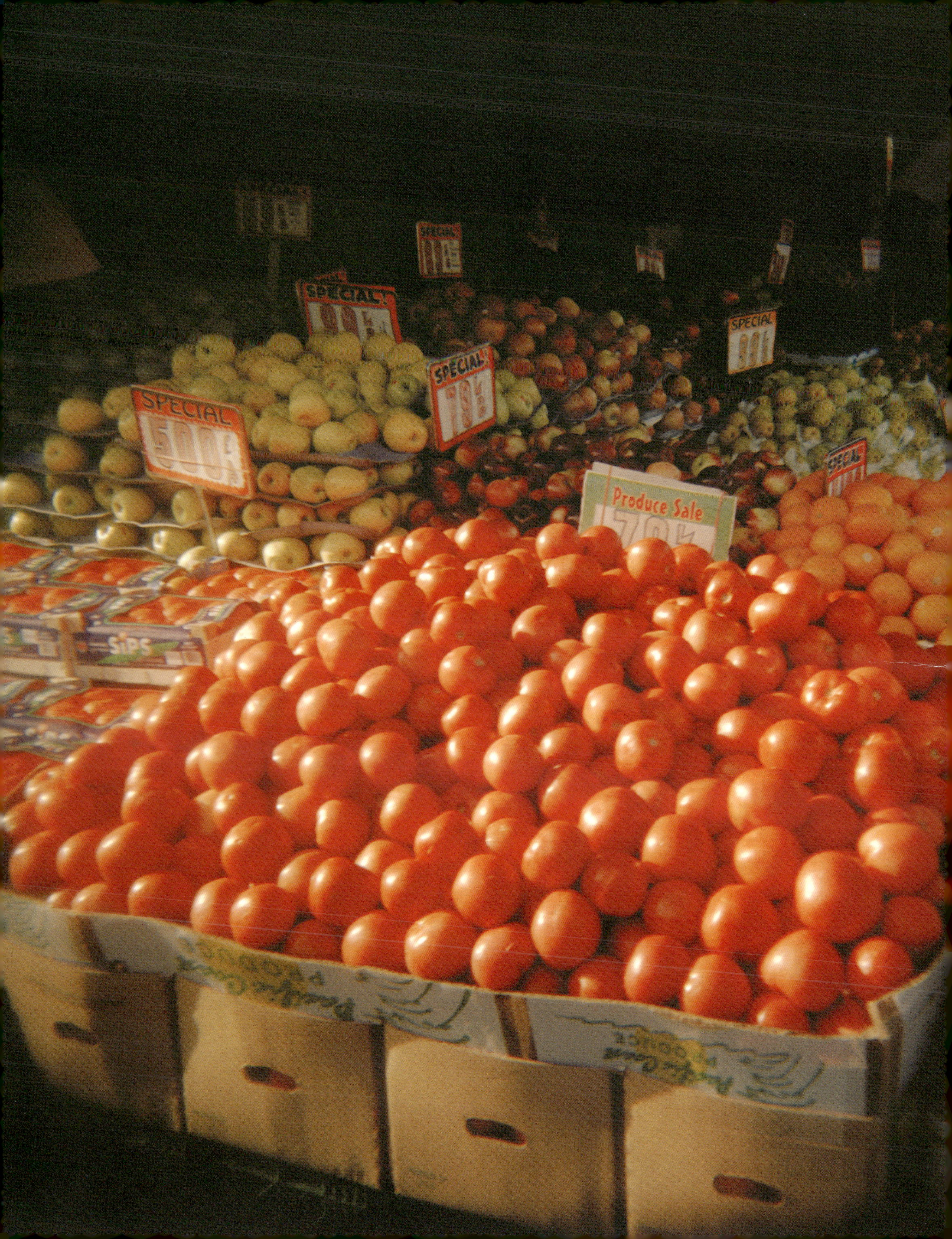

SPECIAL!
SPECIAL
SPECIAL
SPECIAL
SPECIAL
Produce Sale
SiPS

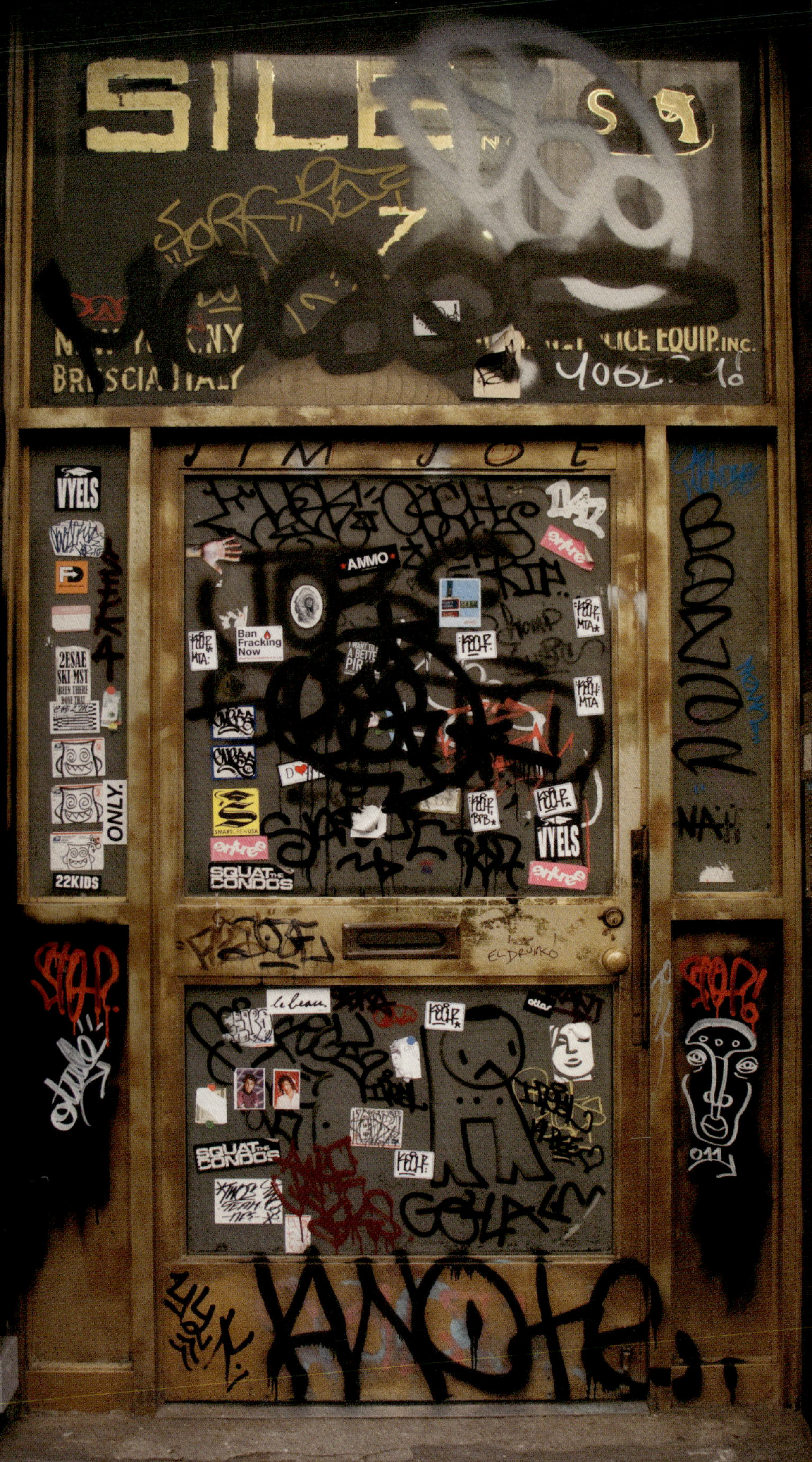
VYELS
AMMO
Ban Fracking Now
SQUAT THE CONDOS
22KIDS
ONLY.
VYELS
SQUAT THE CONDOS

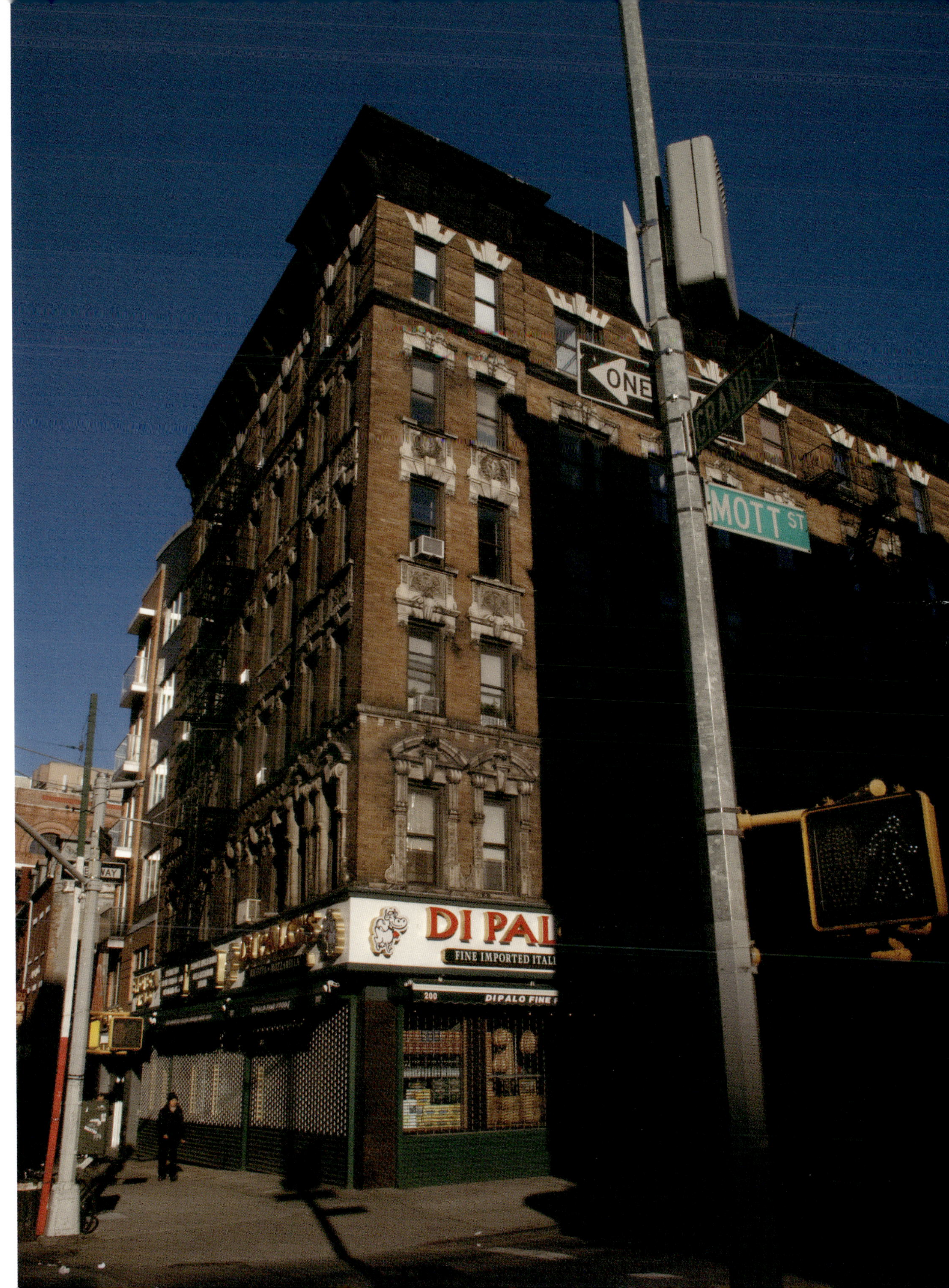
ONE
GRAND ST
MOTT ST
DI PAL
FINE IMPORTED ITALI
200

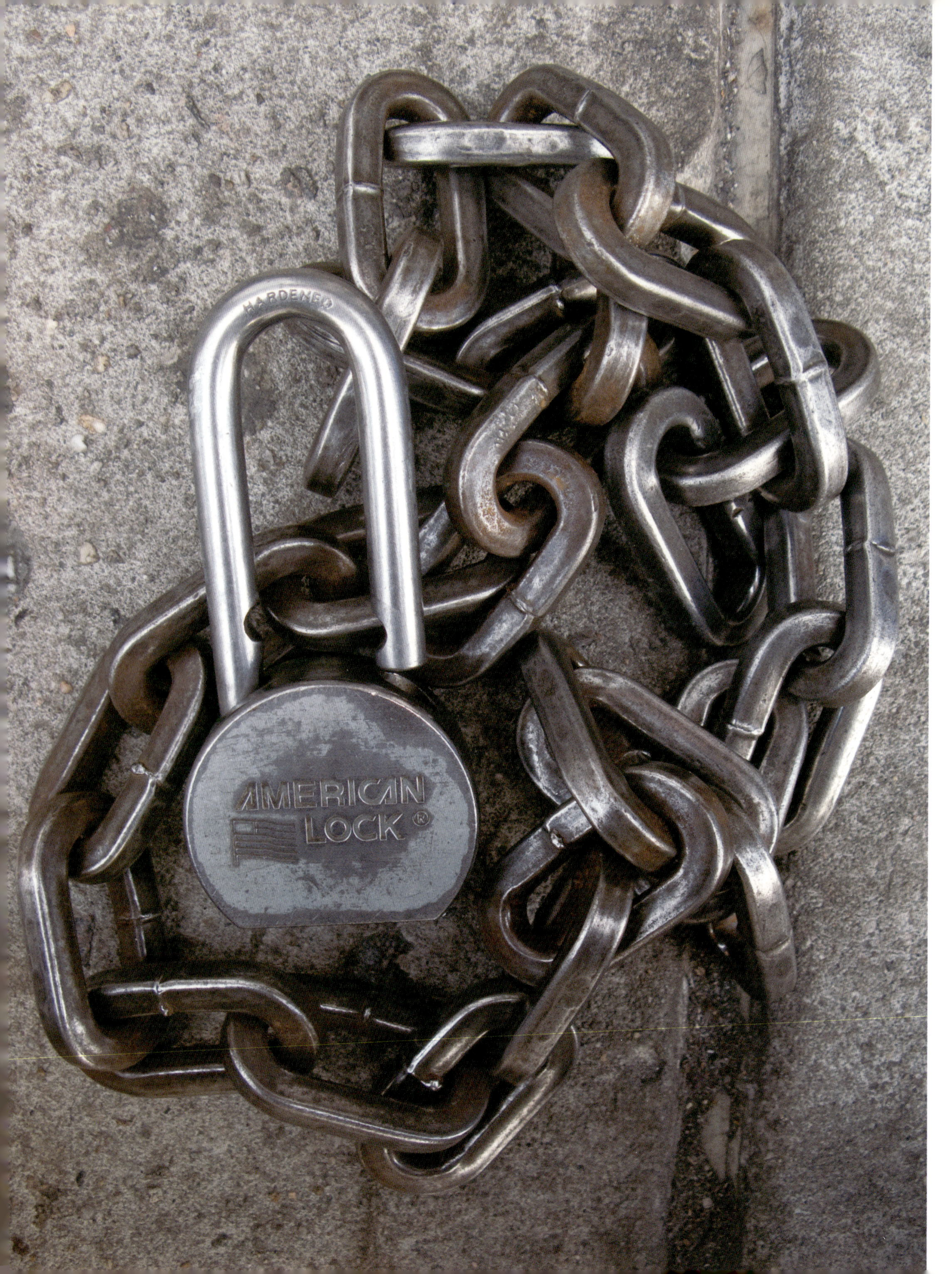
HARDENED
AMERICAN
LOCK ®

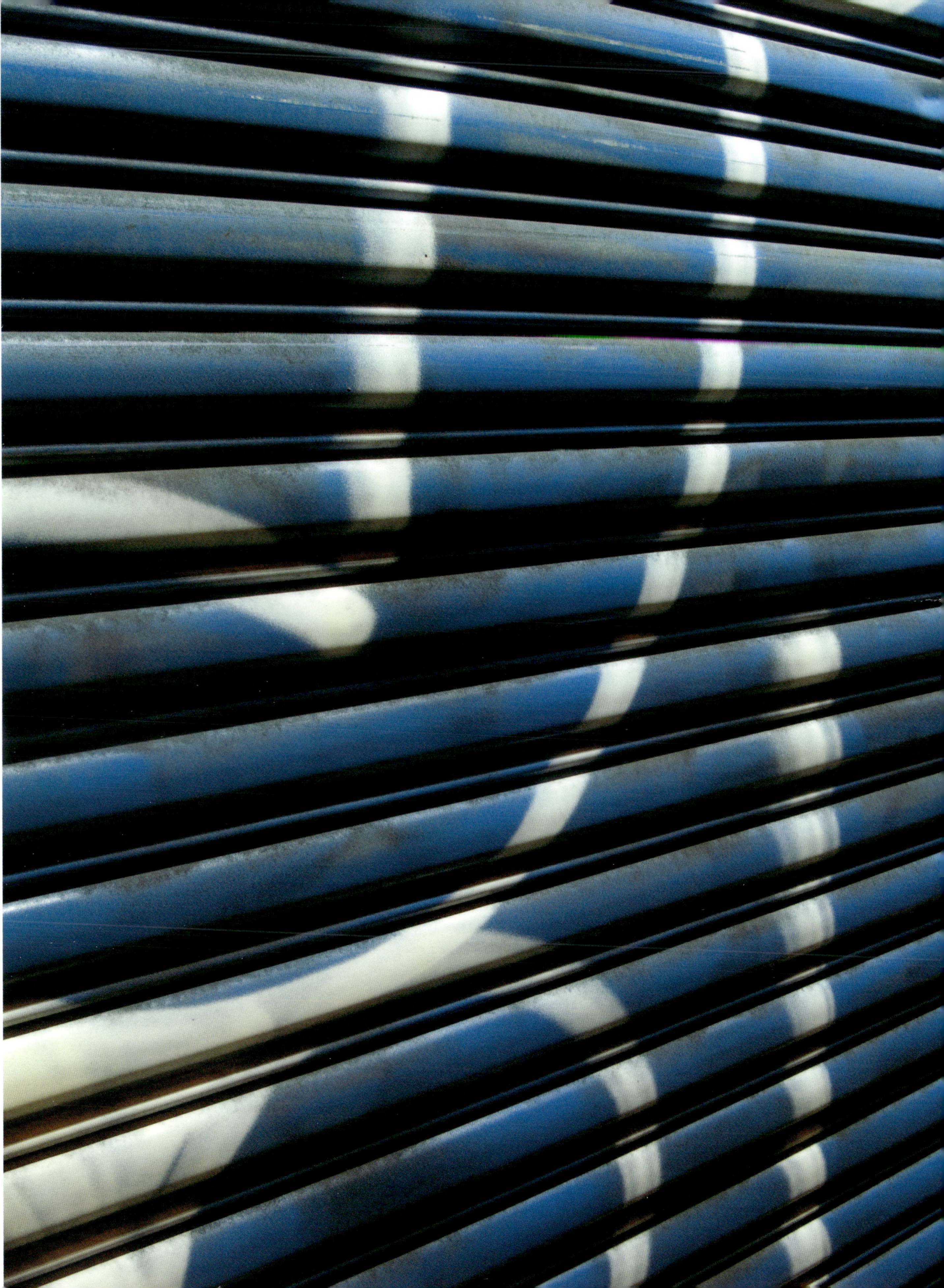

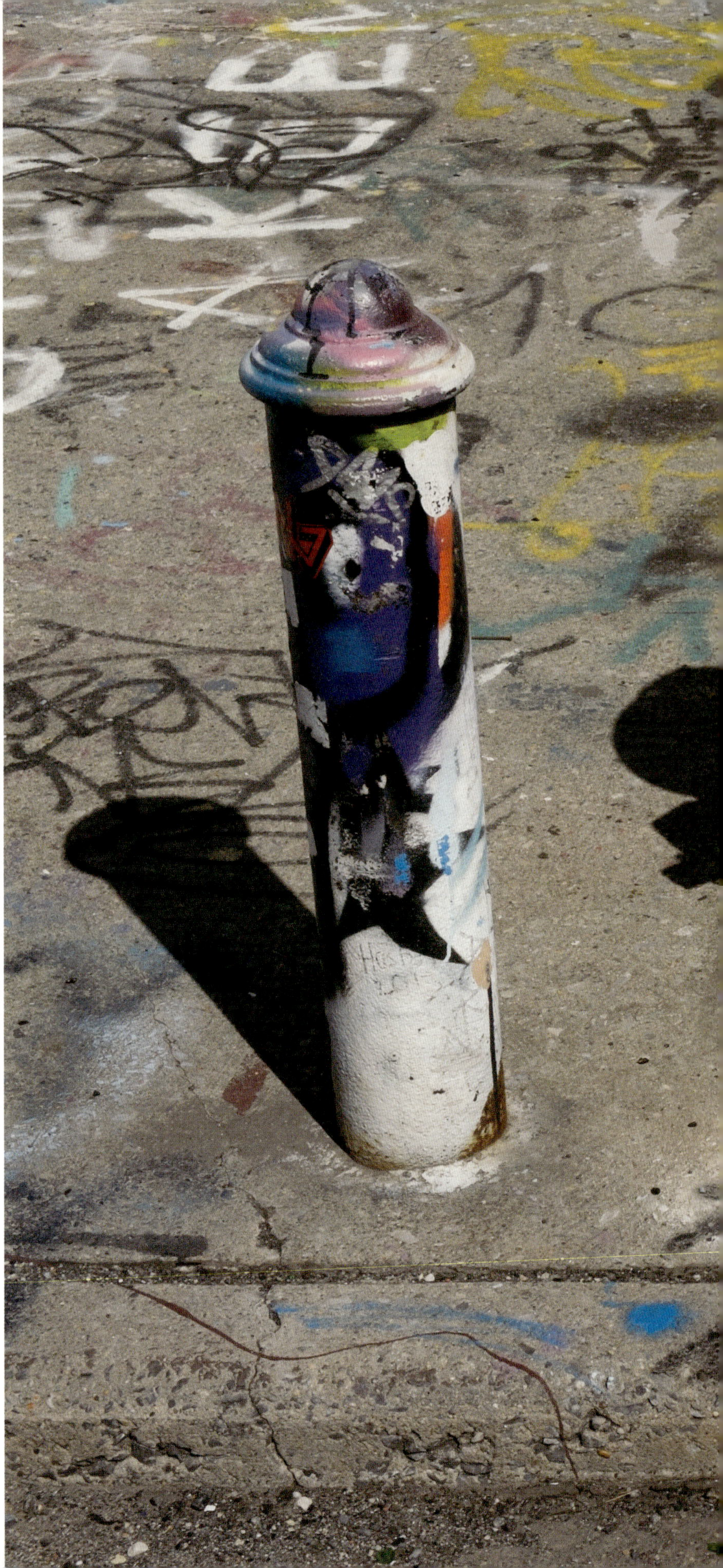

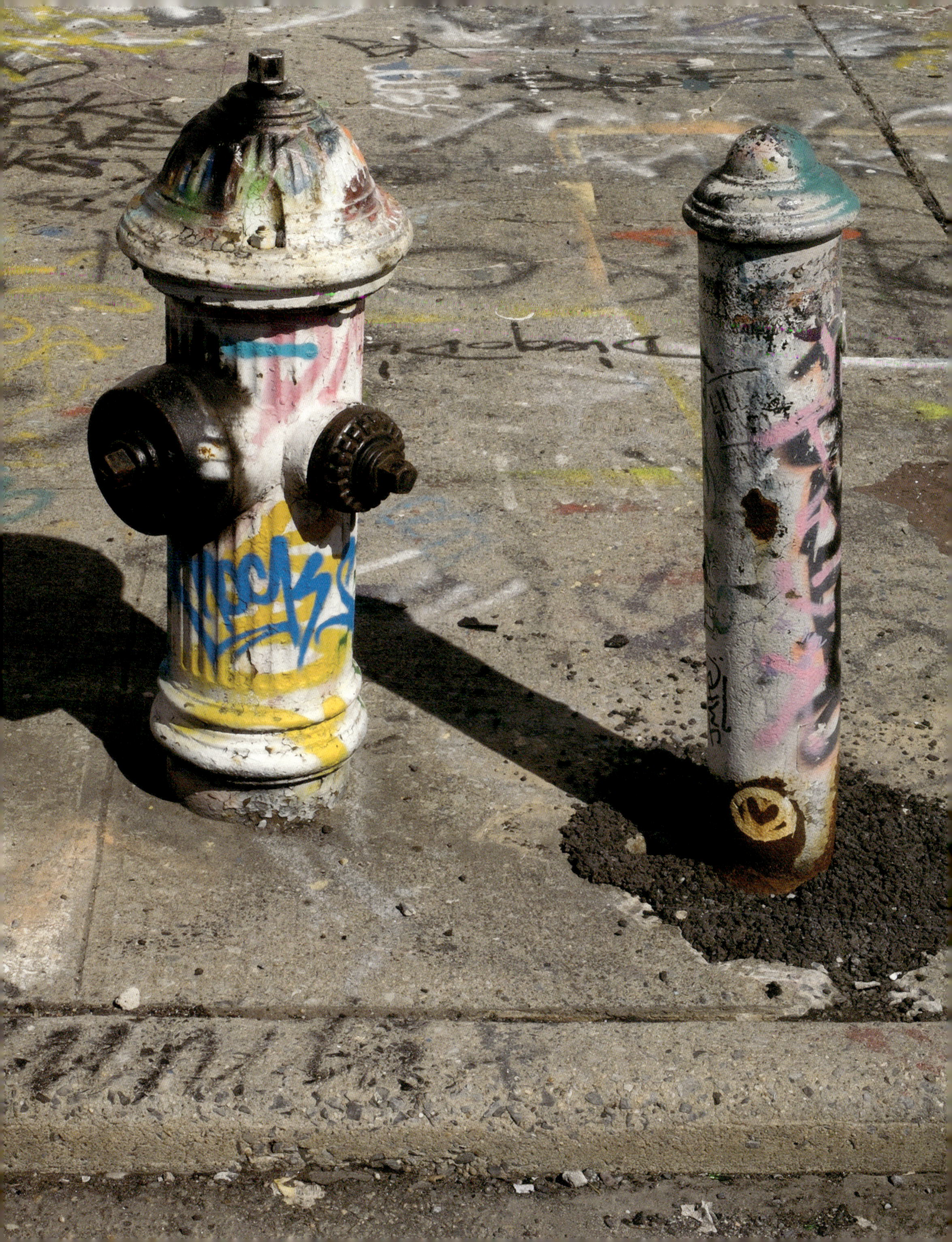

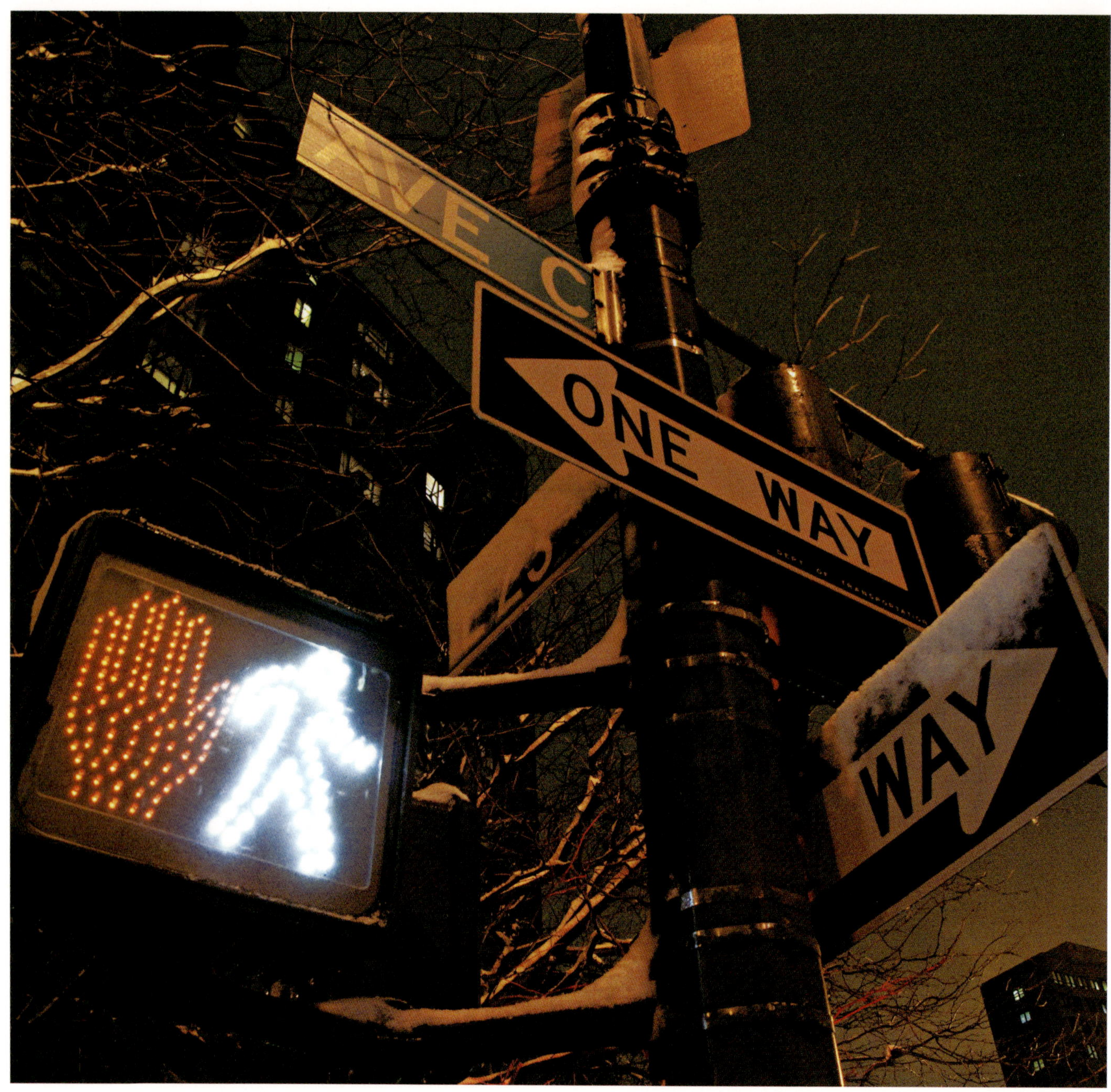

WHEN SNOW FALLS IN THE CITY, it changes the whole atmosphere. First it dampens the acoustics so the traffic noise and sirens sound much farther away. Then as it accumulates, fresh snow blankets the garbage and rough sidewalks. As the snow plow struggle to keep the streets clear, they create massive mounds of snow at the intersections. Never the most patient of people, New Yorkers trudge across these man-made obstacle courses, muttering as they plunge into unexpected pockets of slush. Still there can be a cozy vibe for those who brave the elements to congregate in local bars and restaurants—a friendliness that can be quite surprising for a big city.

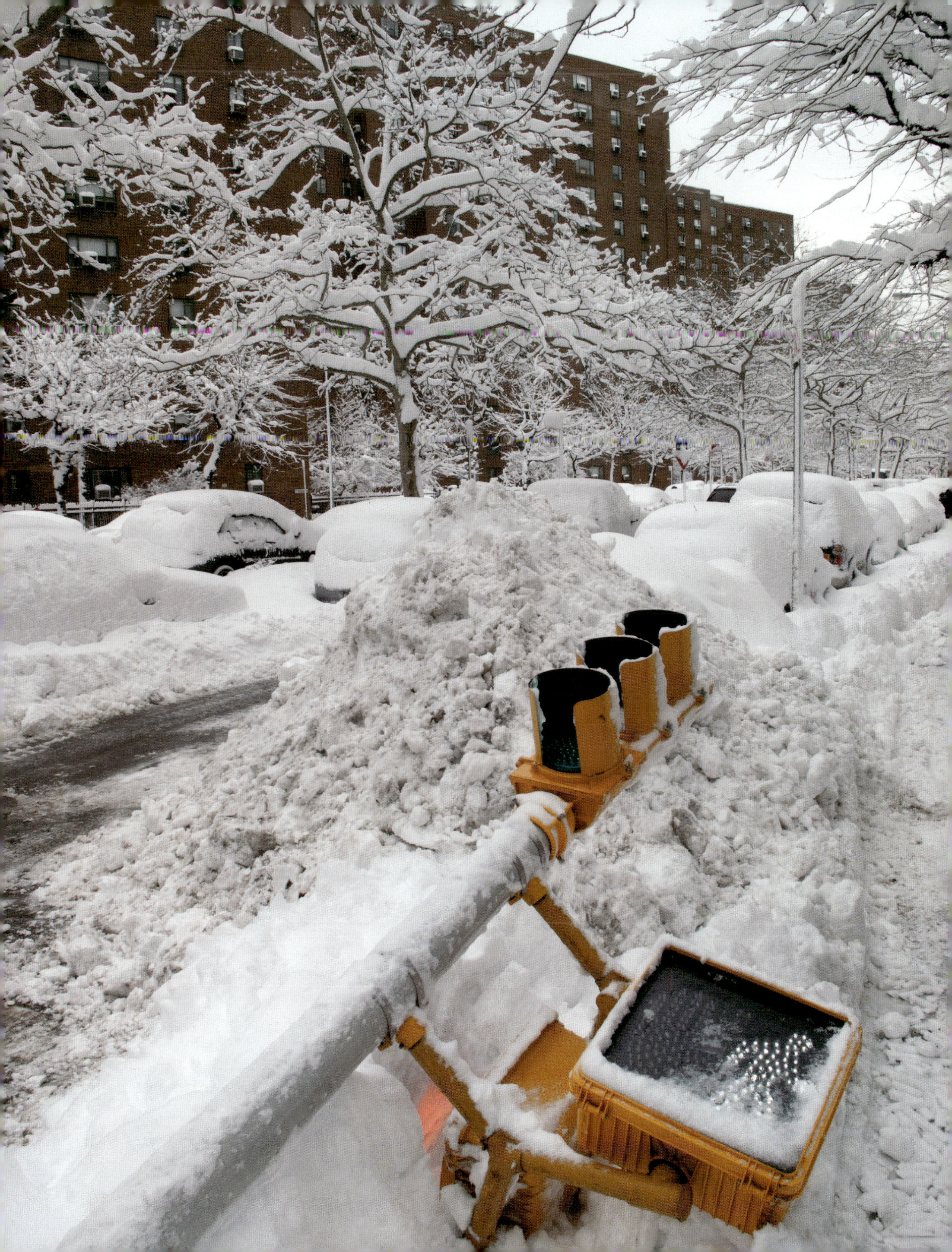

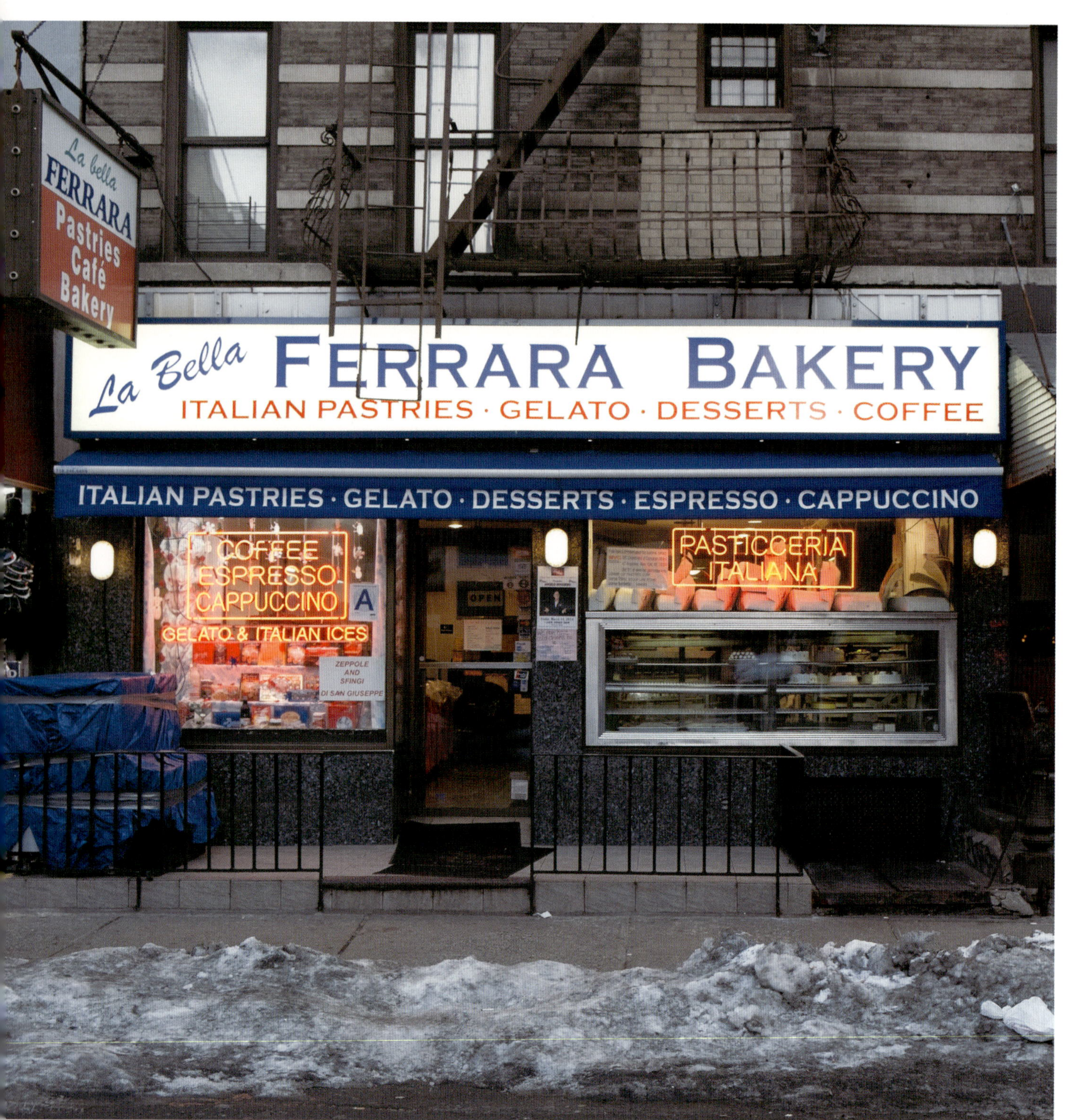
La bella
FERRARA
Pastries
Café
Bakery
La Bella FERRARA BAKERY
ITALIAN PASTRIES · GELATO · DESSERTS · COFFEE
ITALIAN PASTRIES · GELATO · DESSERTS · ESPRESSO · CAPPUCCINO
COFFEE
ESPRESSO
CAPPUCCINO
GELATO & ITALIAN ICES
ZEPPOLE
AND
SFINGI
DI SAN GIUSEPPE
OPEN
PASTICCERIA
ITALIANA

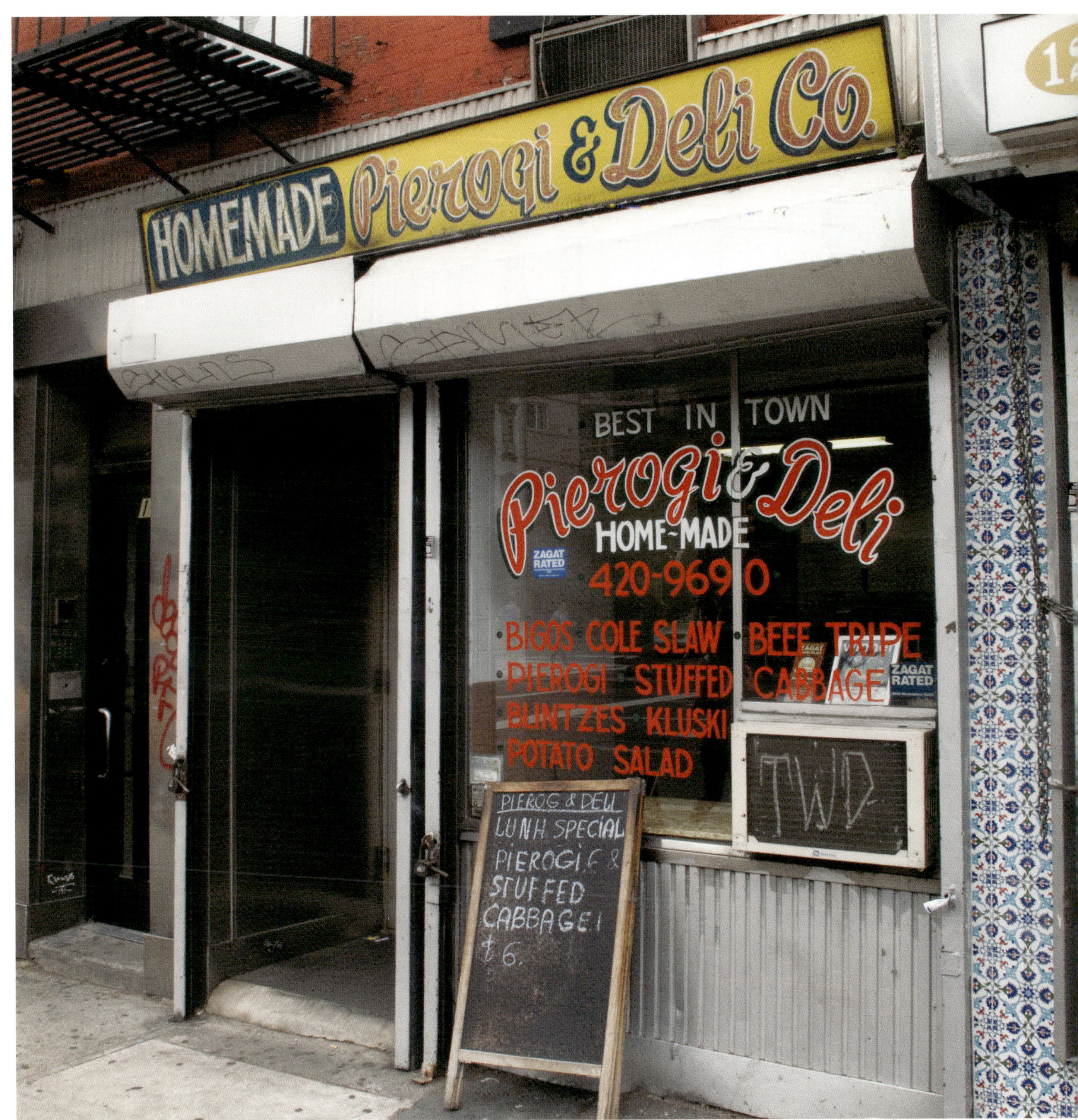
HOMEMADE Pierogi & Deli Co.
BEST IN TOWN
Pierogi & Deli
HOME-MADE
ZAGAT RATED
420-9690
BIGOS COLE SLAW BEEF TRIPE
PIEROGI STUFFED CABBAGE
BLINTZES KLUSKI
POTATO SALAD
PIEROG & DELI
LUNH SPECIAL
PIEROGI &
STUFFED
CABBAGE
$6.
TWD

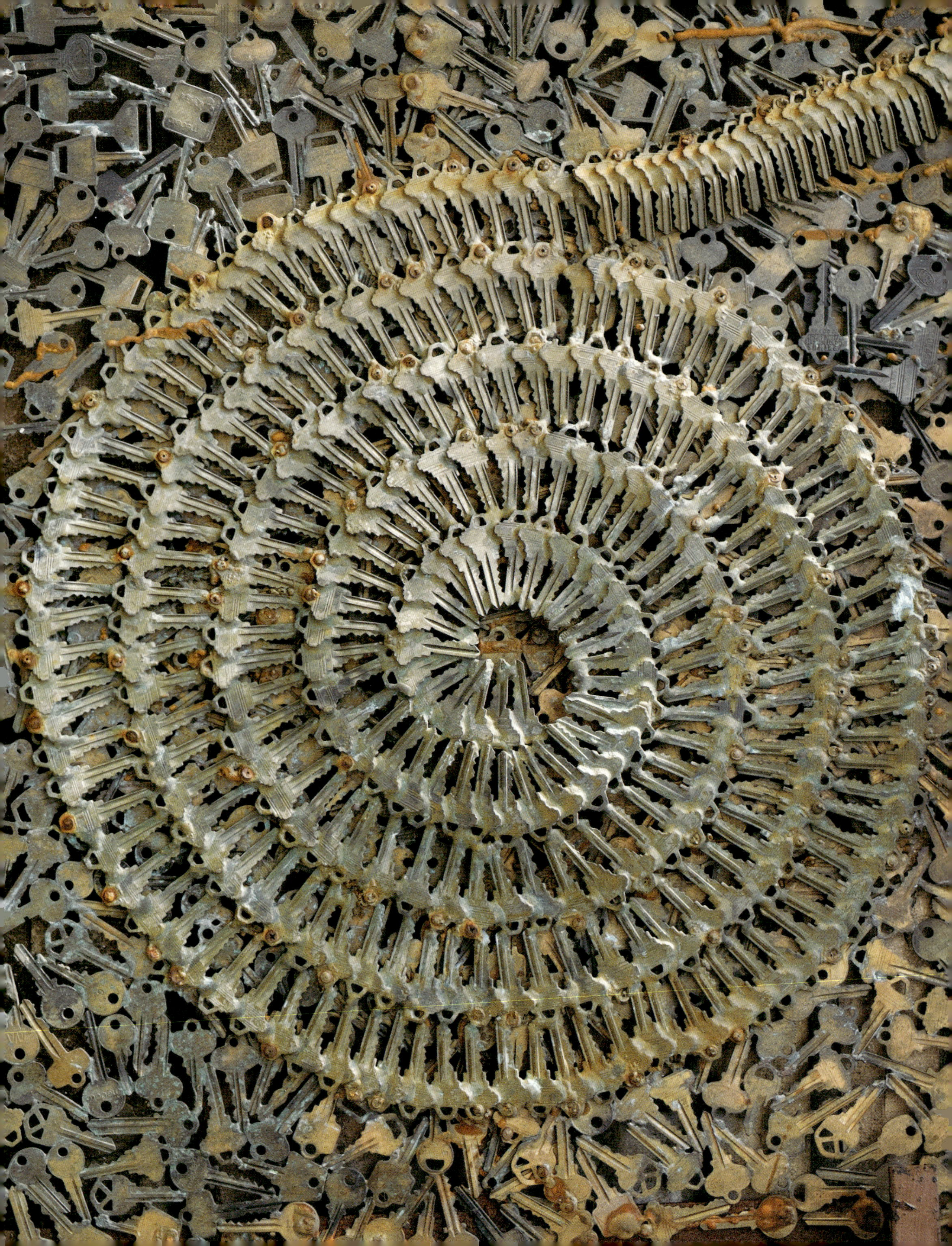

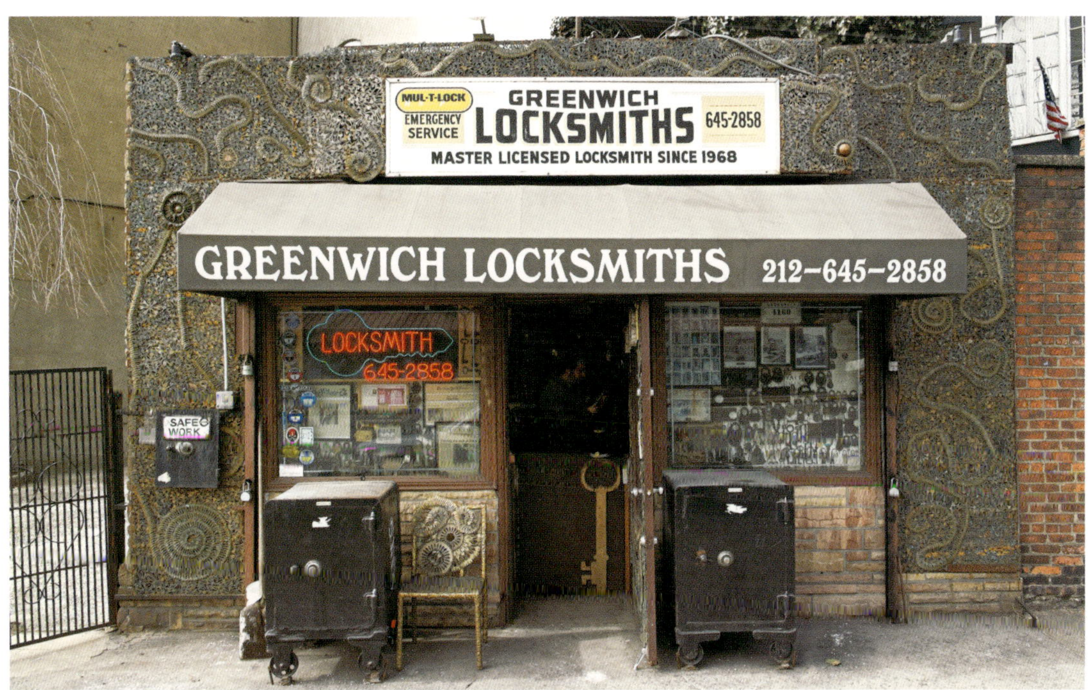

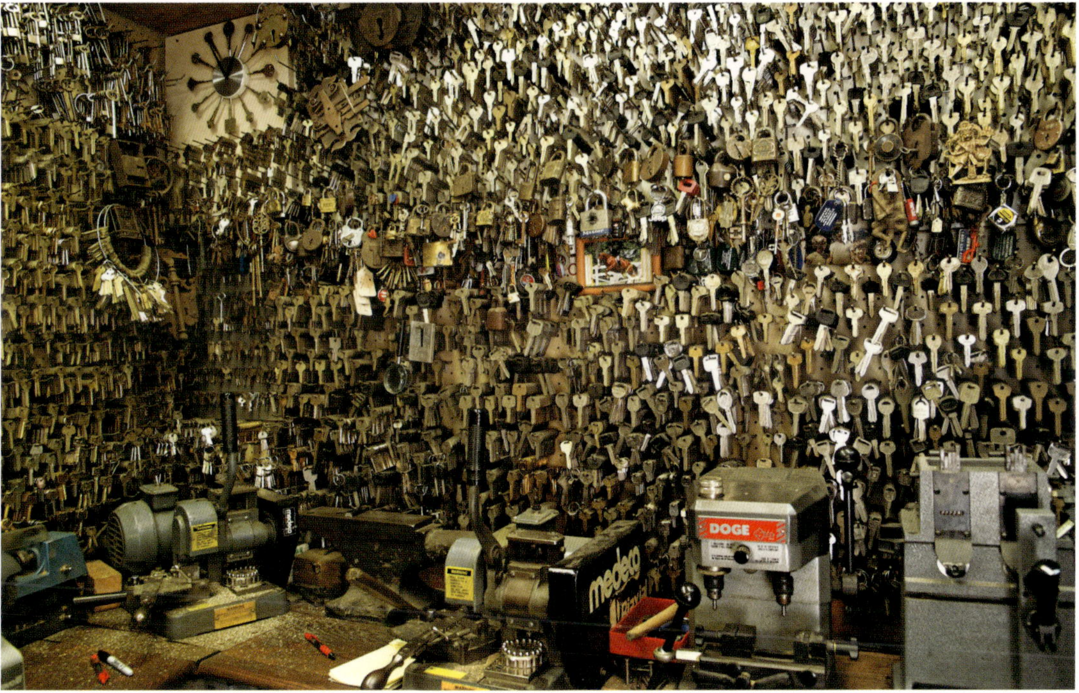

EVEN IN THIS HIGH-TECH AGE, keys are some of the most important objects we own. Lose one and you might be out on the streets or find that there's no way your fancy new bike is ever coming unchained from that railing. Greenwich Locksmiths has been helping New Yorkers get into their apartments and ride on their bikes for over thirty years. Along with their technical expertise, owner Phil and his son (also named Phil) have created a monument to this humble tool so necessary to all our lives. Every inch, inside and out, is covered with hundreds and hundreds of keys, all arranged precisely into swirling, complicated patterns that decorate every surface. I love this unique shrine to keys and locksmiths—an ancient trade that's just as important now as it ever was.

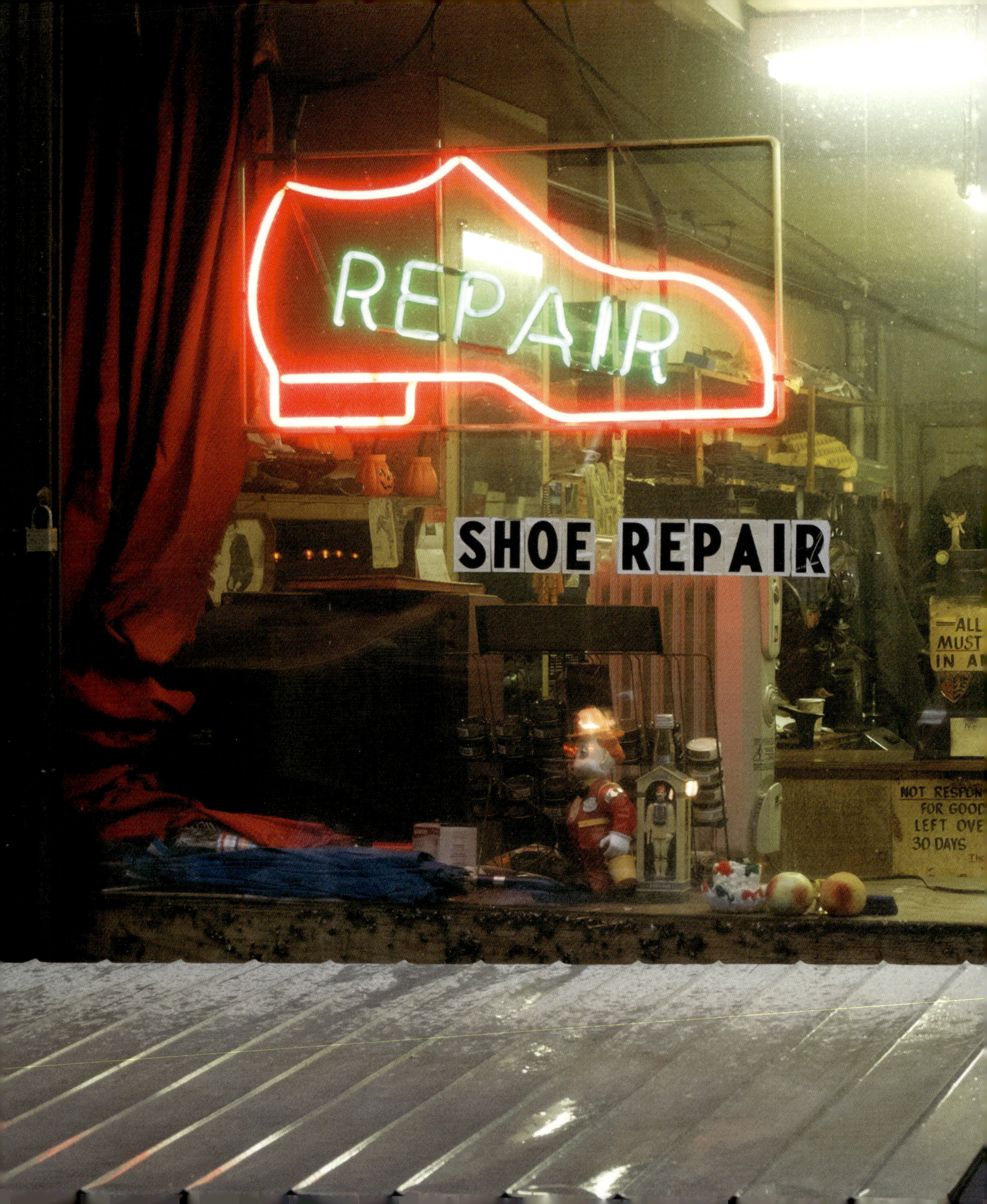
REPAIR
SHOE REPAIR

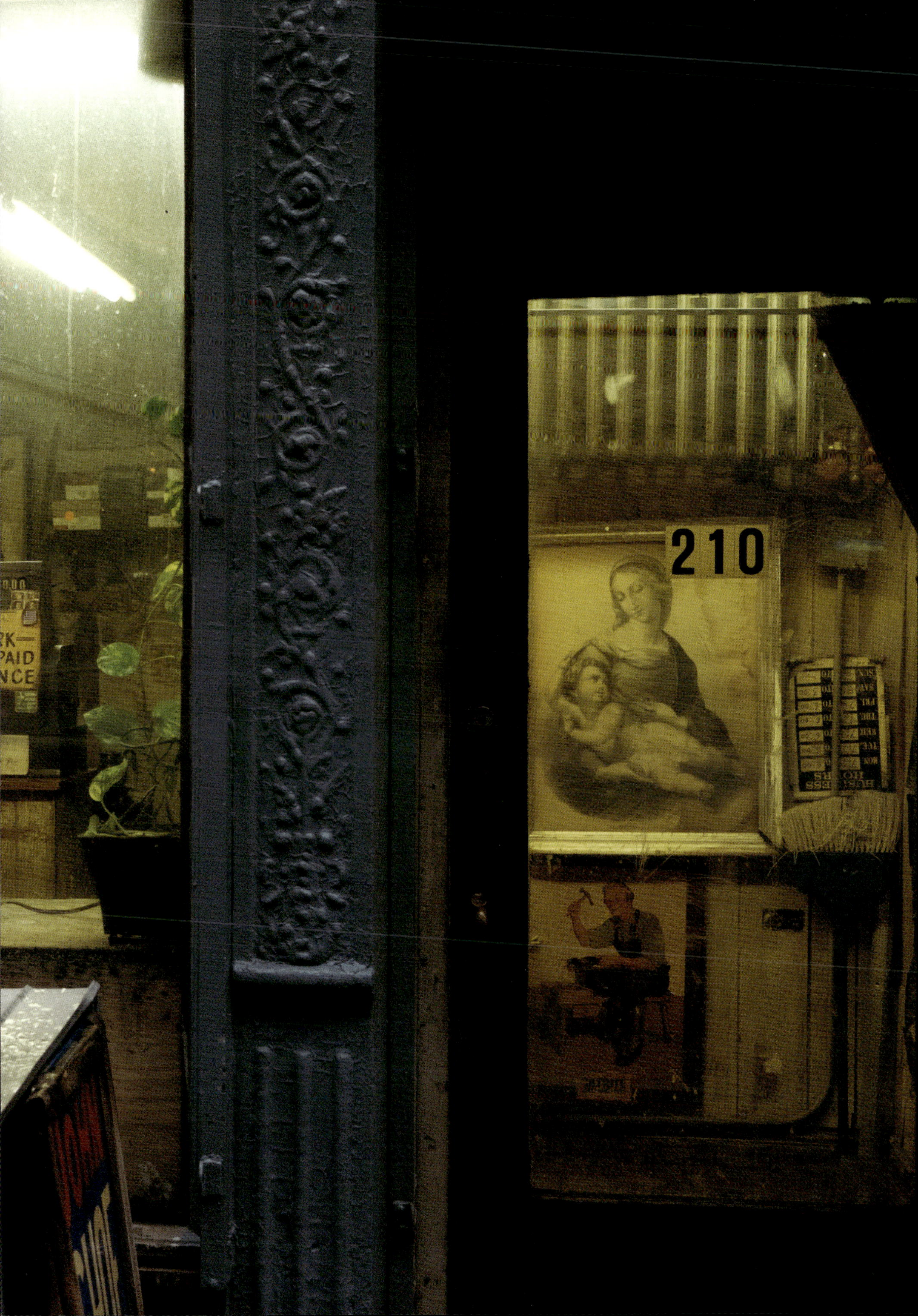
PAID
210

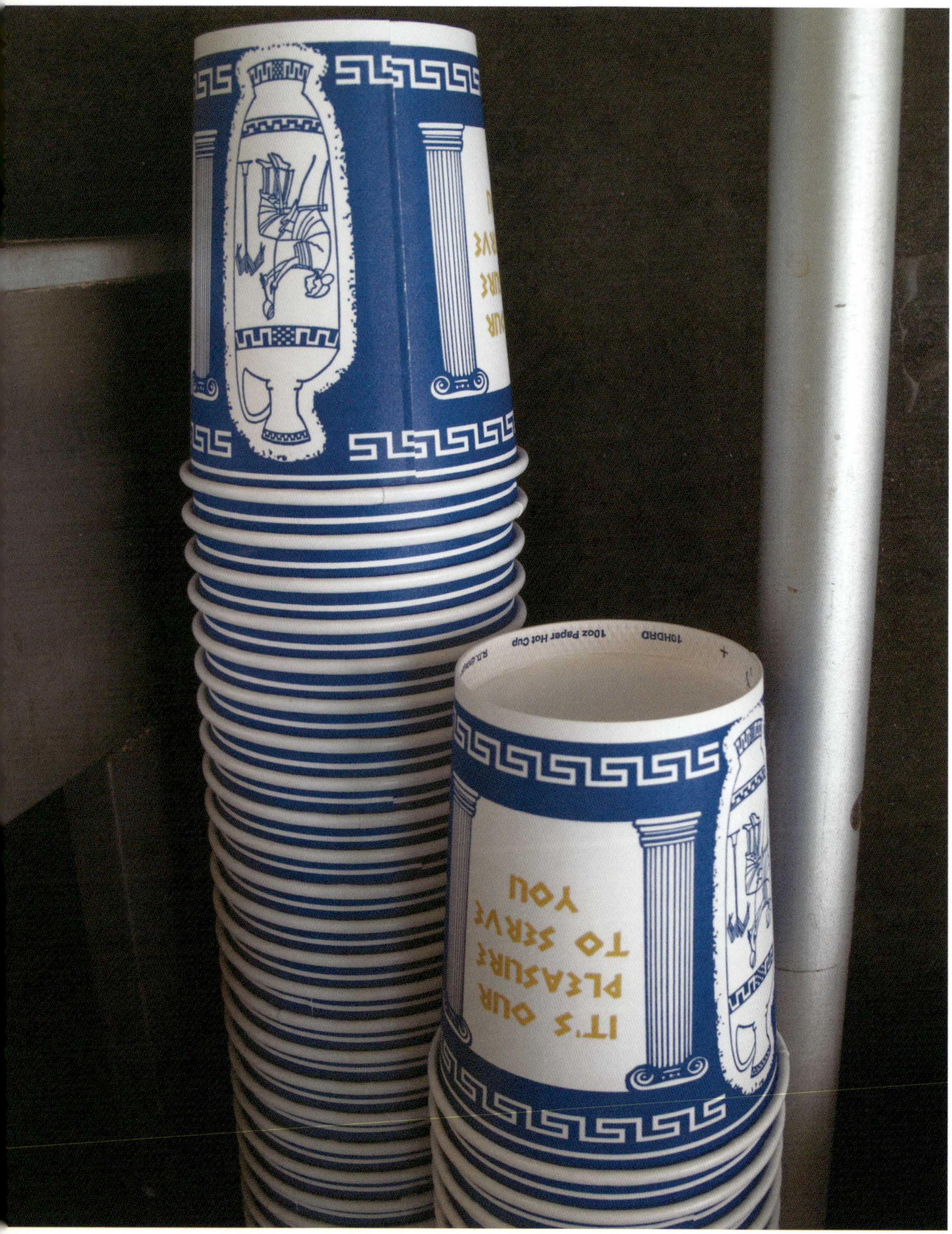

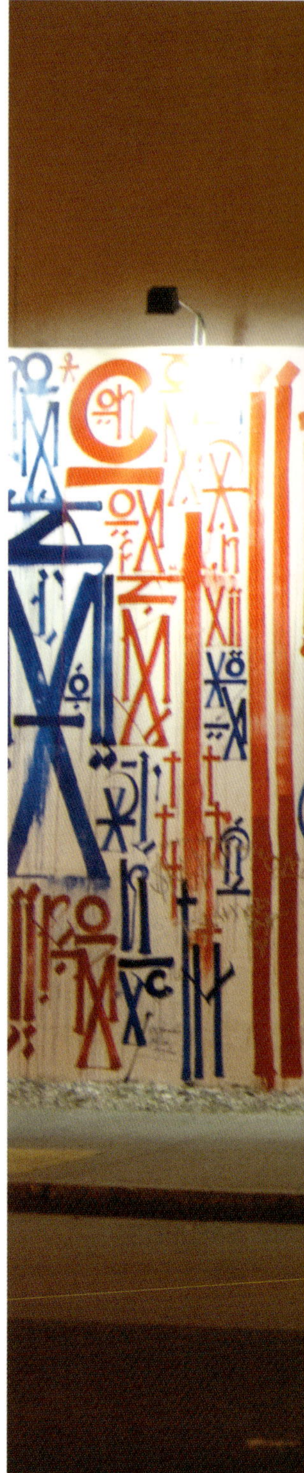

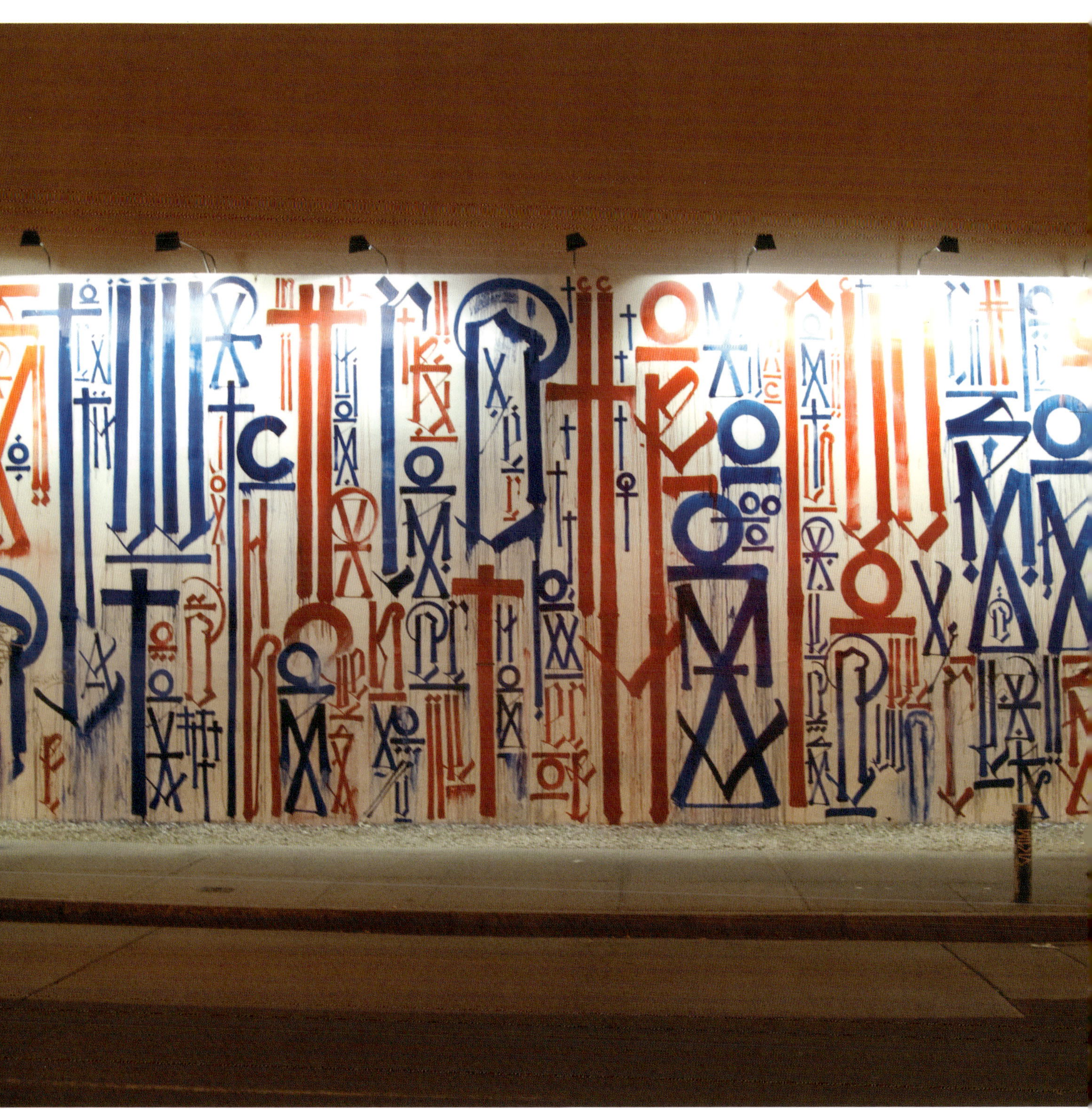

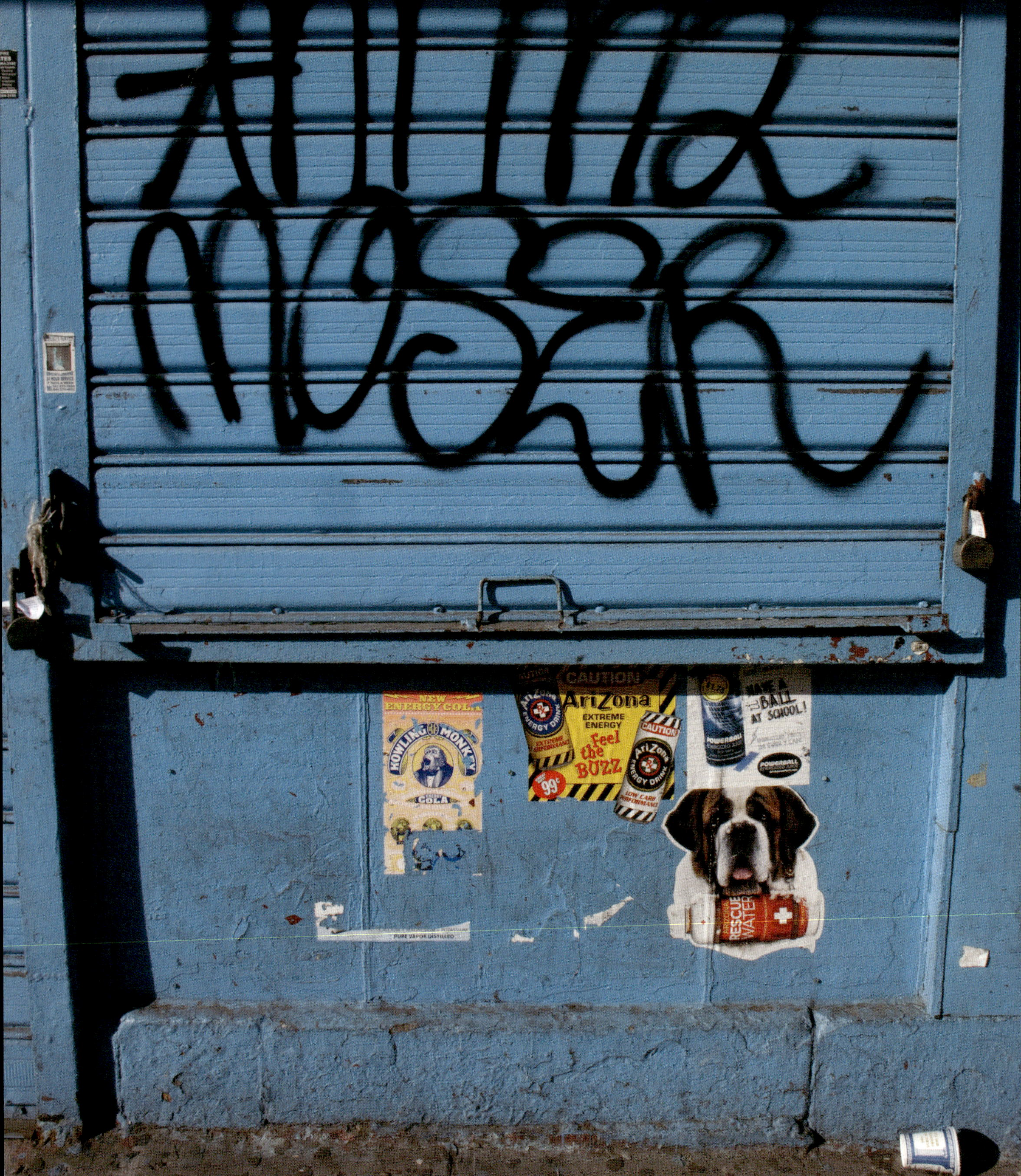
NEW
ENERGY COLA
HOWLING MONKEY
COLA
CAUTION
AriZona
EXTREME
ENERGY
Feel
the
BUZZ
99¢
AriZona
ENERGY DRINK
EXTREME PERFORMANCE
CAUTION
AriZona
ENERGY DRINK
LOW CARB
PERFORMANCE
HAVE A BALL AT SCHOOL!
POWERBALL
ARIZONA
RESCUE
WATER
PURE VAPOR DISTILLED

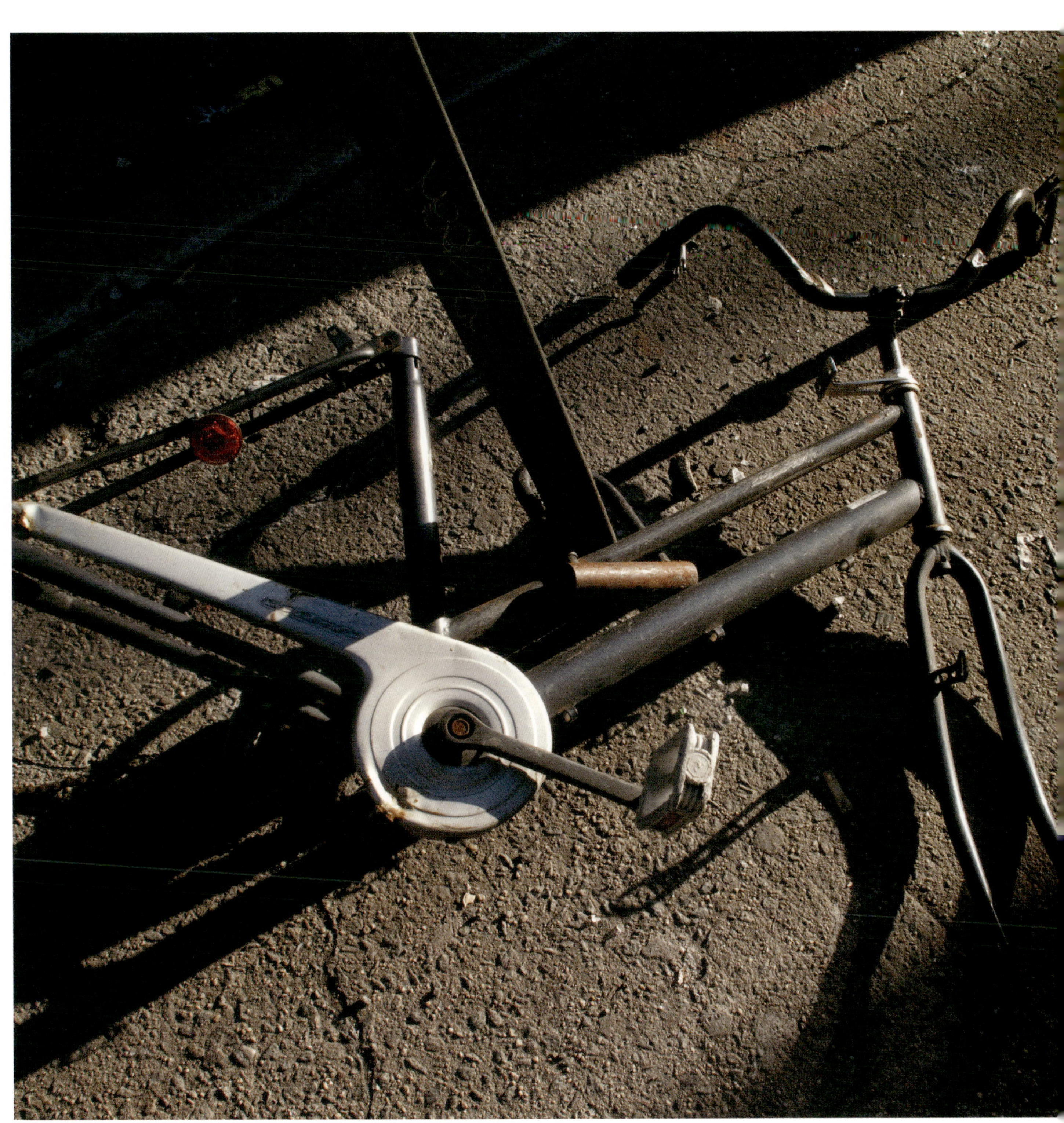

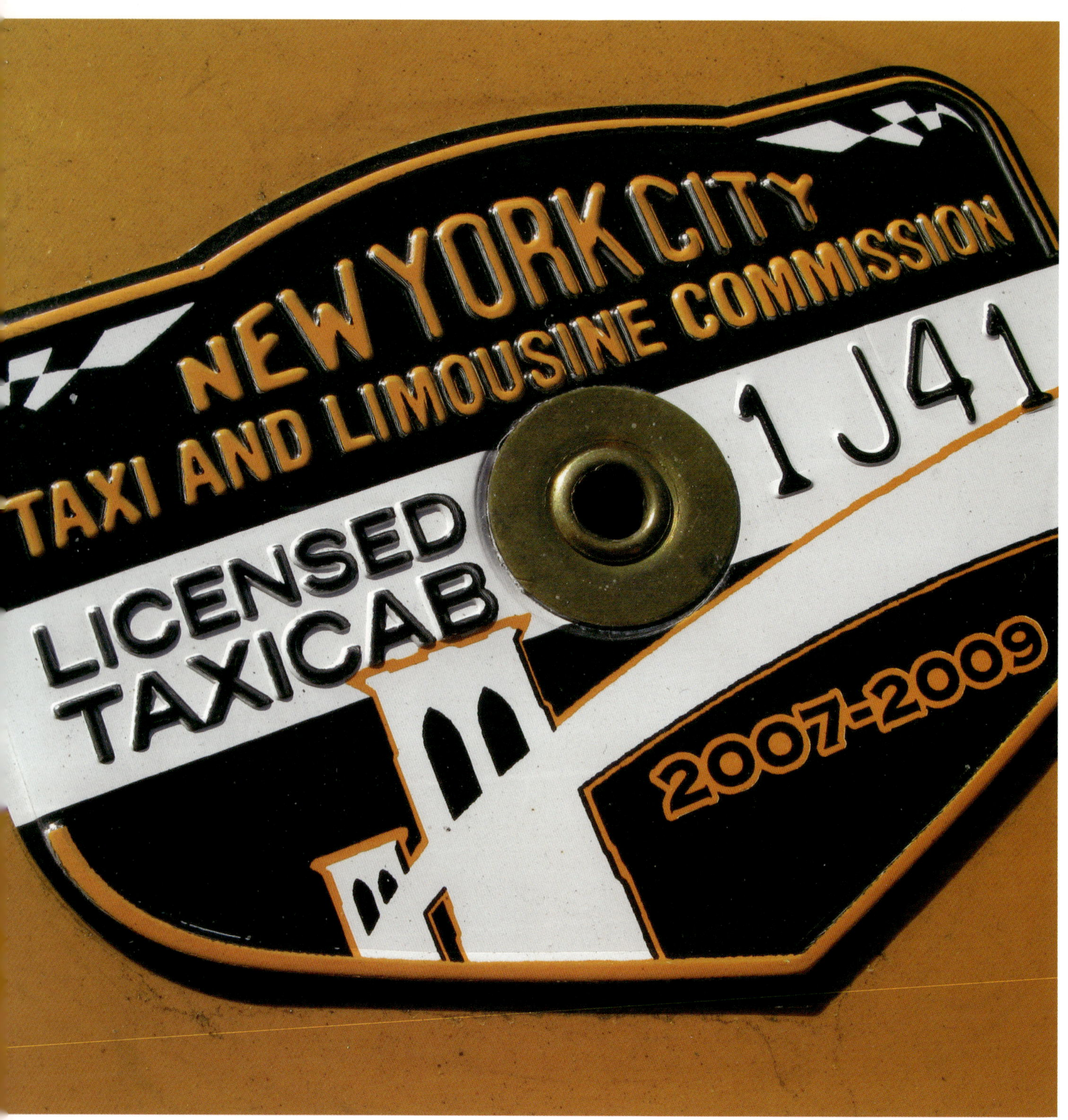
NEW YORK CITY
TAXI AND LIMOUSINE COMMISSION
1J41
LICENSED
TAXICAB
2007-2009

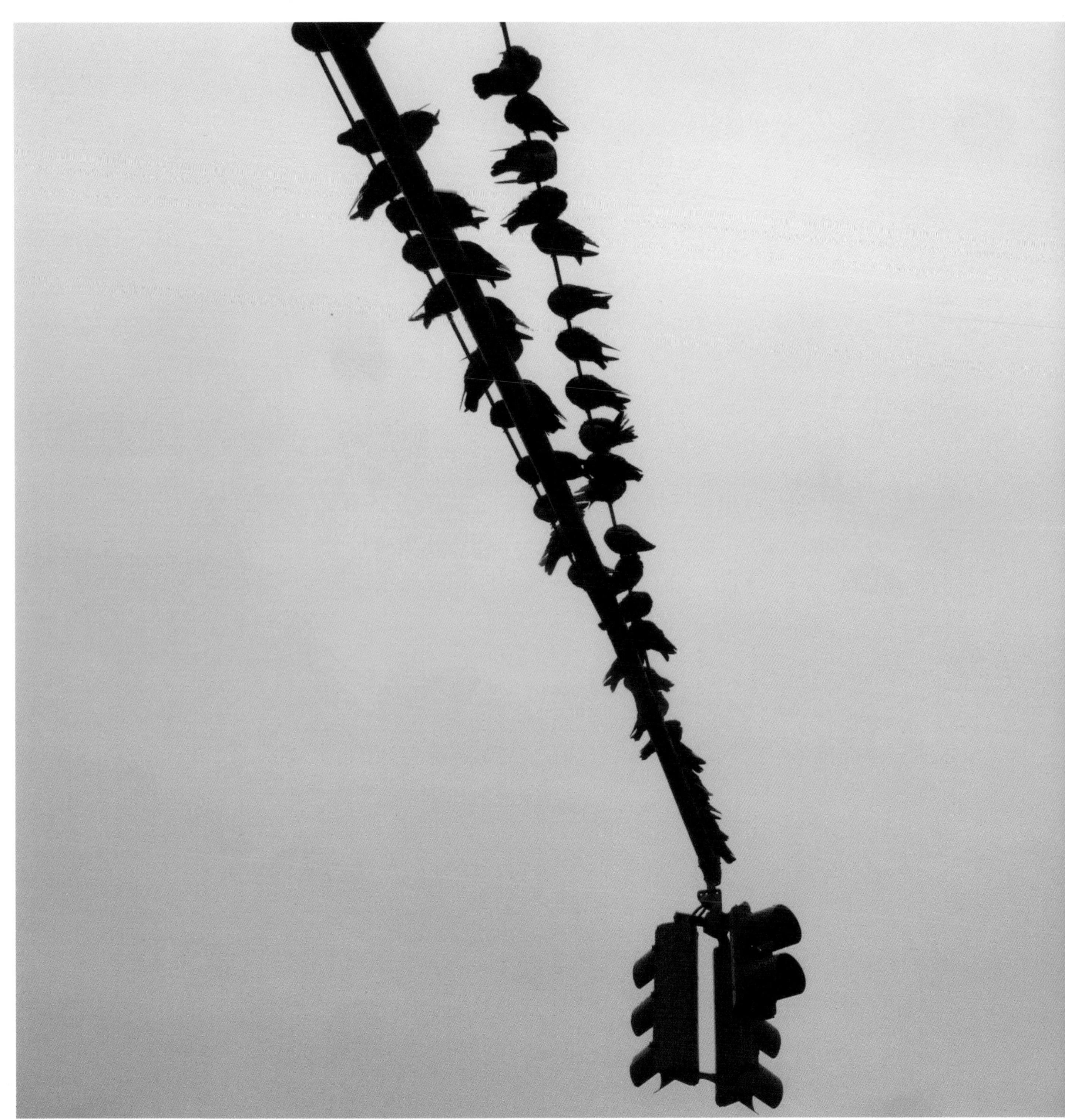

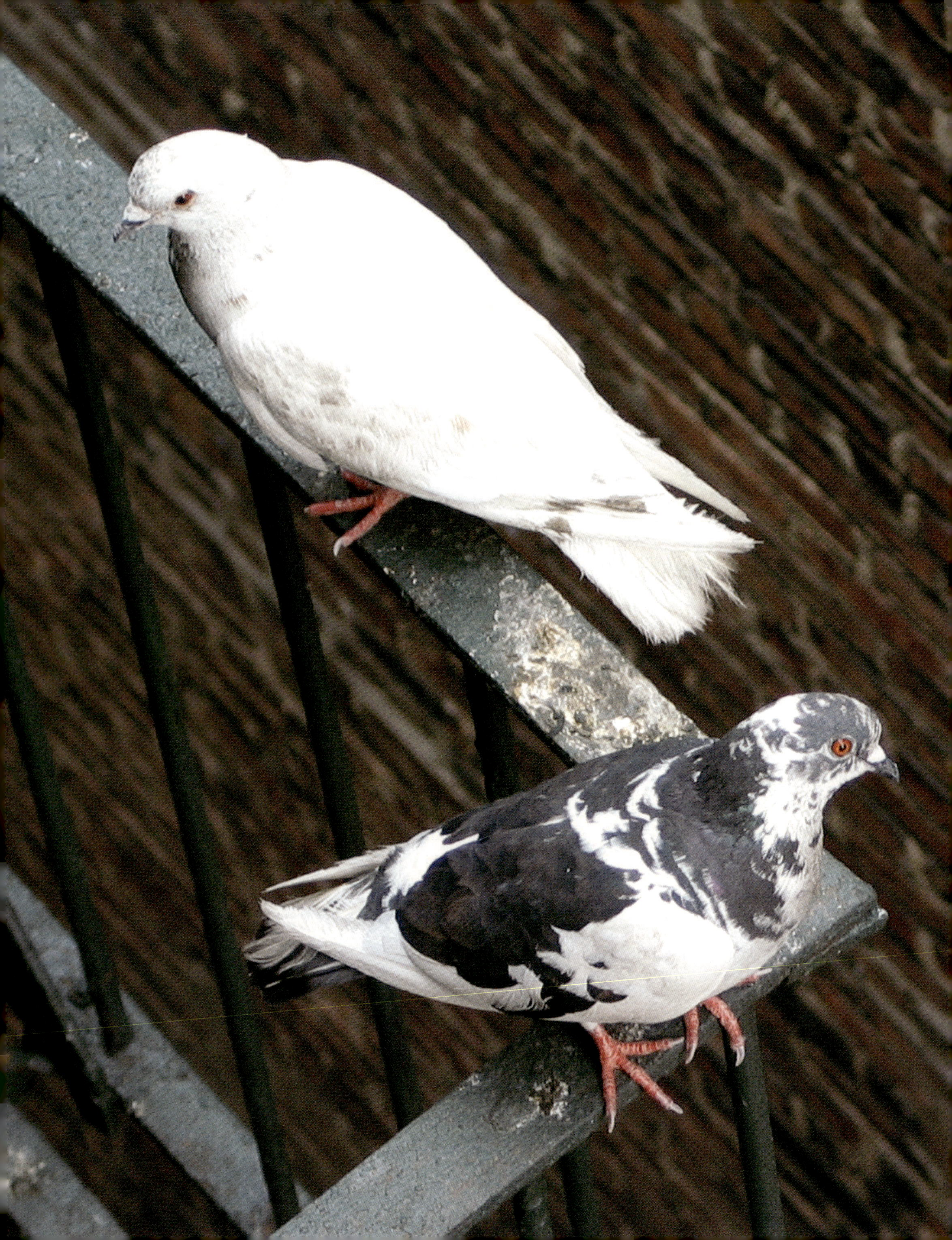

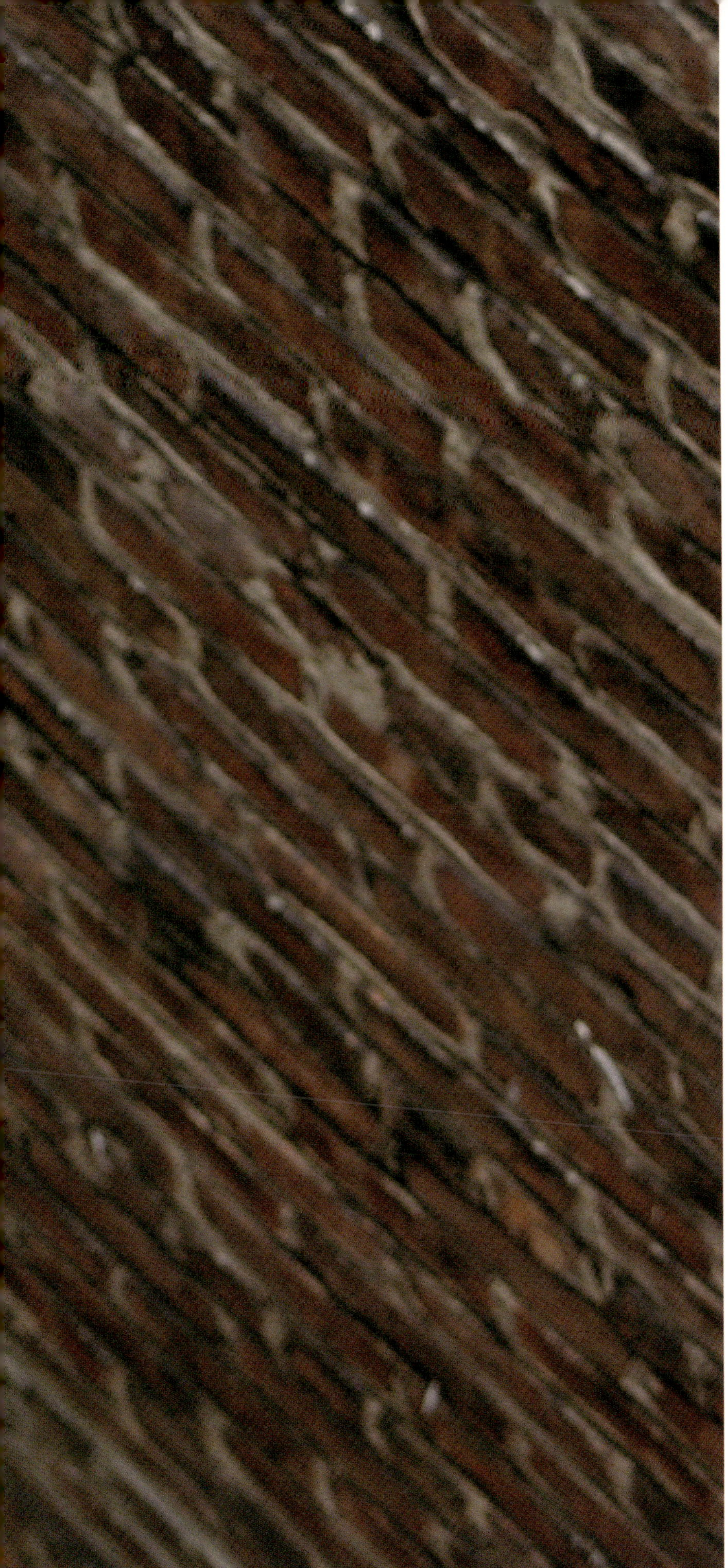

THERE'S ALWAYS A NEARBY CREATURE to keep you company in this city. When answering e-mails I was inspired by the elegant coloring of these pigeons on my fire escape. Their striking feathers rival some of the fine fabrics I've seen on the runways. I can't help thinking these birds knew that posing against the symmetrical pattern of the brick wall made them look even more stunning.

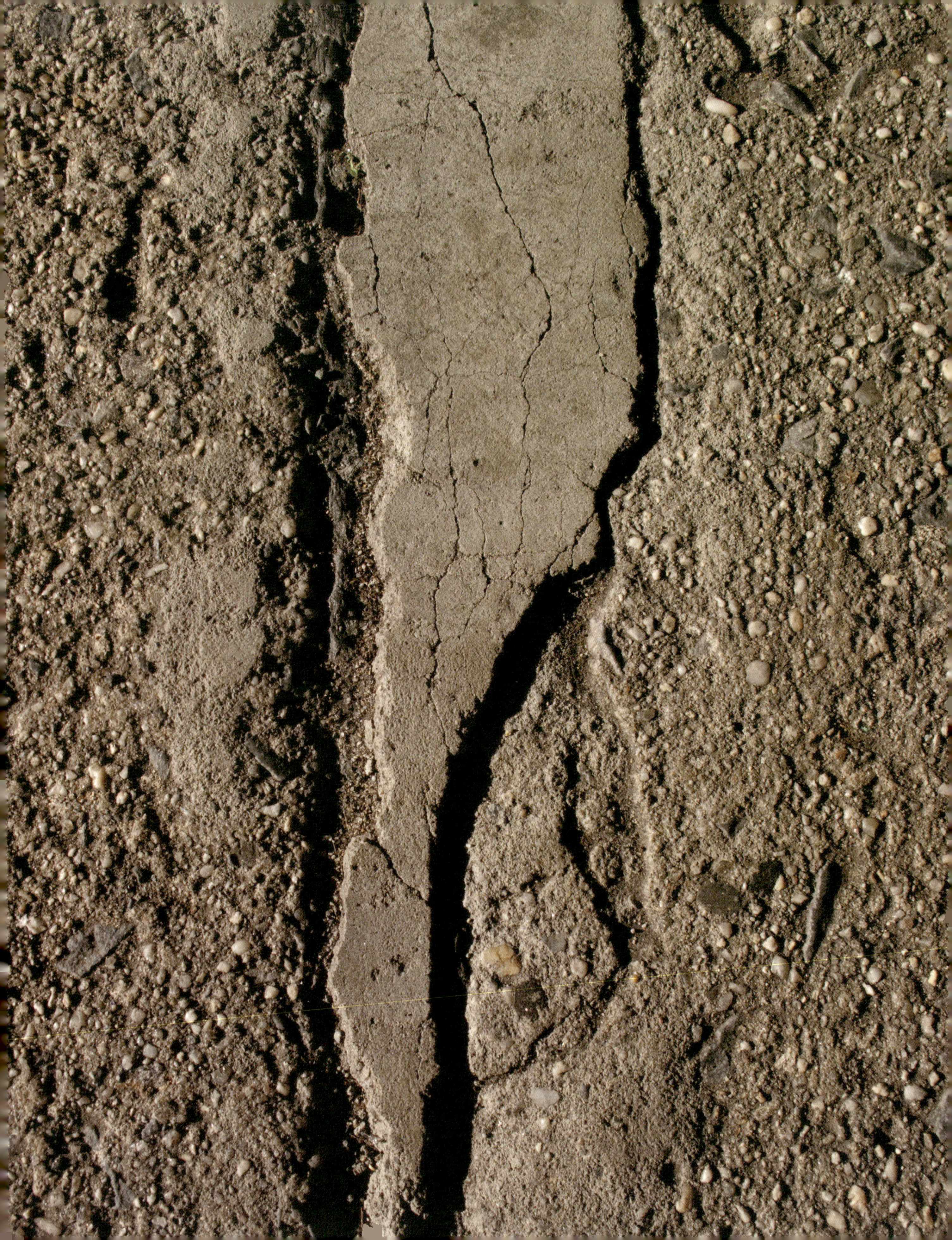

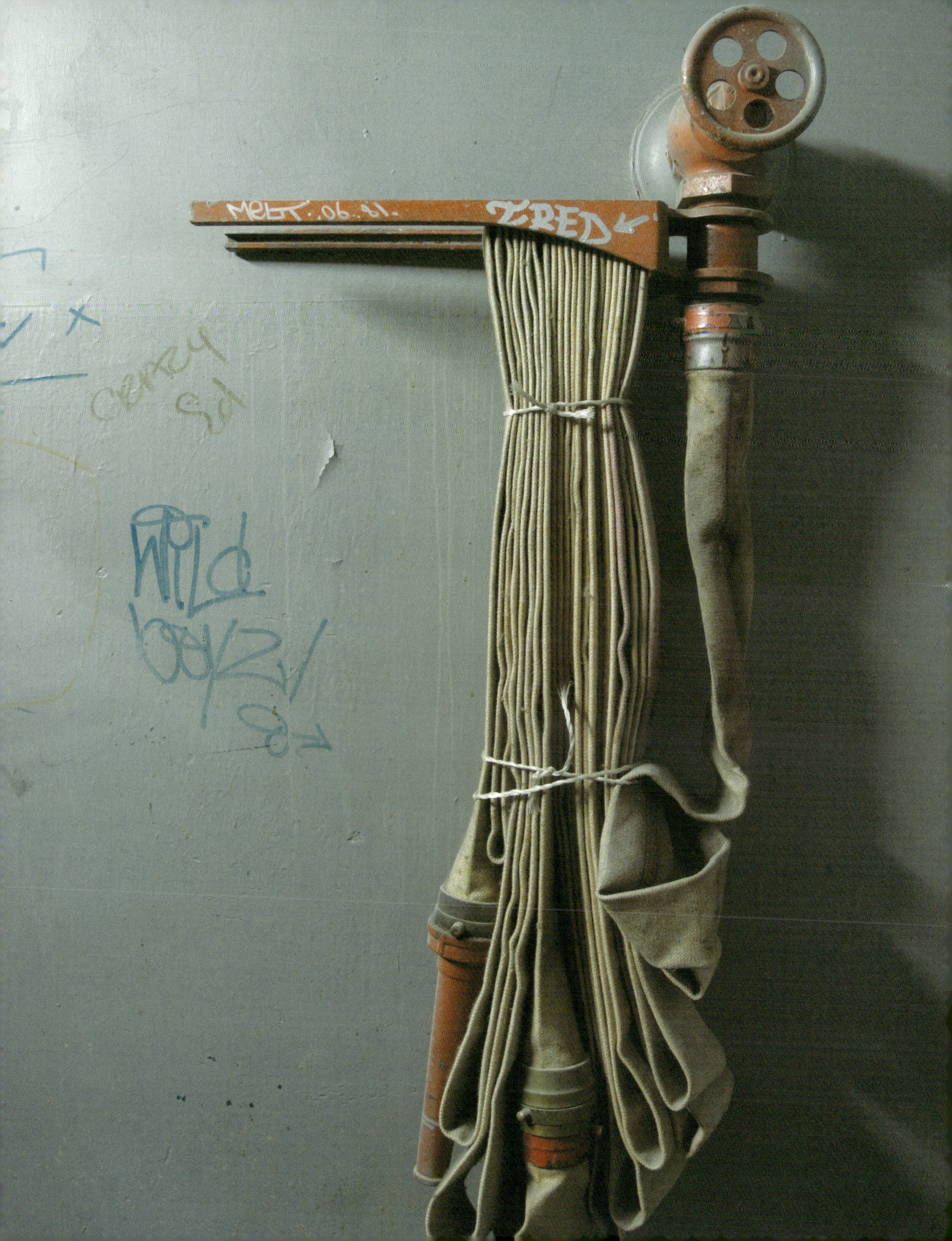

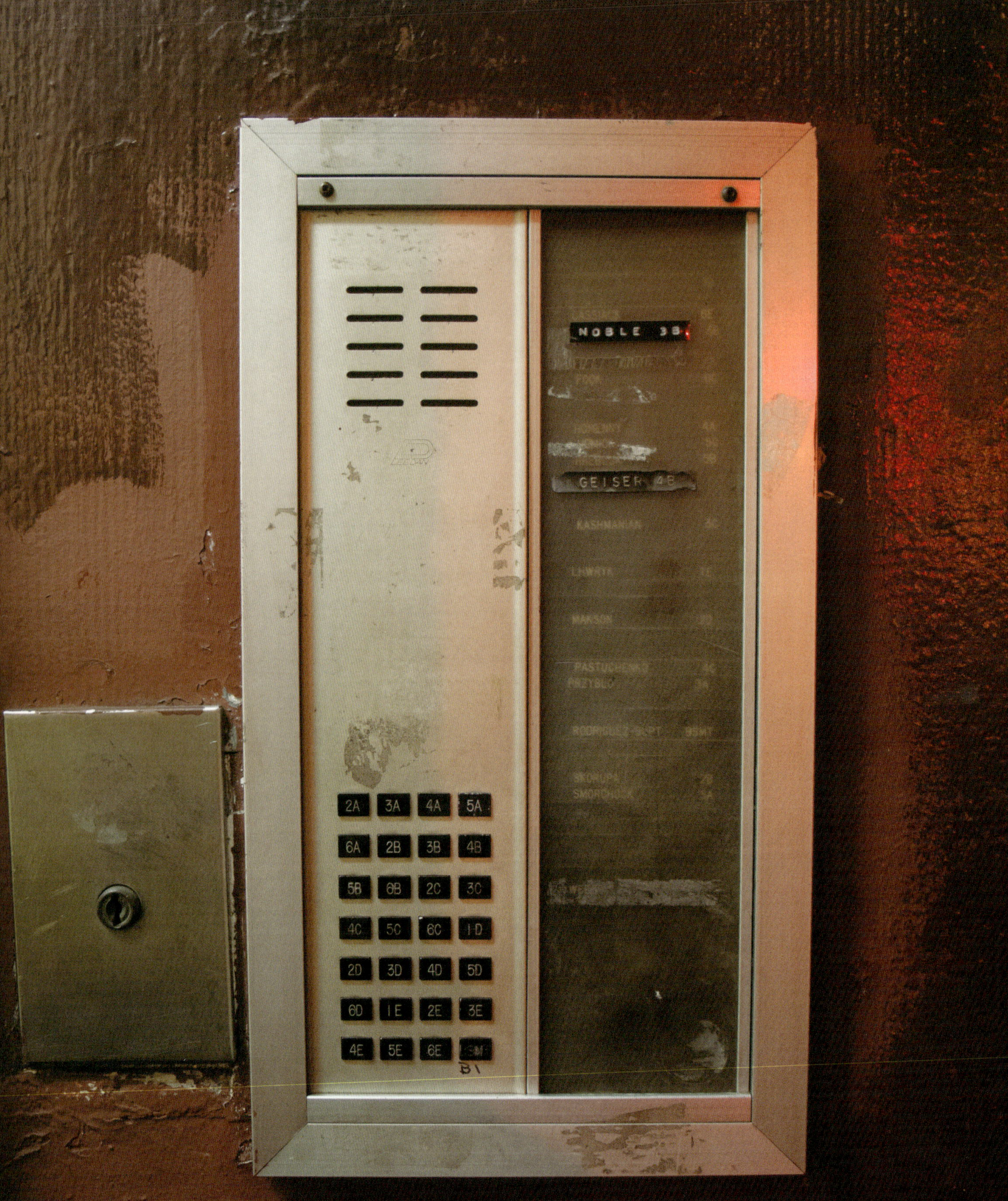
NOBLE 3B
GEISER 4B
2A 3A 4A 5A
6A 2B 3B 4B
5B 6B 2C 3C
4C 5C 6C 1D
2D 3D 4D 5D
6D 1E 2E 3E
4E 5E 6E
B1

JOSH

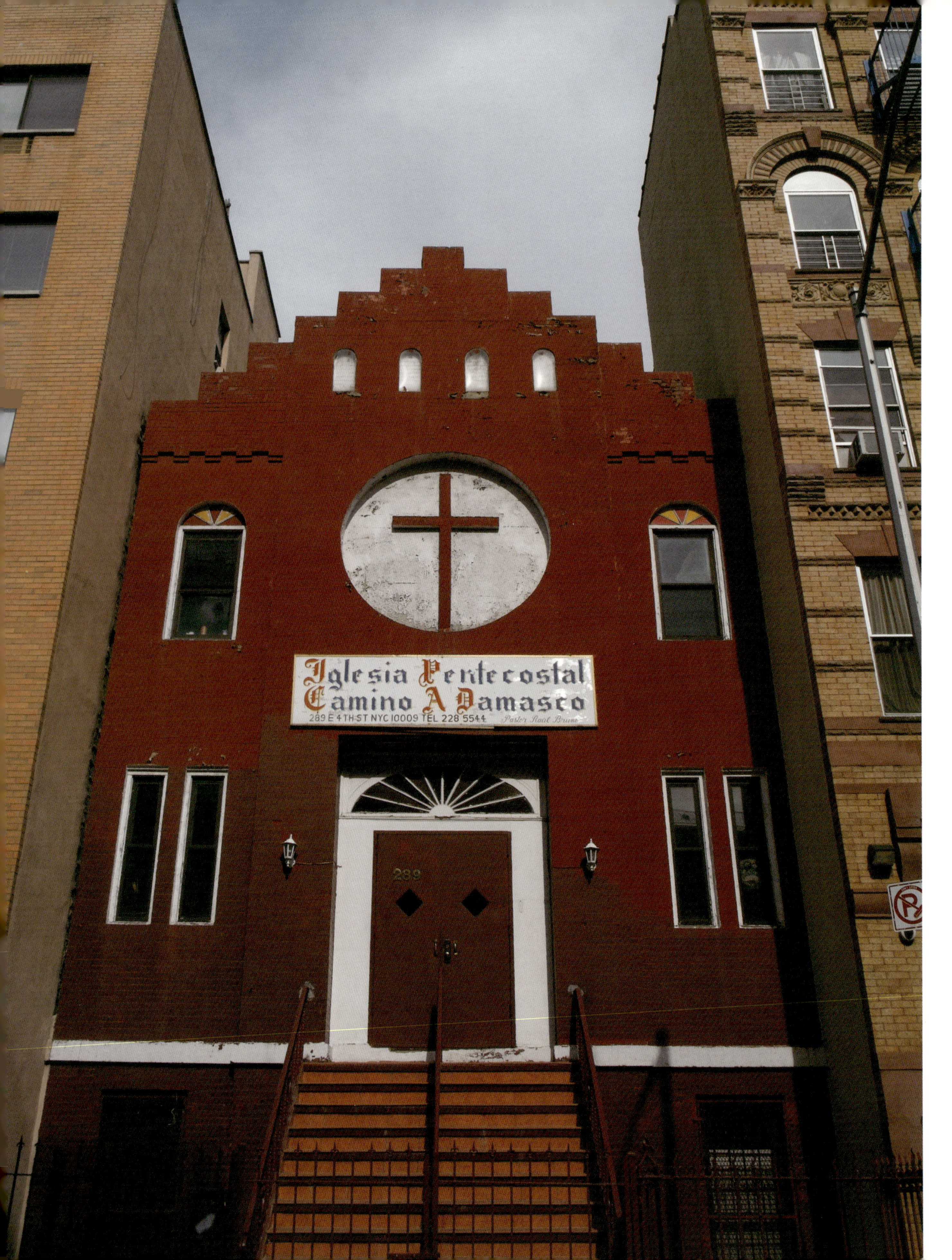
Iglesia Pentecostal
Camino A Damasco
289 E 4TH ST NYC 10009 TEL 228 5544
289

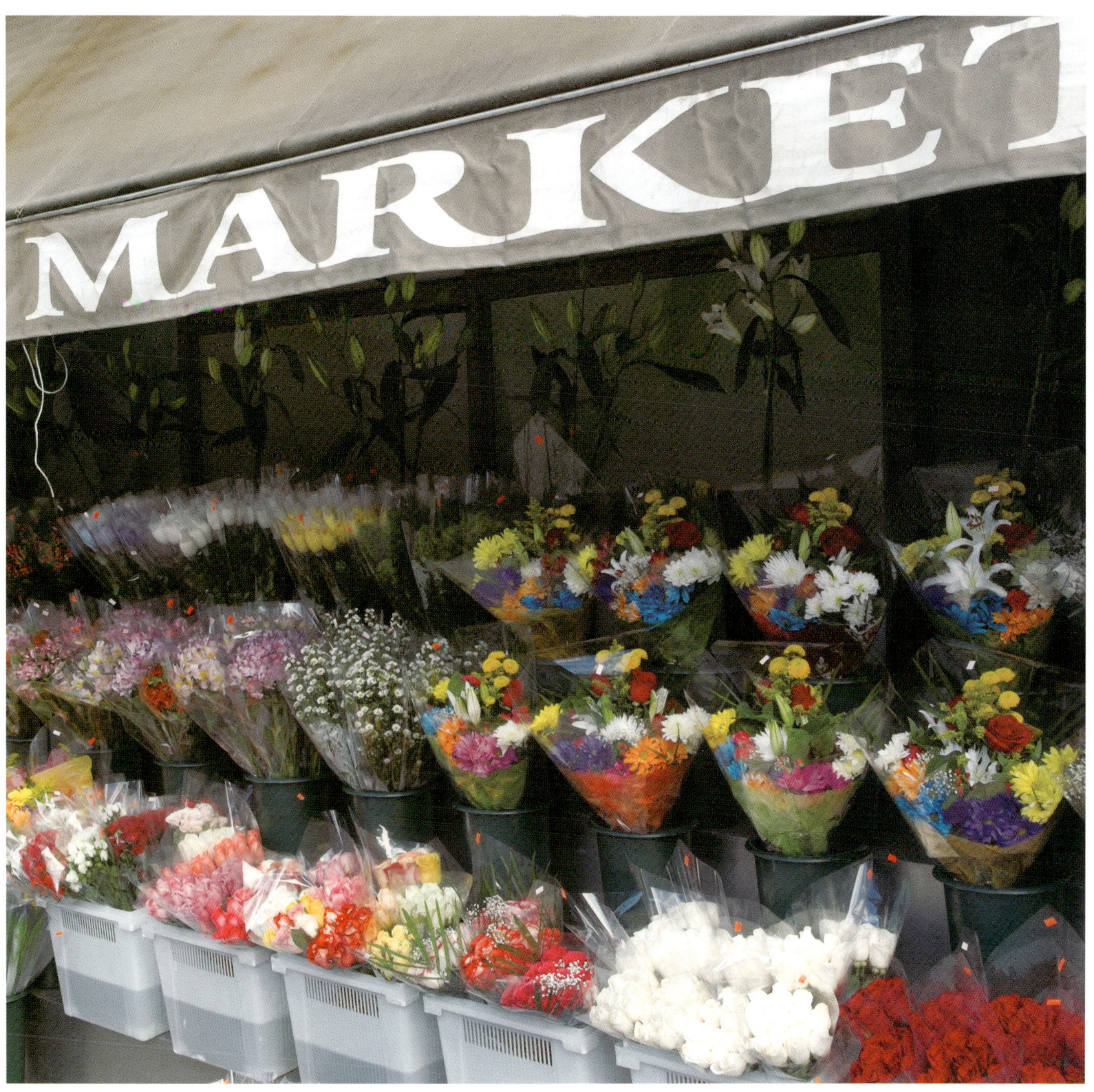

NOT ALL OF NEW YORK is about being big or upmarket. There are many churches that are no wider than a normal house, and normal neighborhood stores offer affordable flowers as well as groceries.

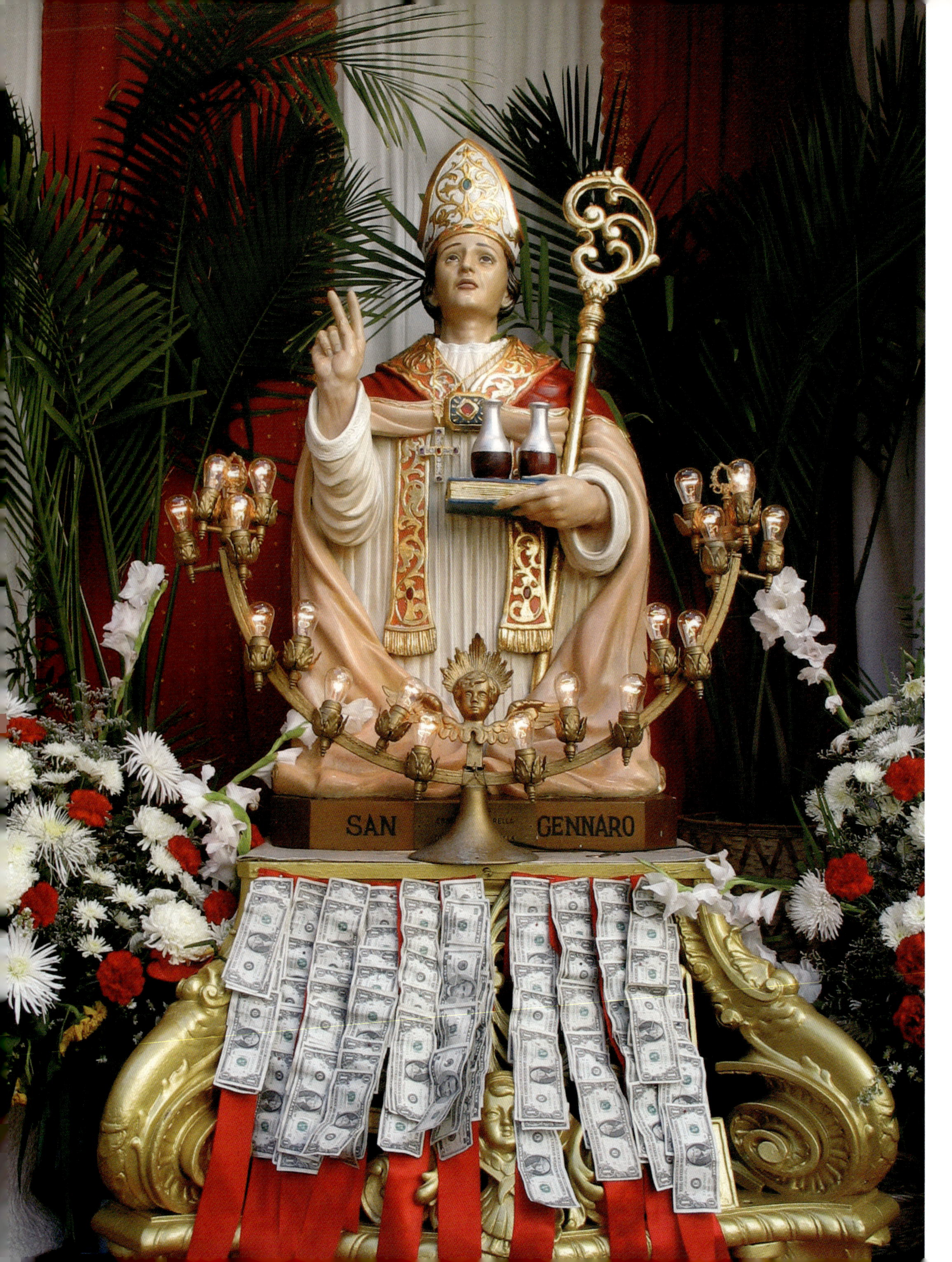
SAN
GENNARO

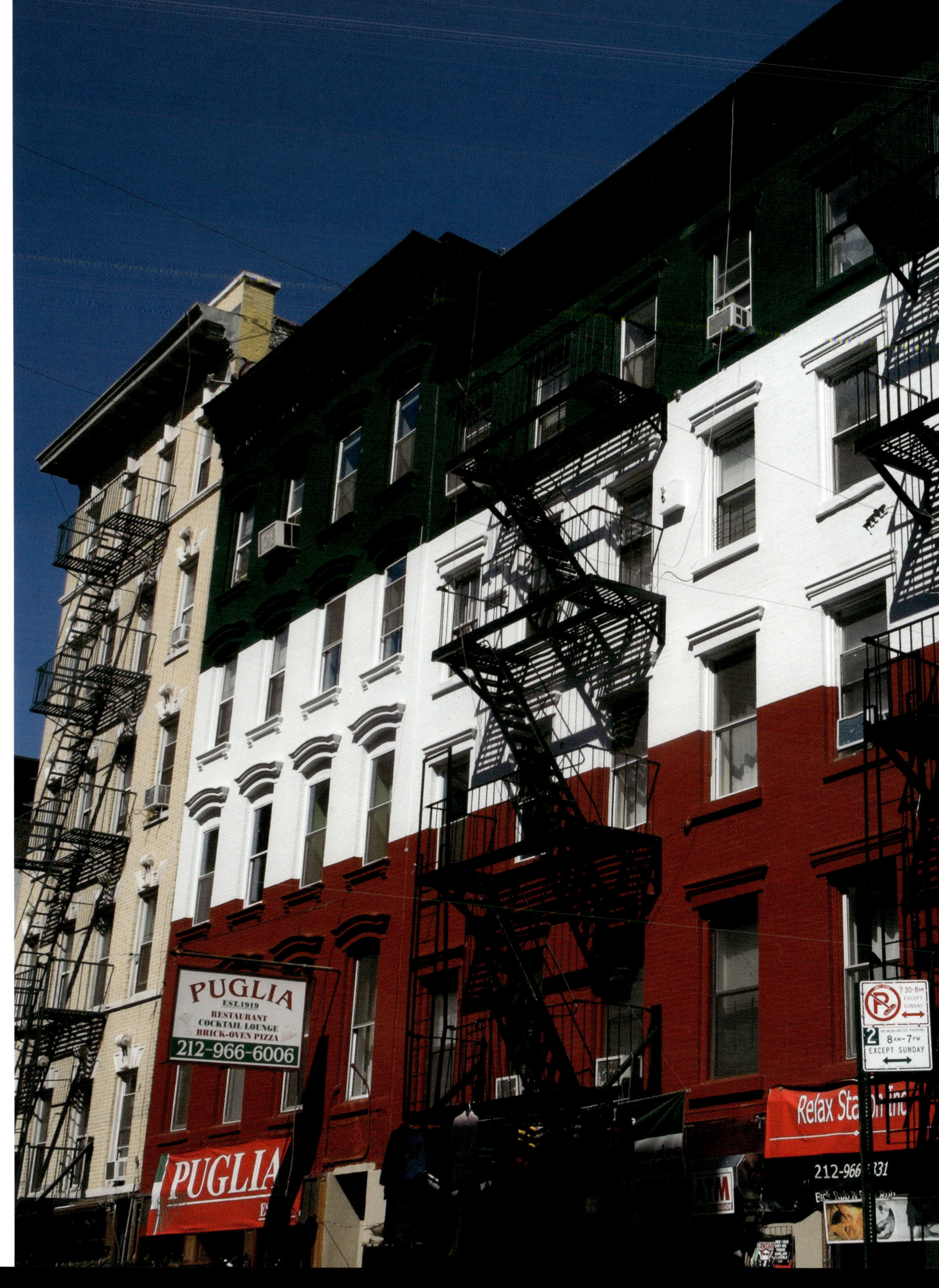
PUGLIA
EST.1919
RESTAURANT
COCKTAIL LOUNGE
BRICK-OVEN PIZZA
212-966-6006
PUGLIA
8AM-7PM
EXCEPT SUNDAY

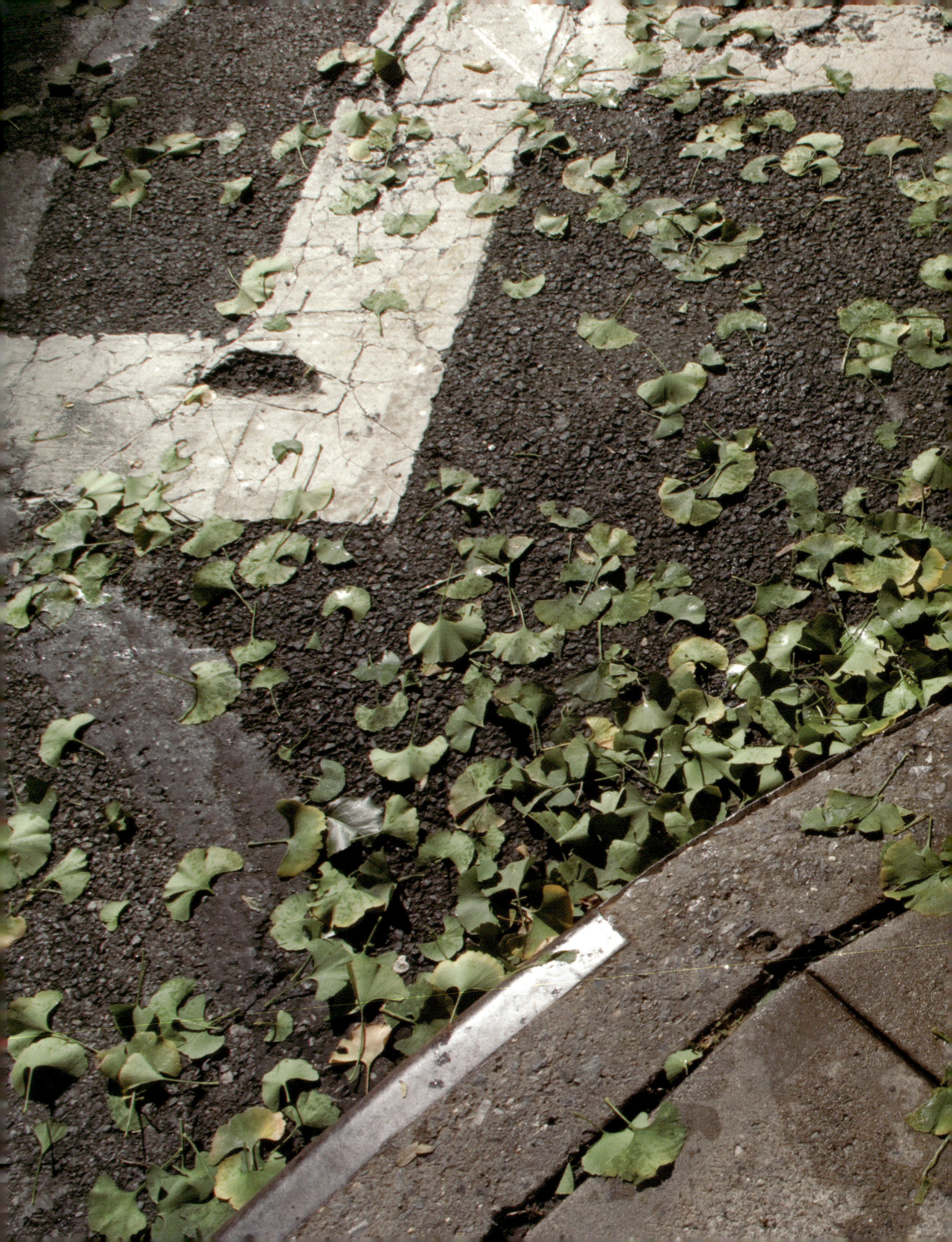

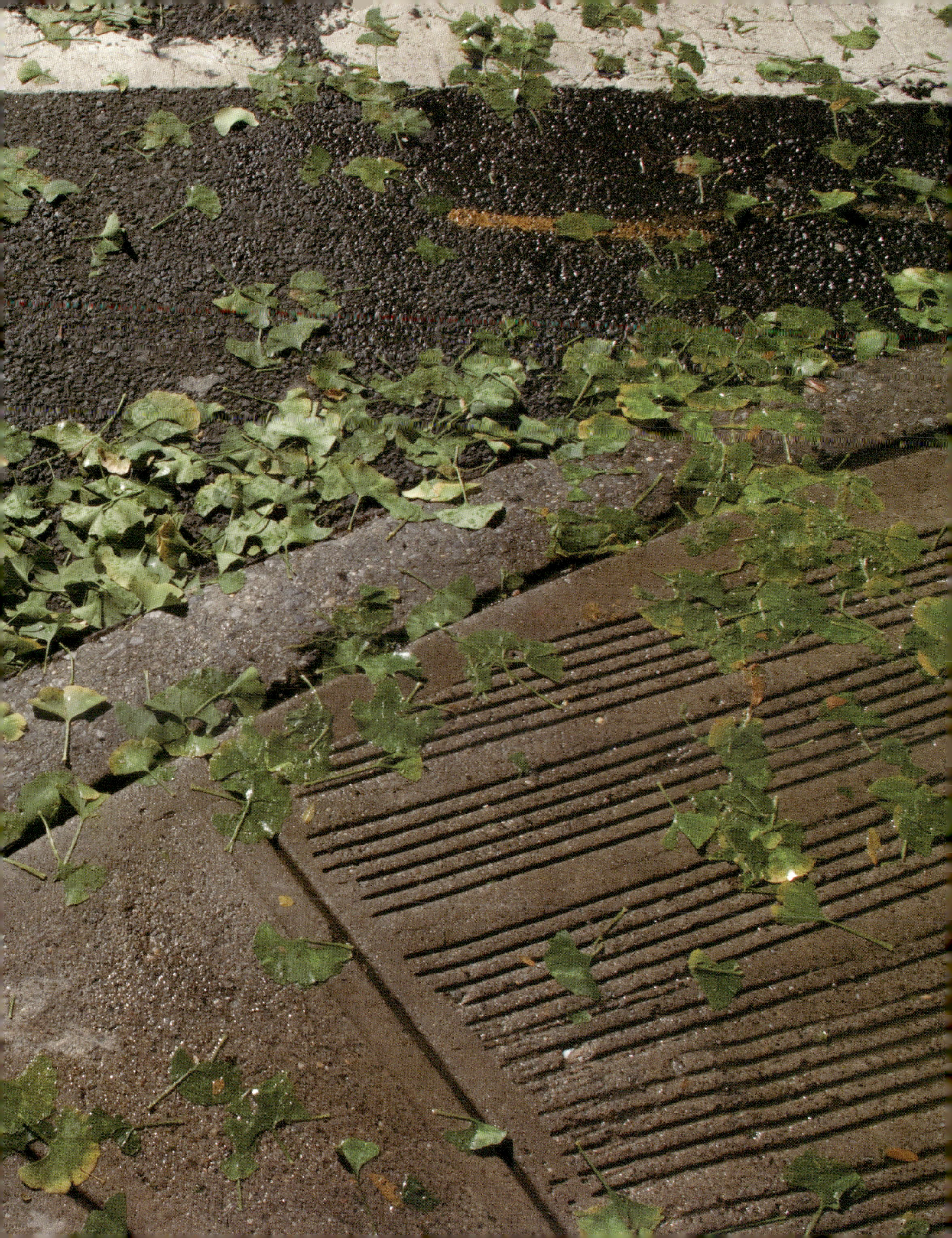

A HANDBALL COURT AND BASEBALL DIAMOND marked on the pavement provide a much-needed space for exercise and team sports. Designated areas like these can be found throughout the city, and are frequently used and much appreciated by the community. What's more, there's no membership or expensive equipment required. Apart from being great amenities for the communities where they are located, I find these areas visually intriguing. Also, for example, if you look at them in the right way, these lines look like a pretty amazing piece of modern art. Like much of the city, people leave their marks on these public venues. The Cosmos were a 1970s–1980s soccer team that featured the immortal sportsman Pelé—but never took hold in this city of asphalt and concrete. I'm not sure if this sticker is a hipster's tribute to a childhood memory or an original that somehow survived. Whichever it was, it brought memories flooding back for me.

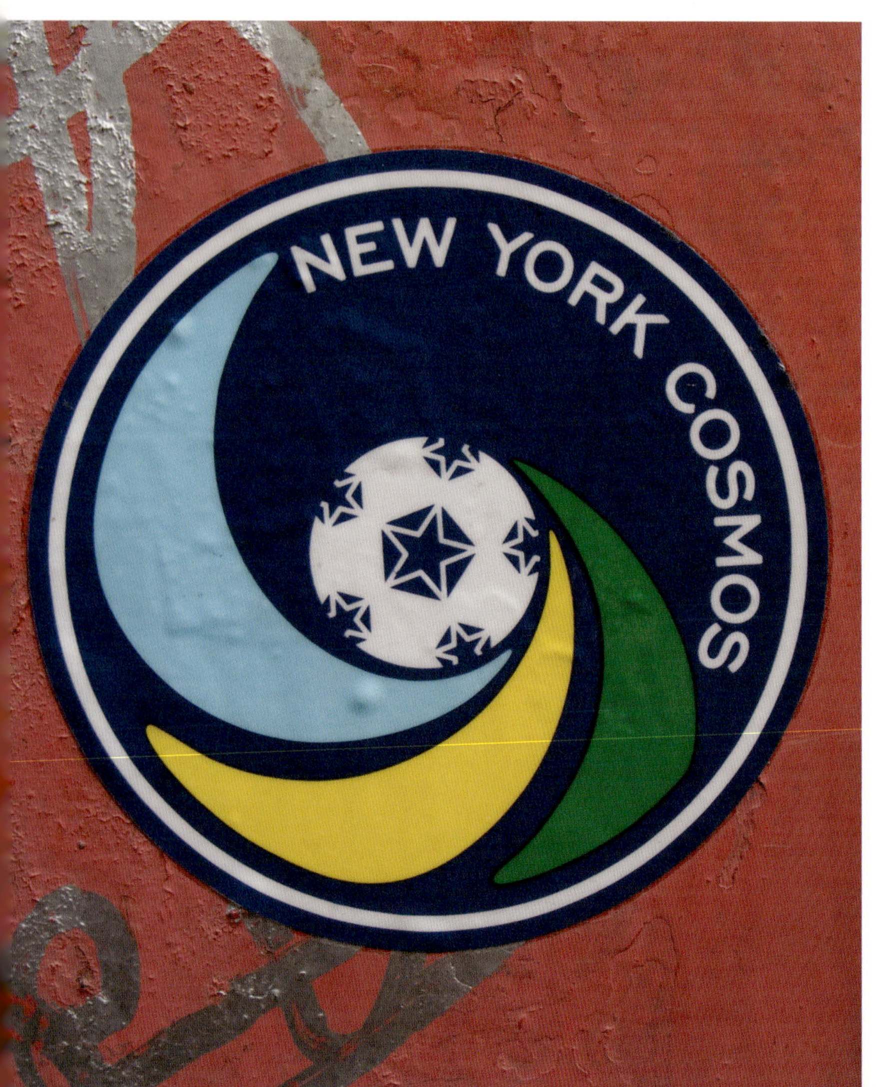

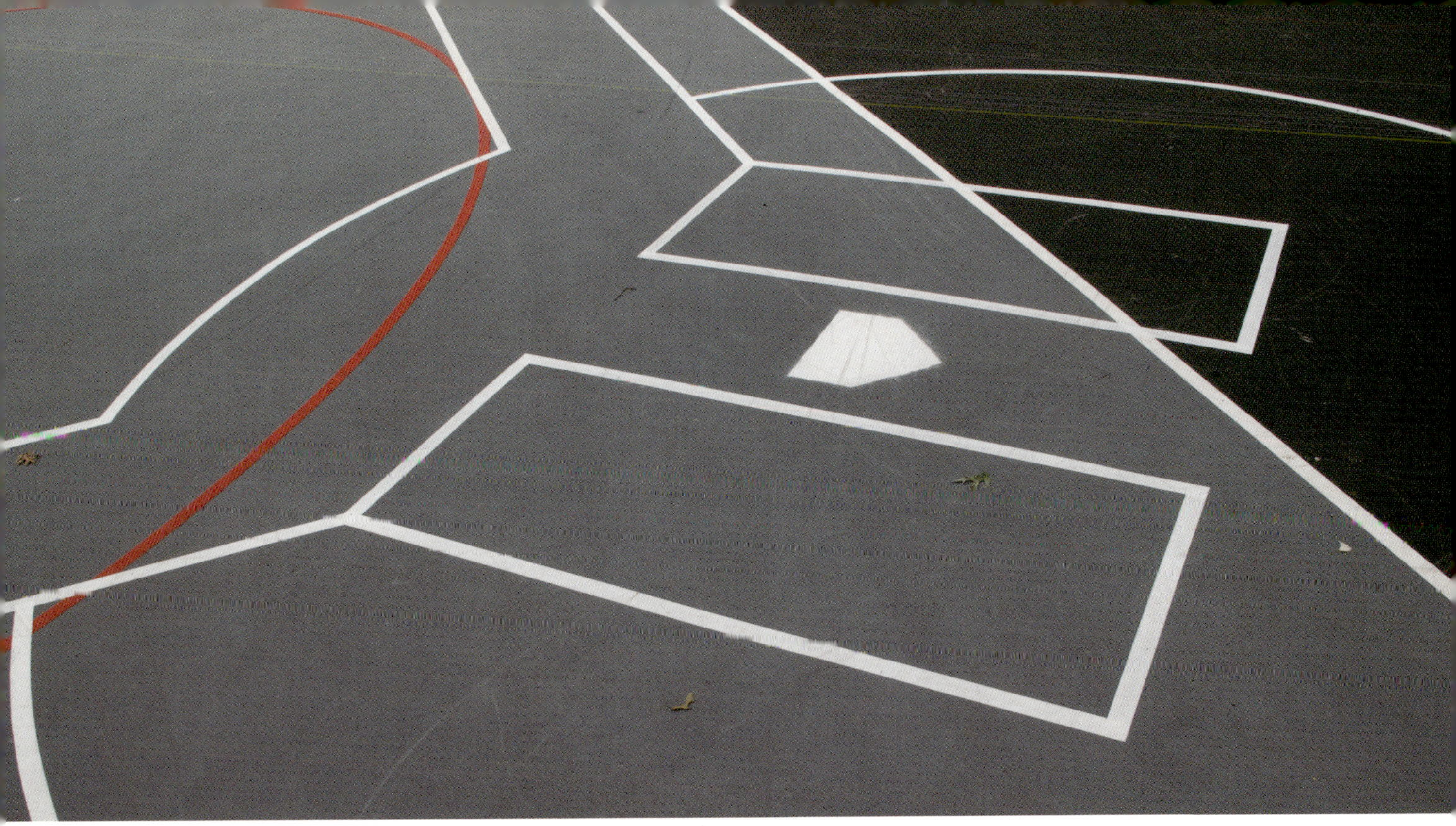

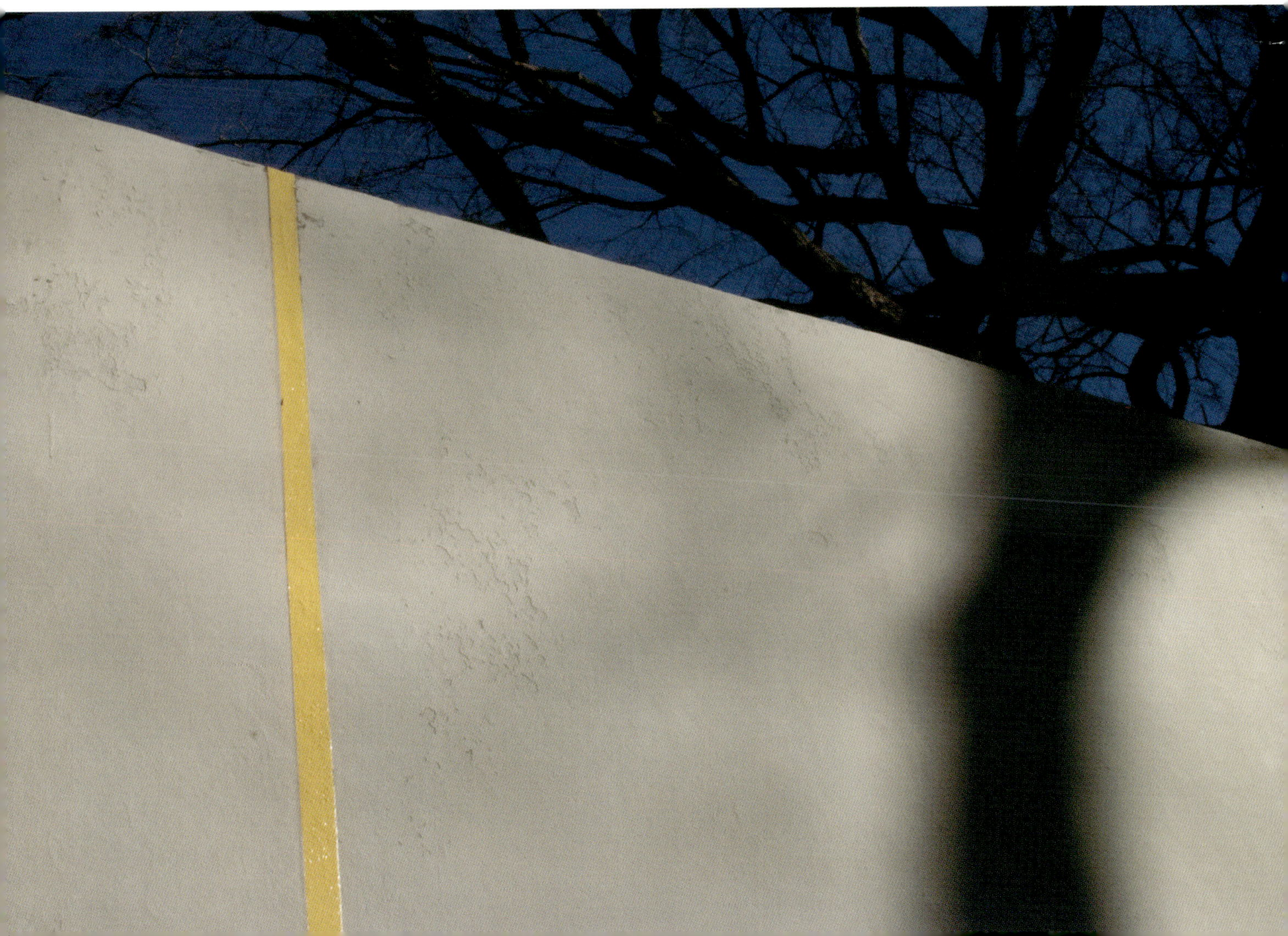

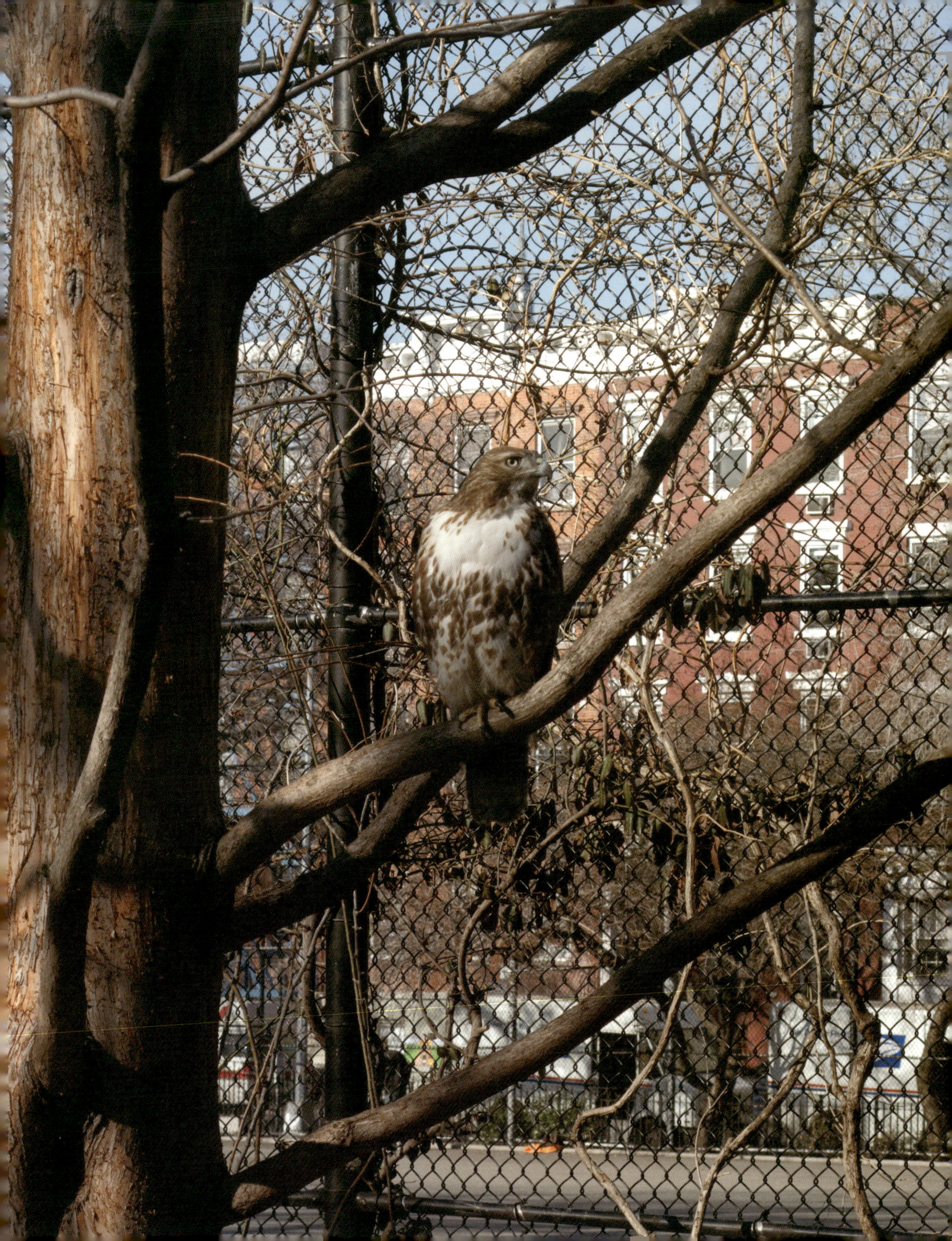

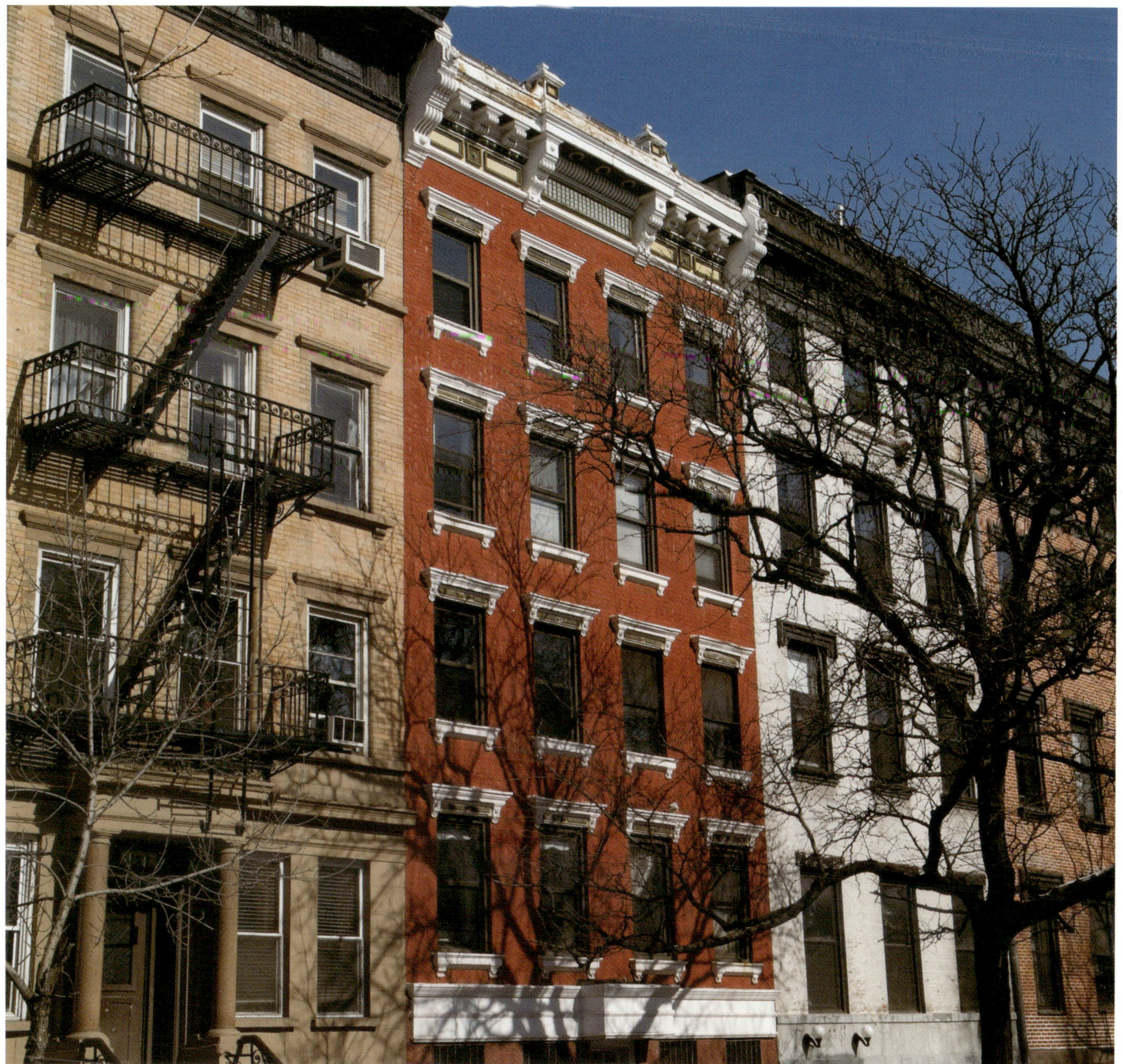

THIS RED-TAIL HAWK was right at eye level—just 7 feet away. Stately birds of prey are symbols of many countries, Poland and the United States just to mention a couple. As the mid-afternoon sun hit the tenements around Tompkins Square Park, I wondered how many immigrants glanced down from their windows, seeing images that reminded them of their homelands.

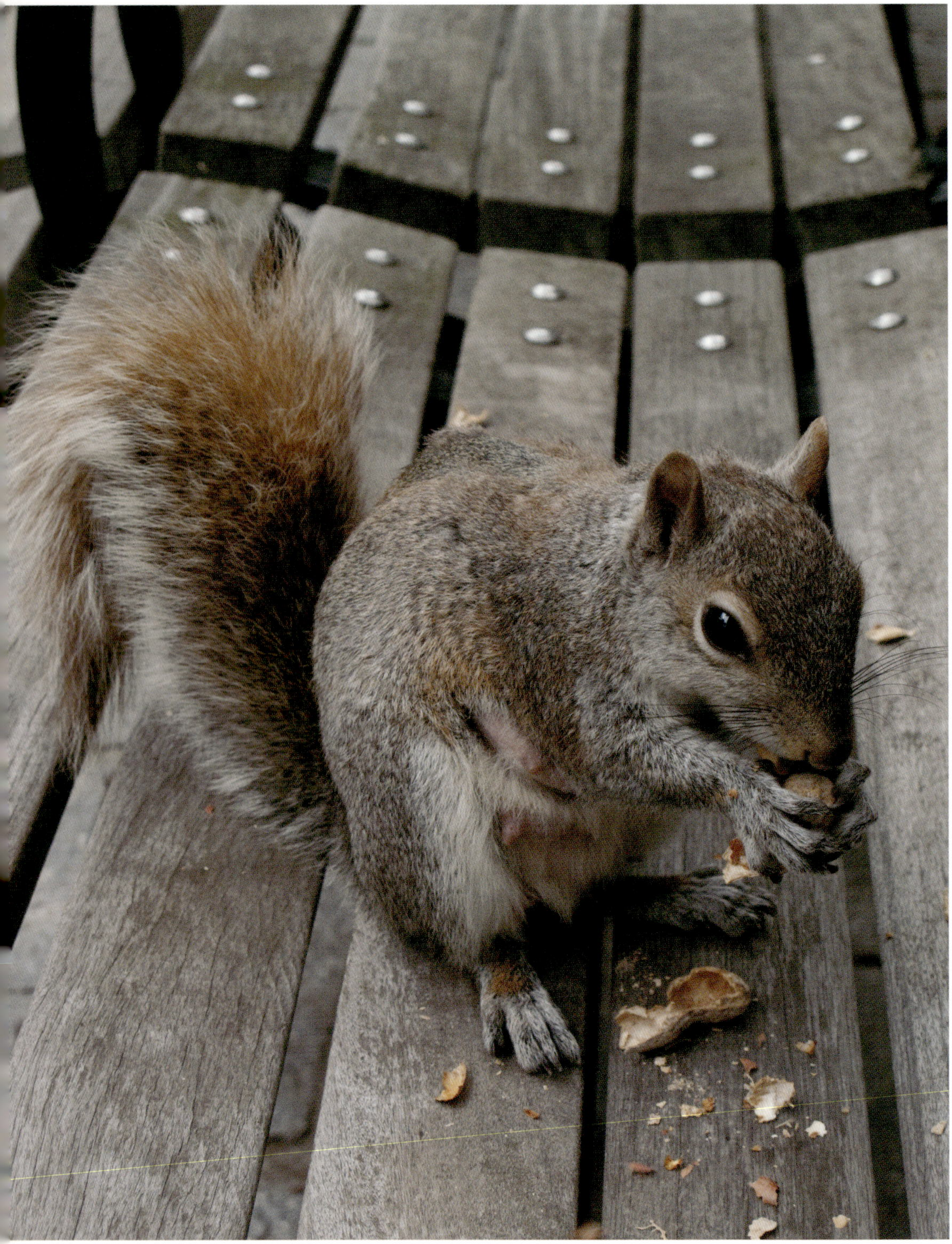

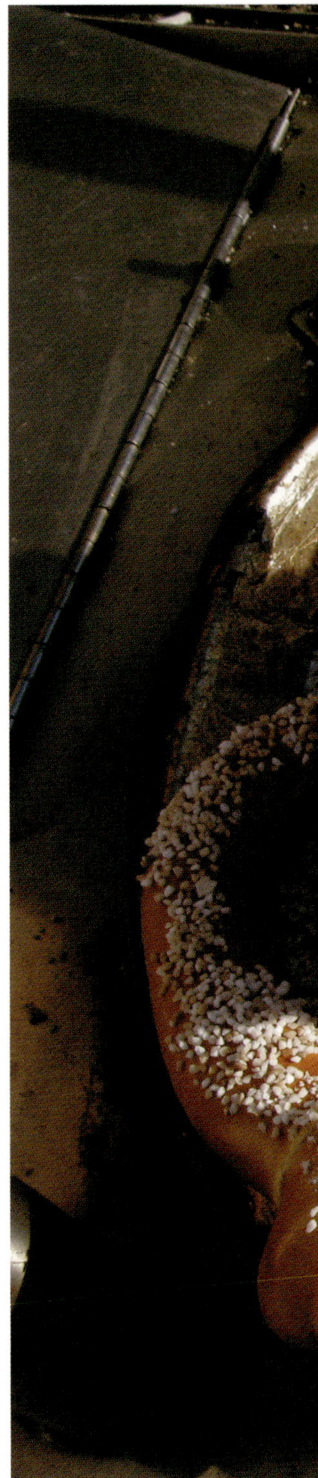

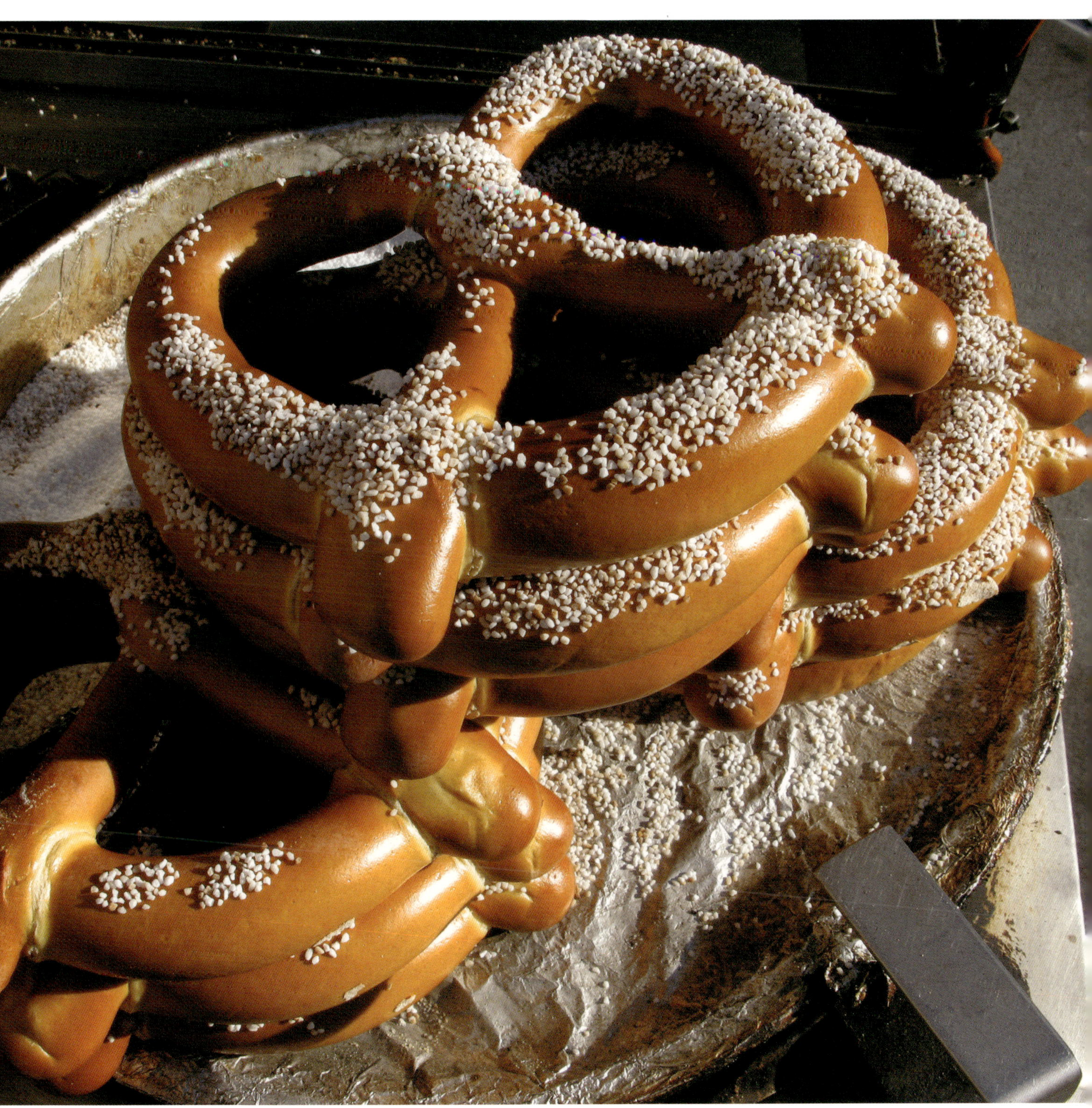

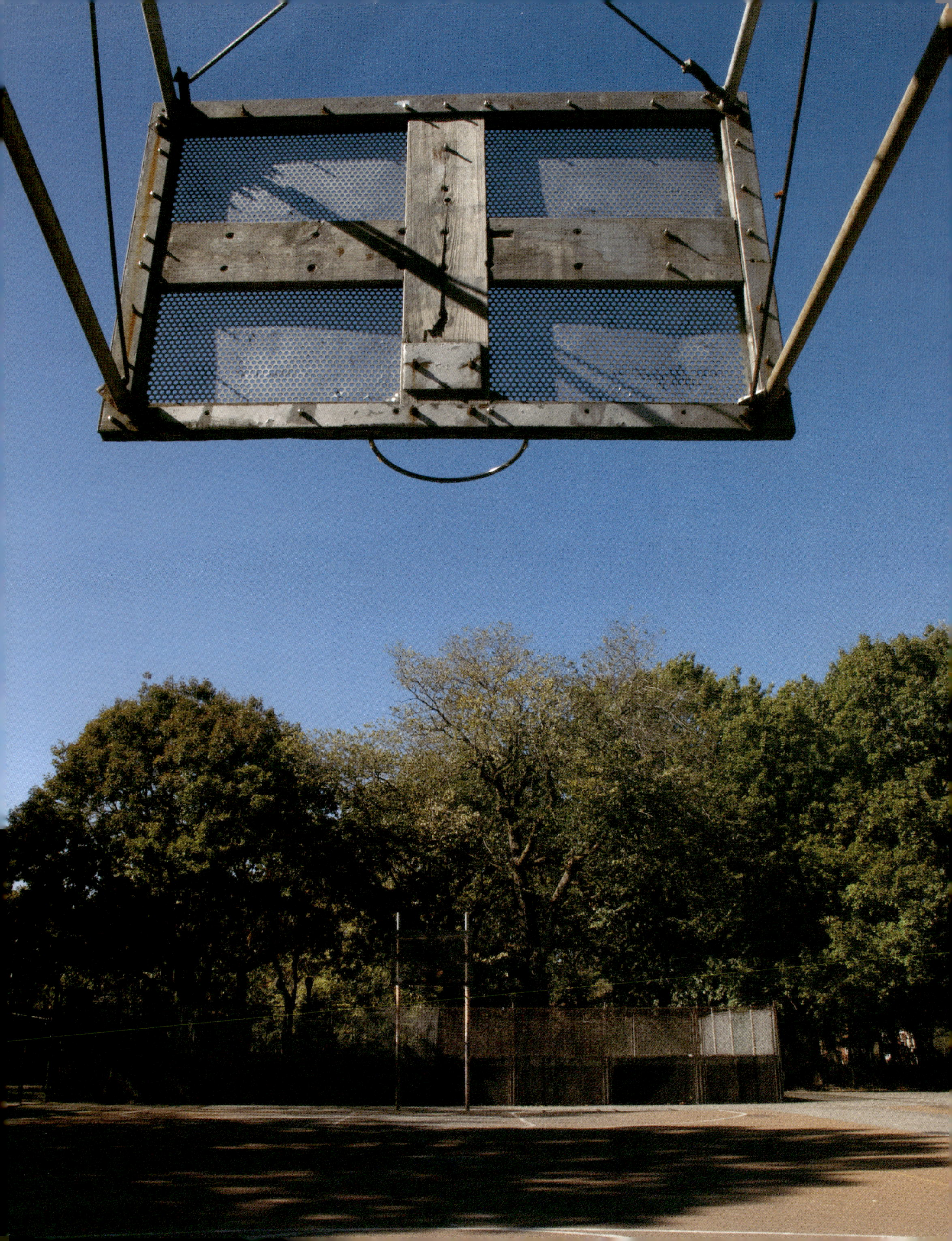

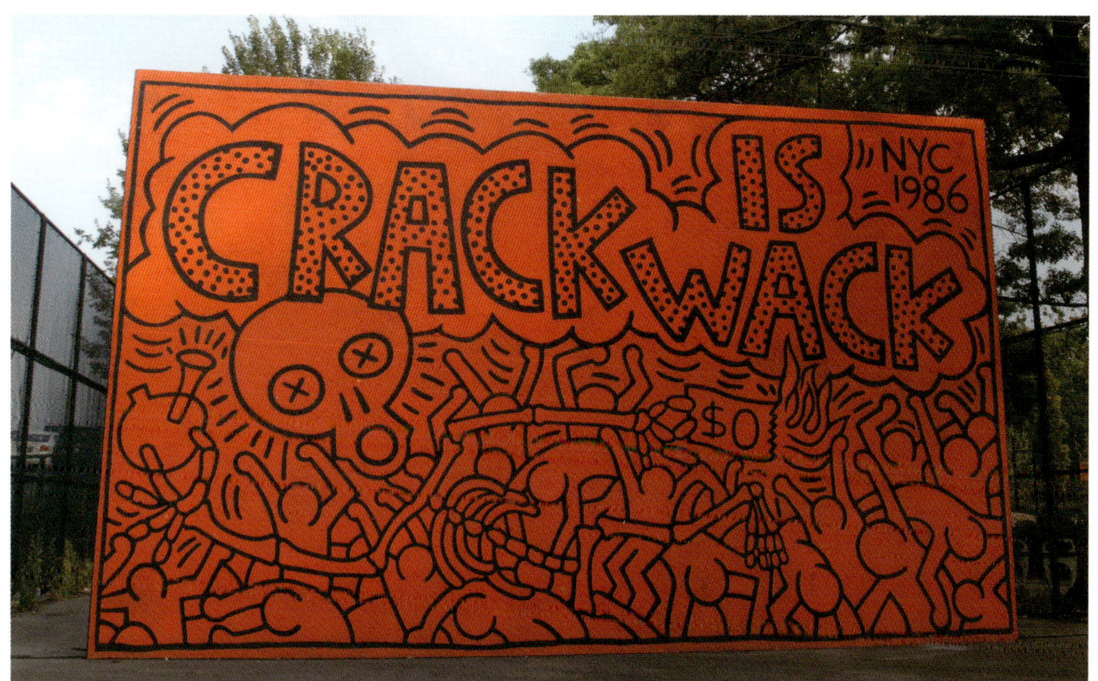

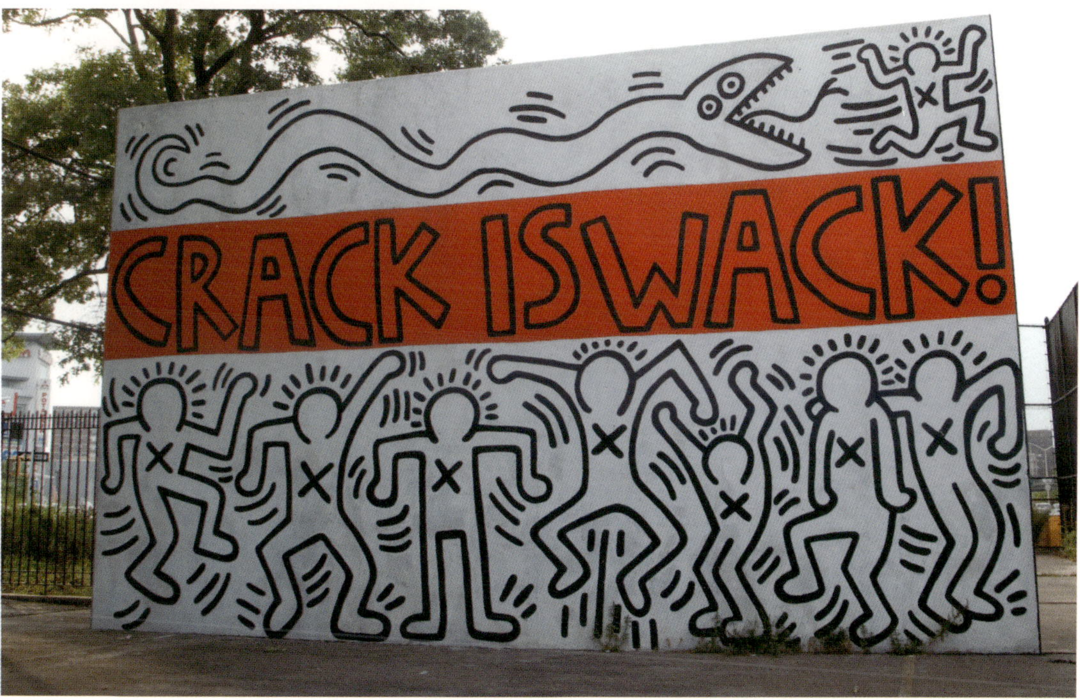

HARING'S 1986 MURALS warn of the perils of crack cocaine, an epidemic that devastated New York in the 1980s and early 1990s. These handball walls—located next to a basketball court—are one of many throughout the city, often the scene of impromptu pick-up games. These players take their game seriously. It's so impressive to watch these hard-core athletes in action—the hoops without nets are typical of this bare-bones city where extras aren't included in the first place, or don't get replaced when they wear out.

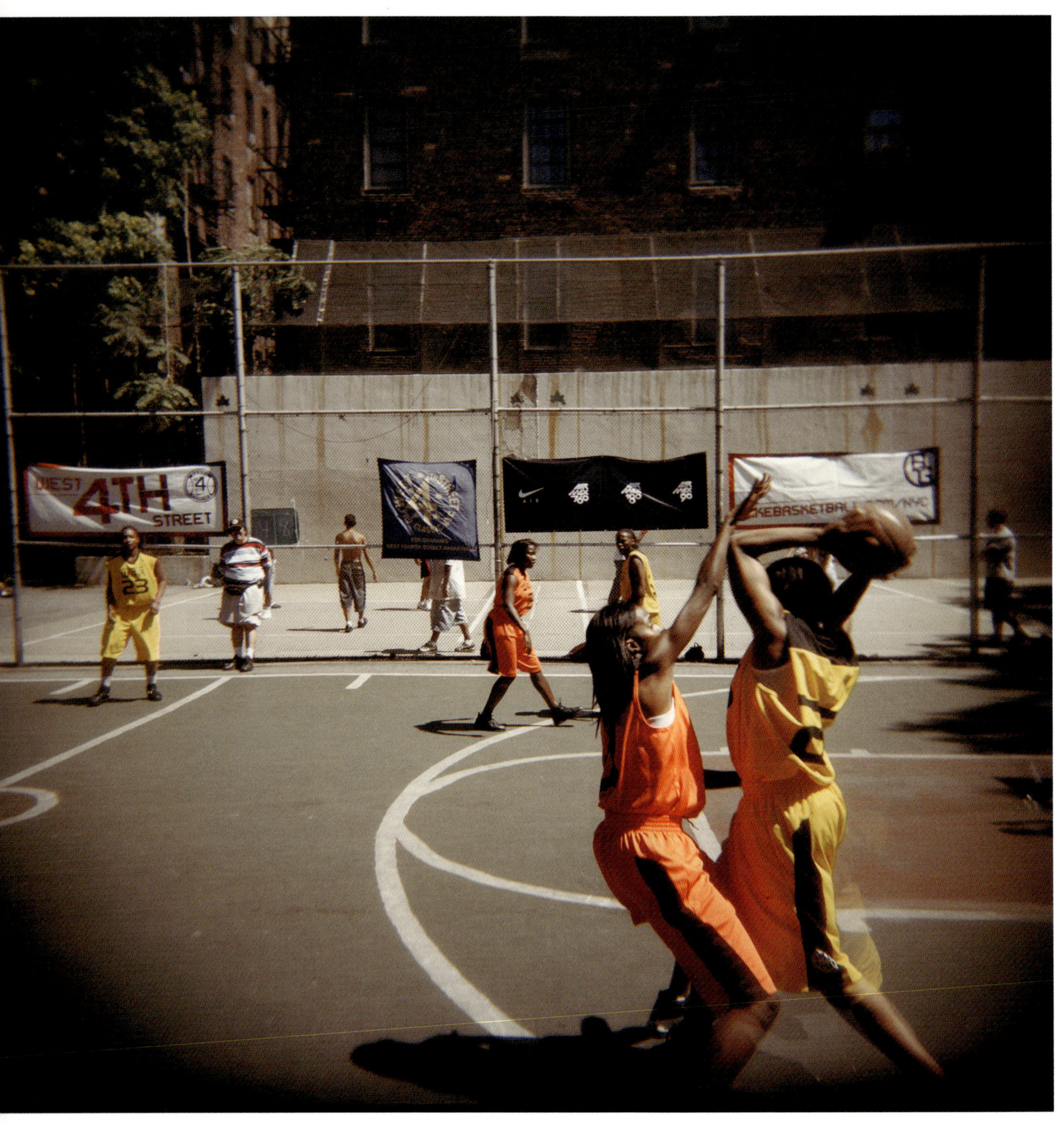
WEST
4TH
STREET
23

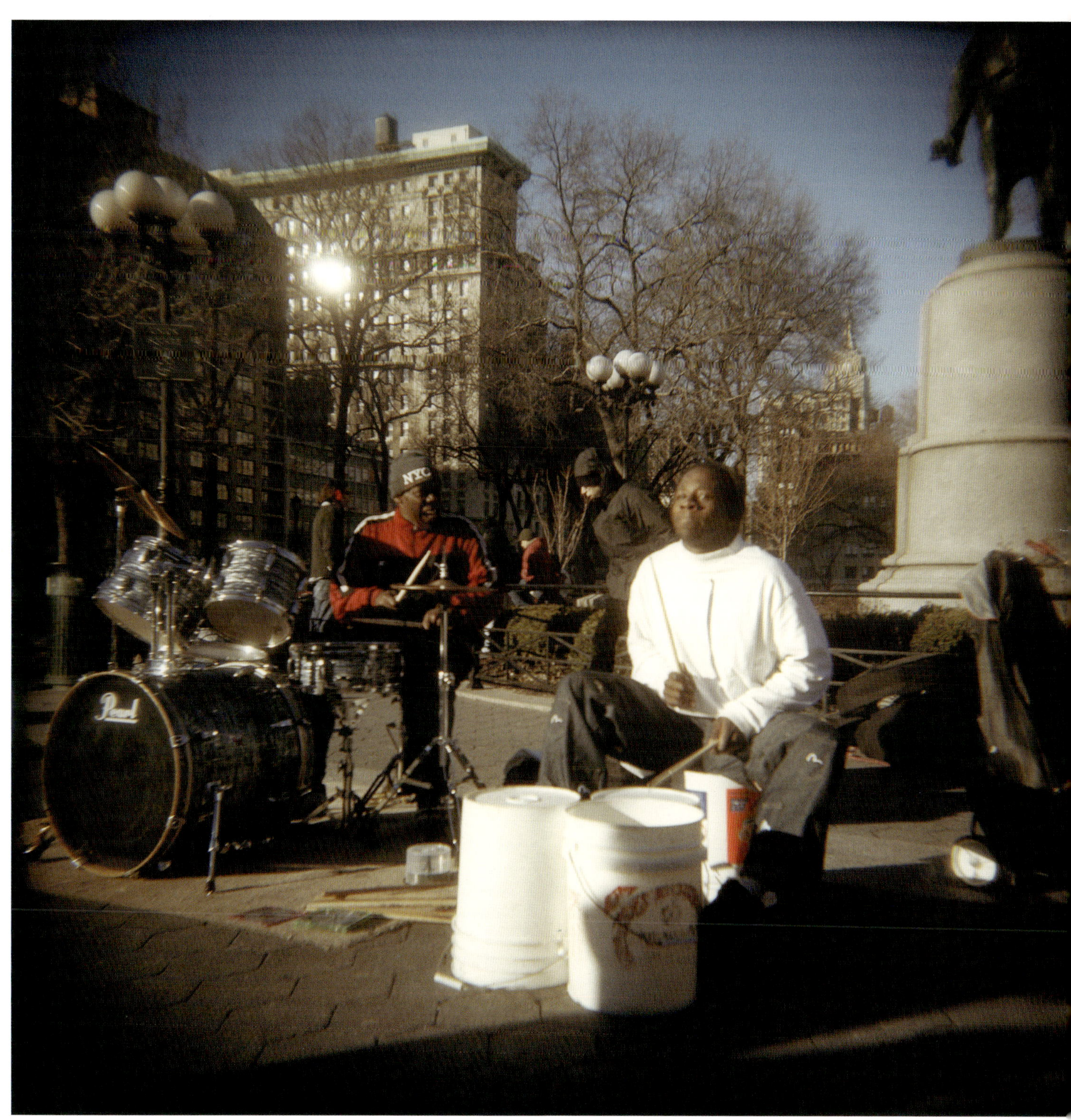
NYC
Pearl

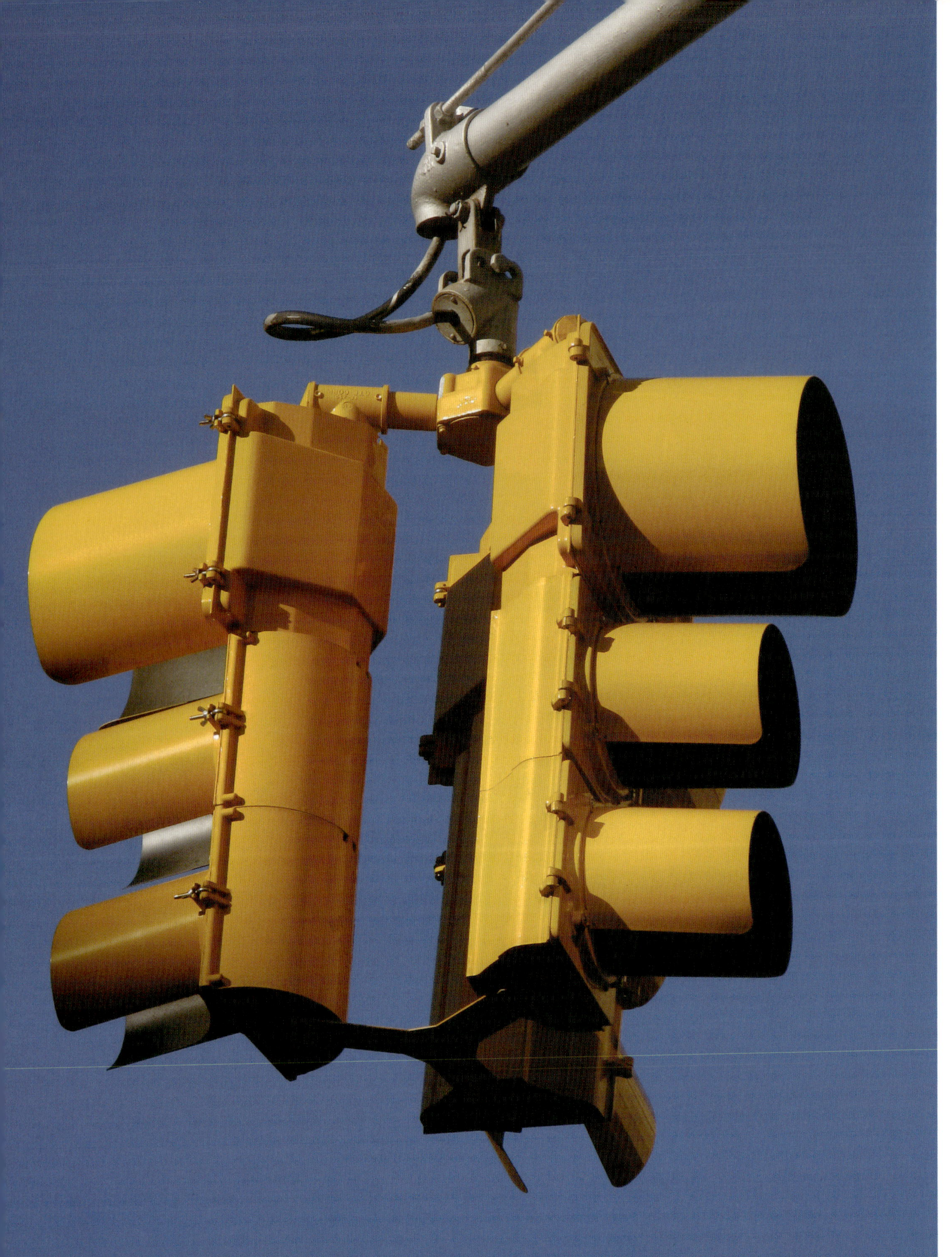

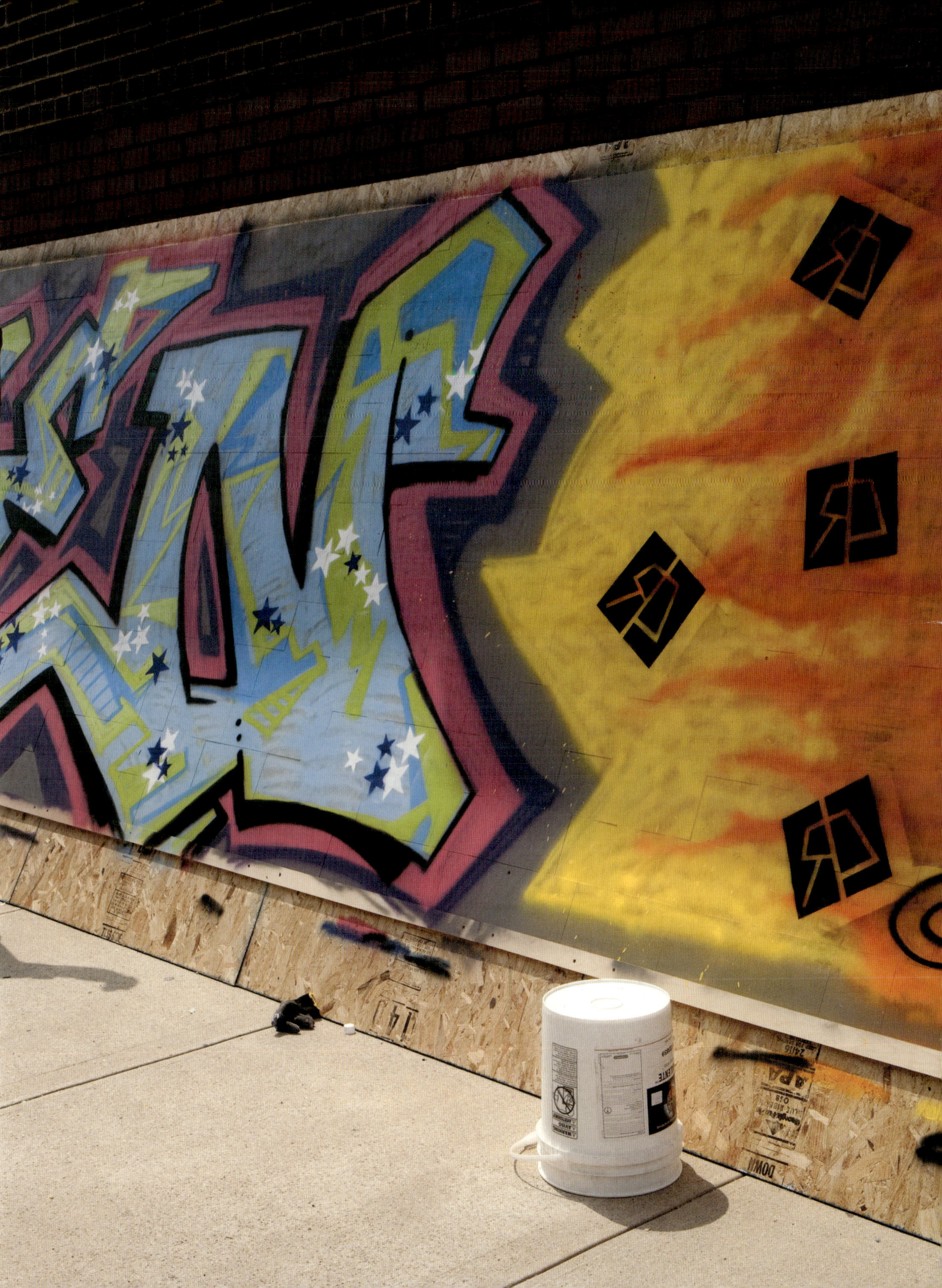

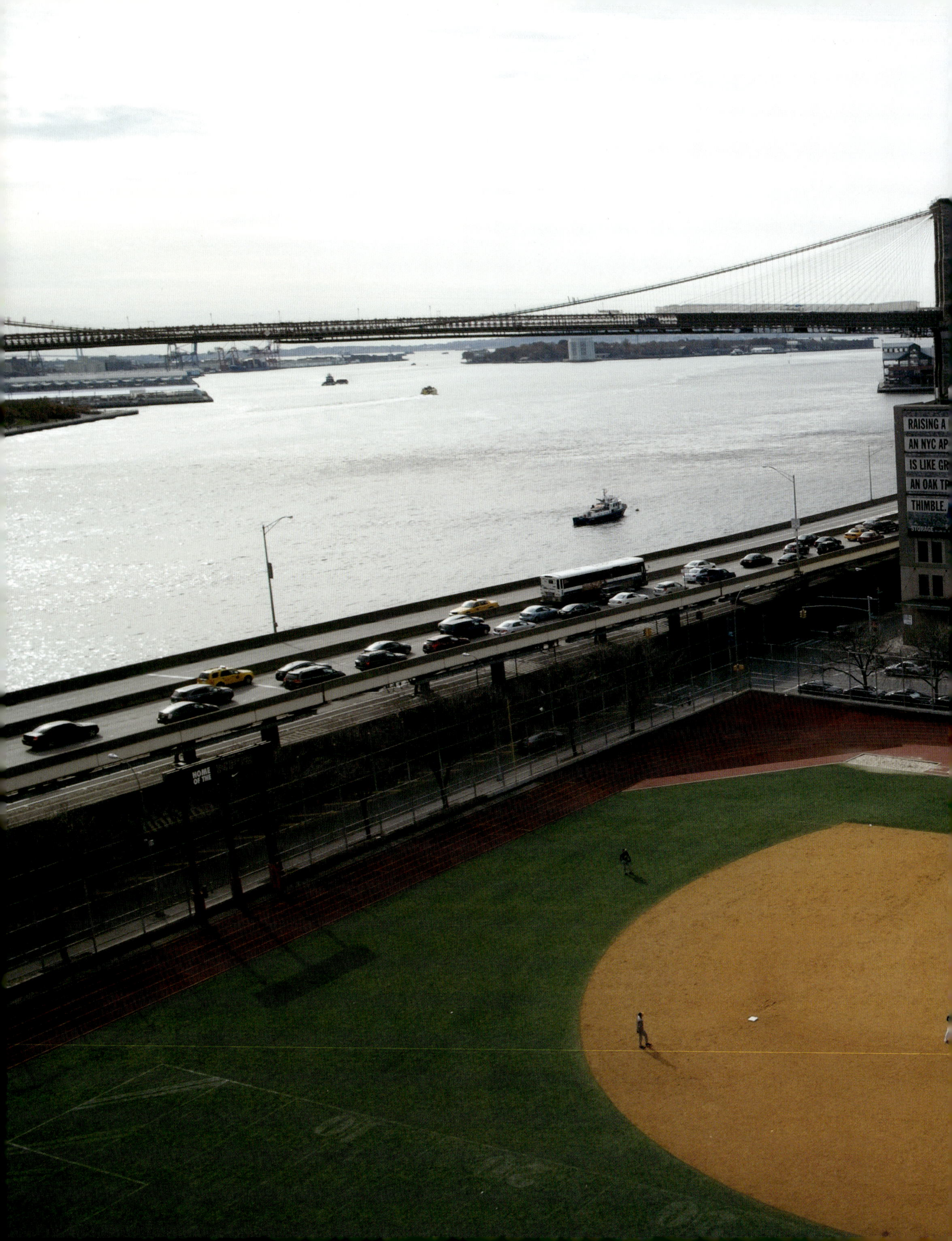
RAISING A
AN NYC AP
IS LIKE GR
AN OAK TR
THIMBLE.

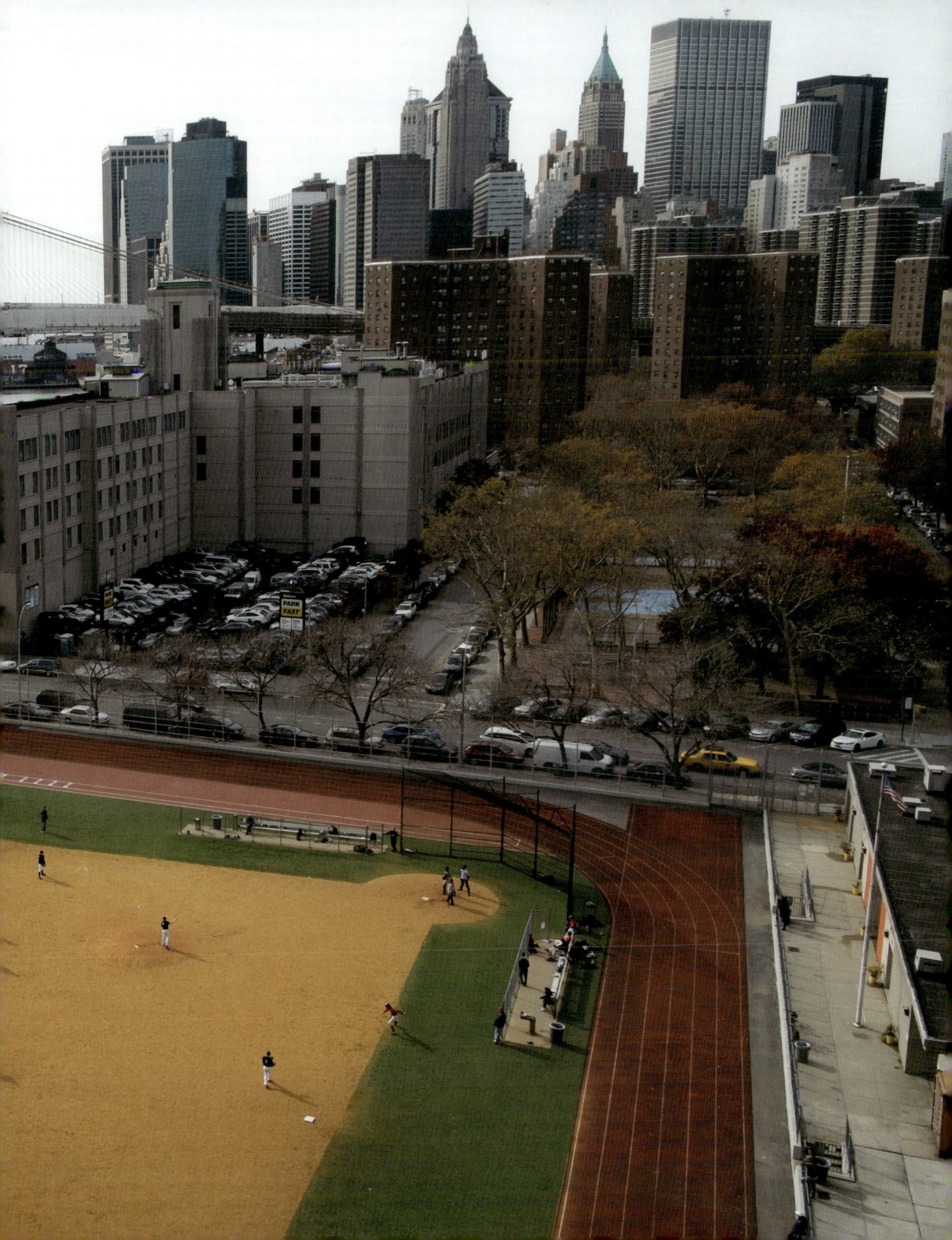
PARK
FAST

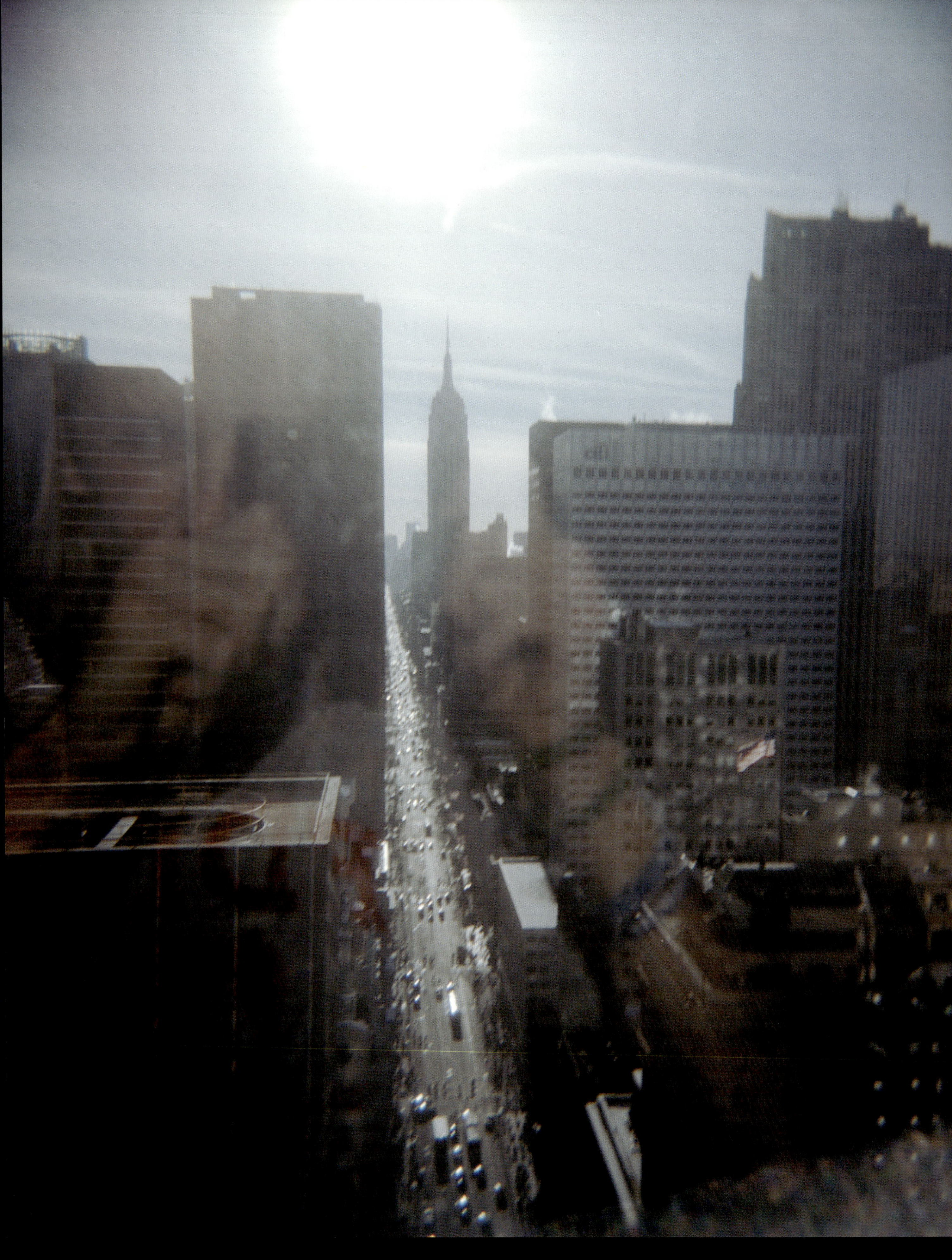

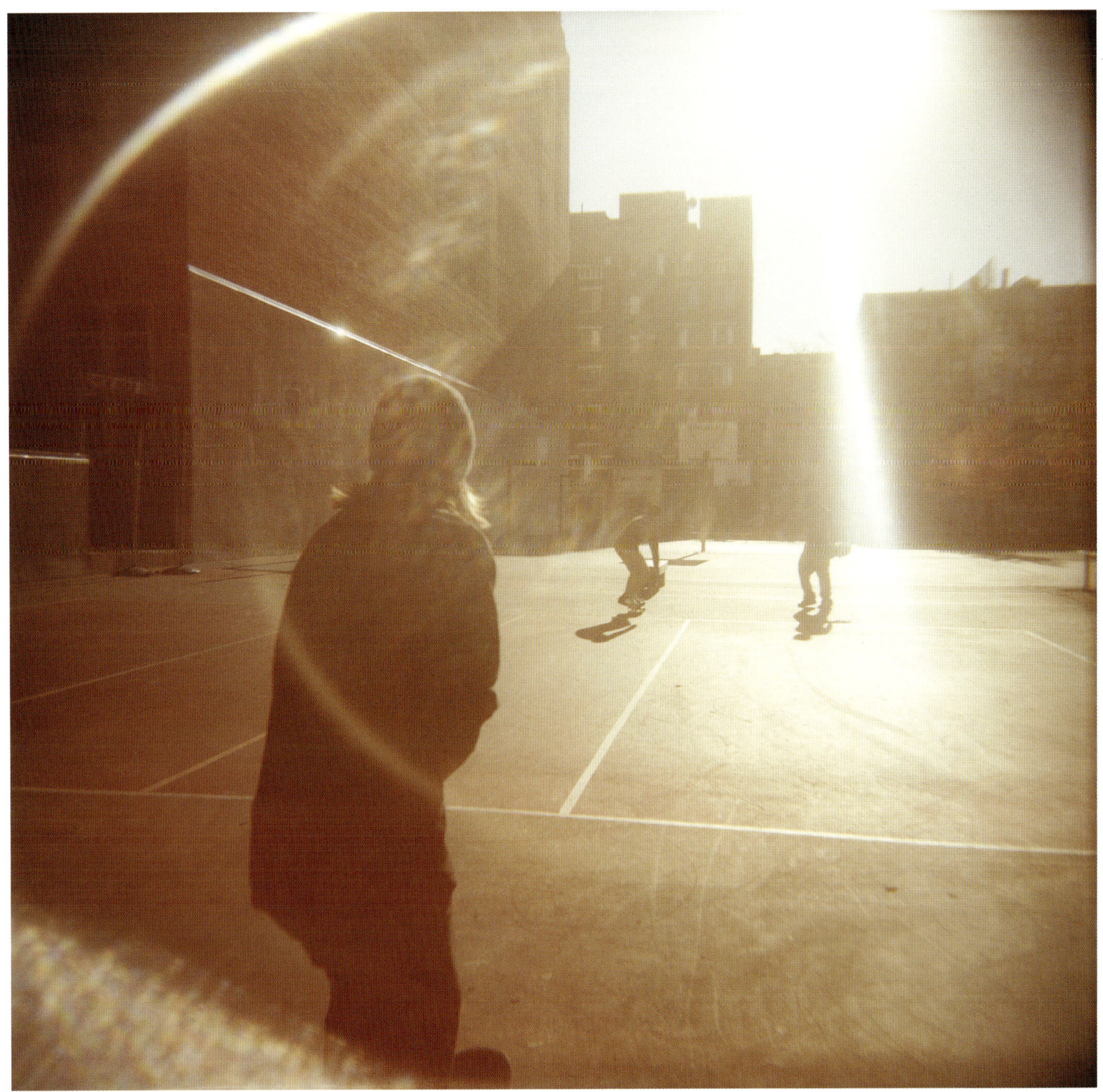

THESE TWO IMAGES were taken with a Holga, an inexpensive plastic camera that is very no-frills. The upside to this simple piece of equipment is that when you get the light right, the images are really hazy—just like in a dream.

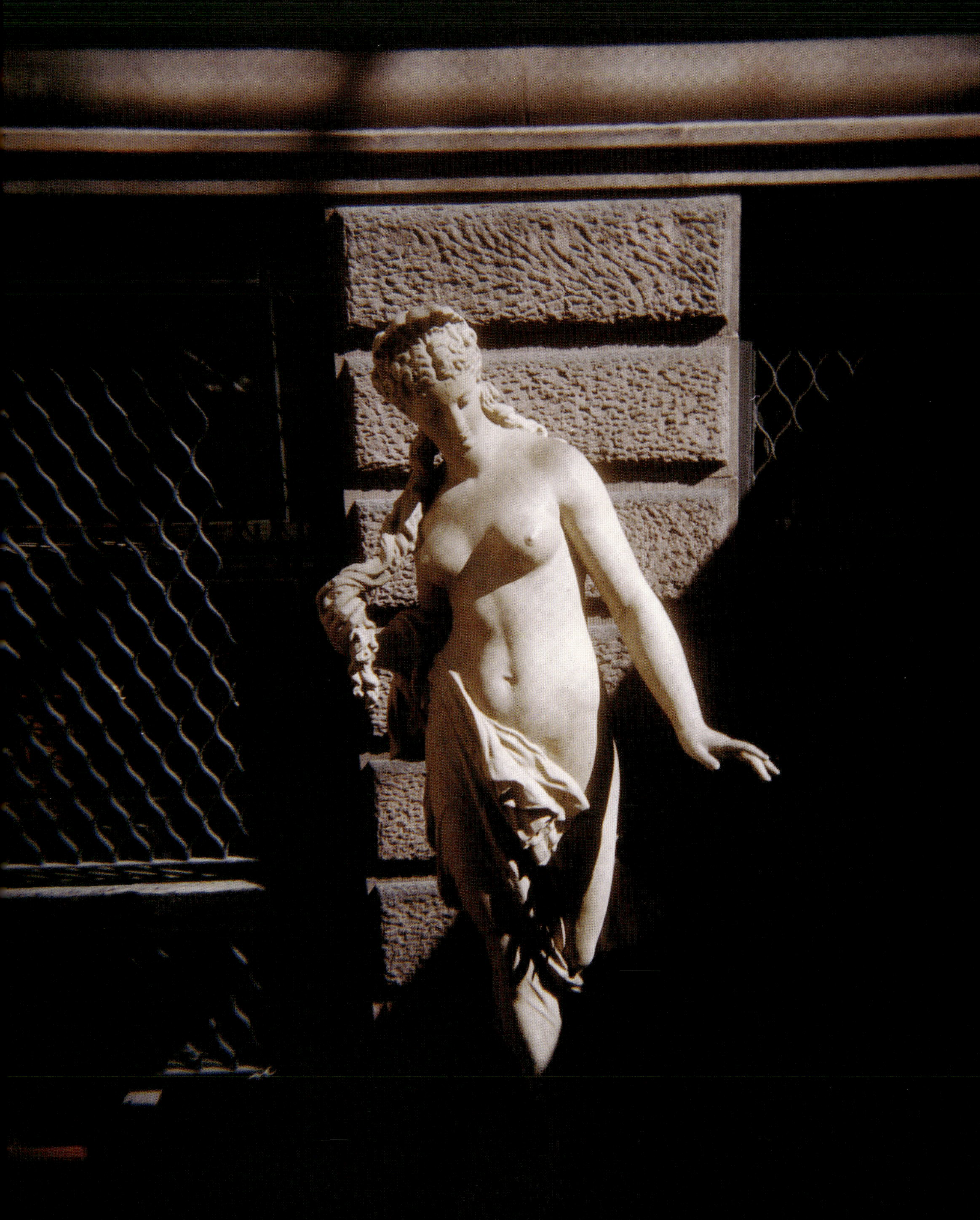

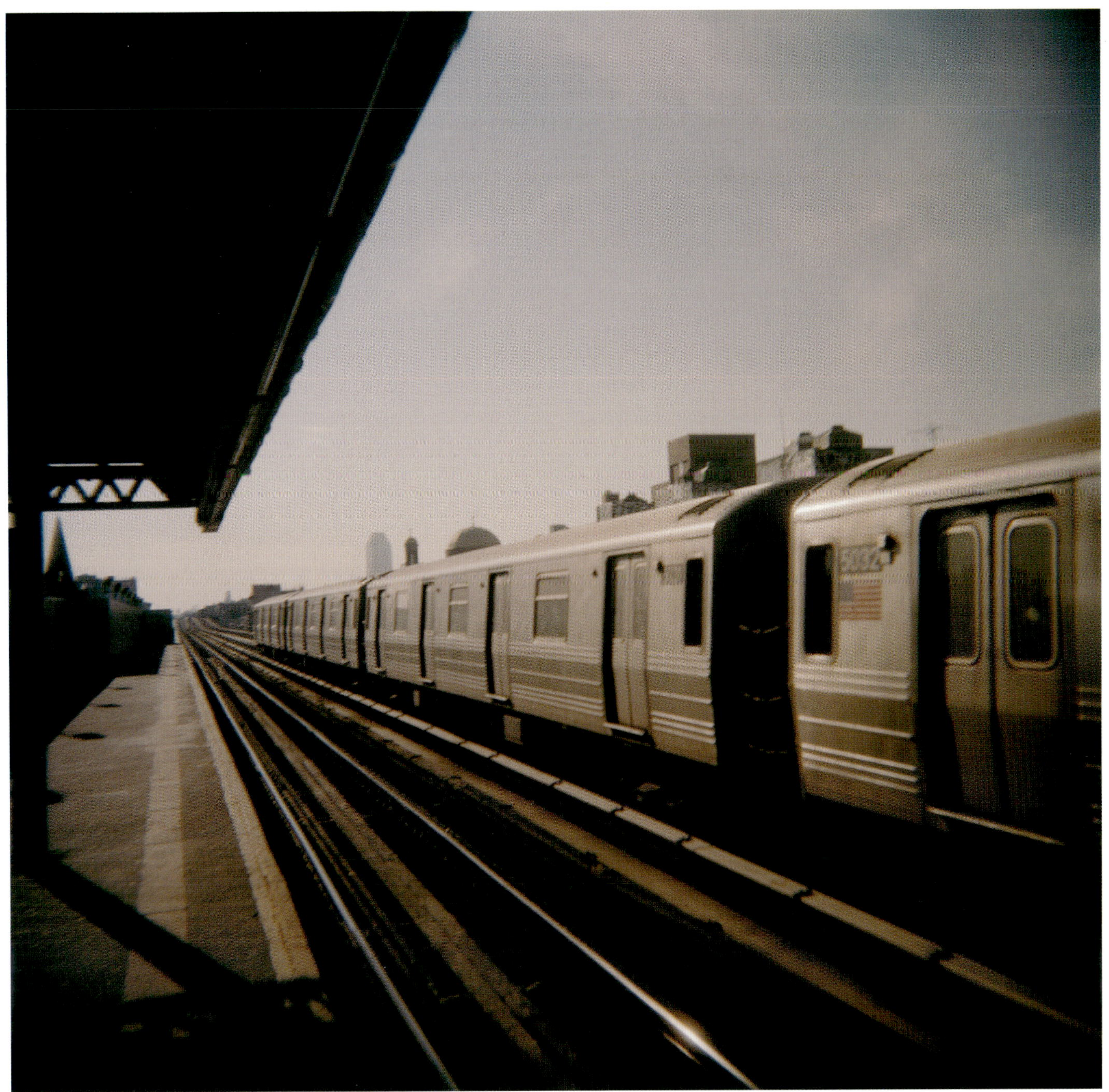

I NOTICED THIS STATUE of Aphrodite off 80th Street between Madison and Park. She's no longer there but when she was, people passing by hardly gave her a second look. You have to do a lot to draw attention to yourself in a town like this. Maybe that's why so many celebrities love New York—an ancient goddess can blend right into the crowd!

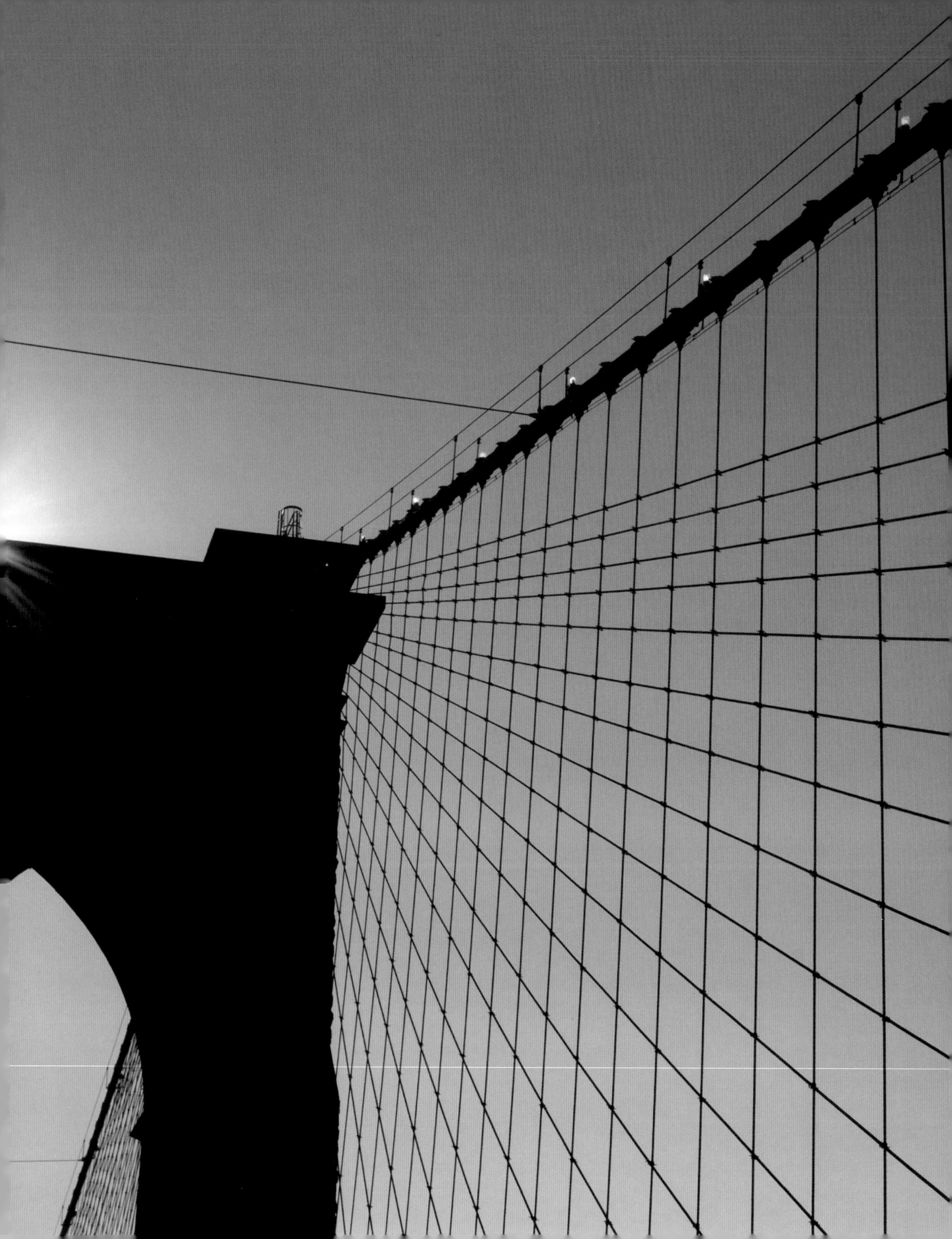

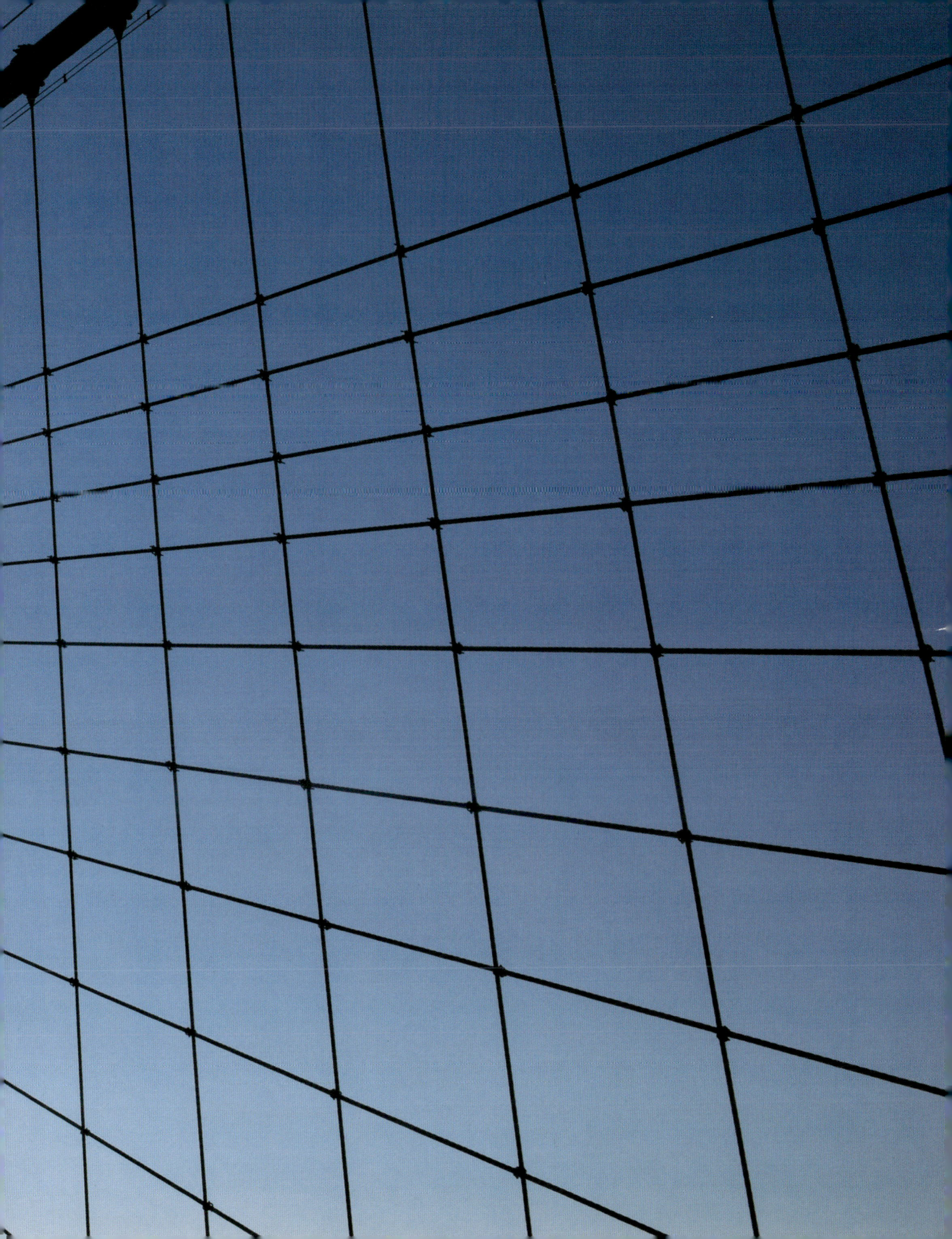

I LIKE TO VISIT CONEY ISLAND in the winter, when there aren't too many people around and I can see the attractions up close and with no distractions. Quite a few of the old amusement park rides are still around—towering like giant robots over the empty boardwalks. There's a totally different vibe to the warmer months when the place is thronged full of people and all the businesses are open. It's hard to imagine you're in the same location. You can hear the sound of the waves and seagulls squawking. Even better, you get the whole beach to yourself—well apart from the occasional guy with a metal detector looking for lost jewelry and probably finding loose change here and there. This place sometimes makes me feel like a teenager cutting out of school. It has that slightly forbidden vibe to it. On days like this, when it's pretty desolate, it's easy to imagine you've stumbled onto a lost part of the city that everyone's forgotten about. I've sometimes felt like an explorer finding the ruins of an ancient civilization, one where the people really knew how to have a good time and built monuments to thrills and excitement.

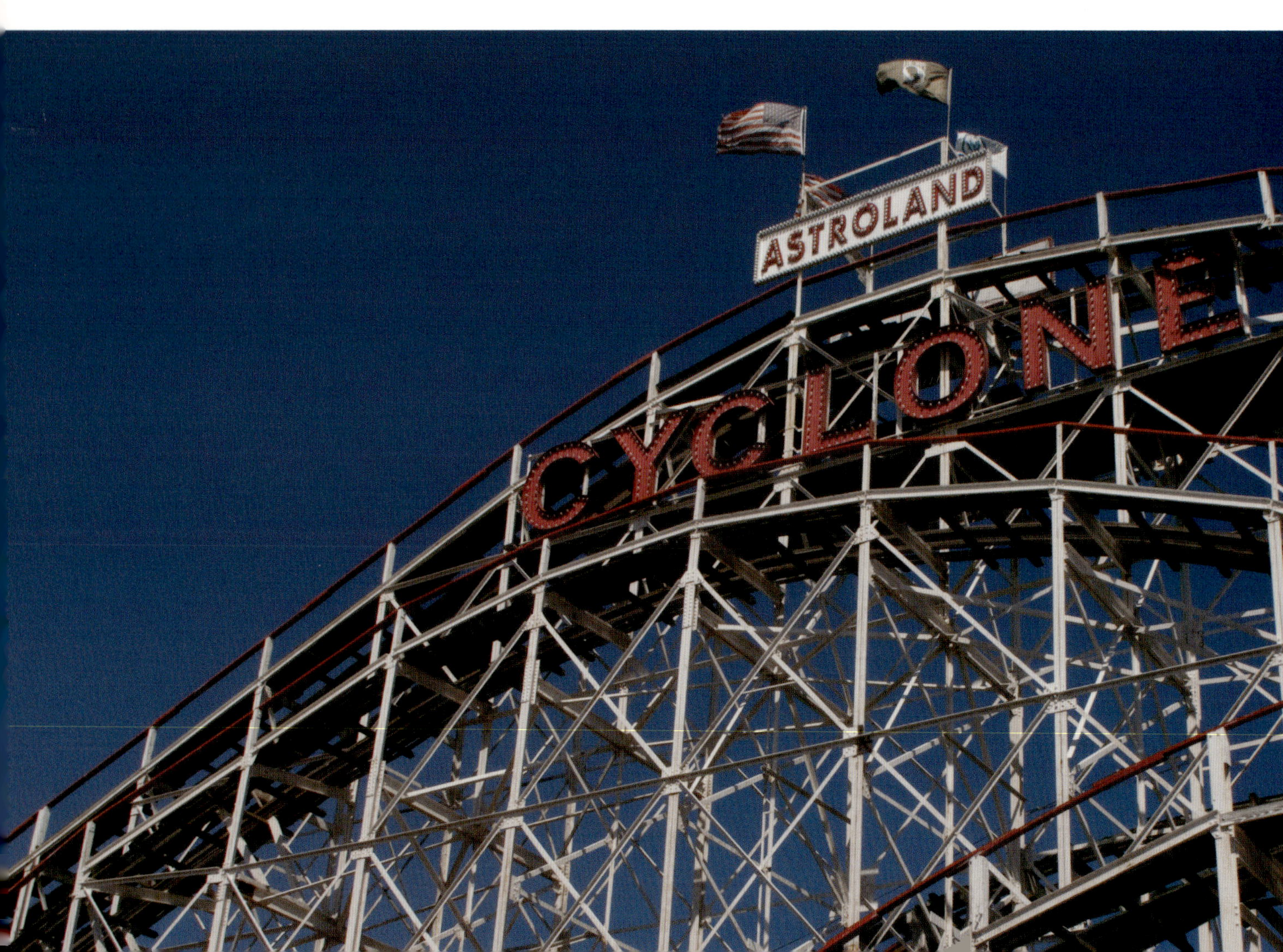

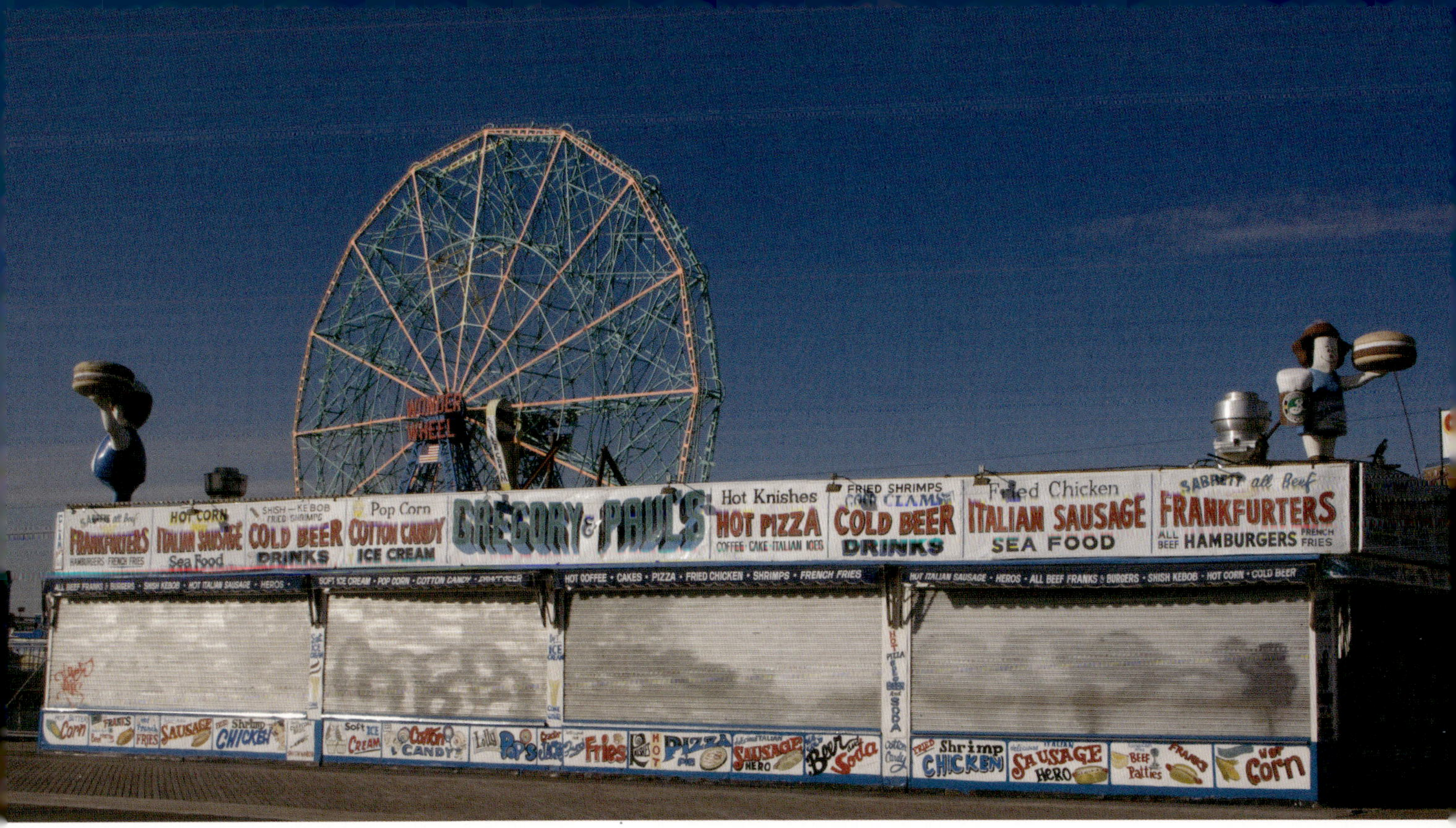

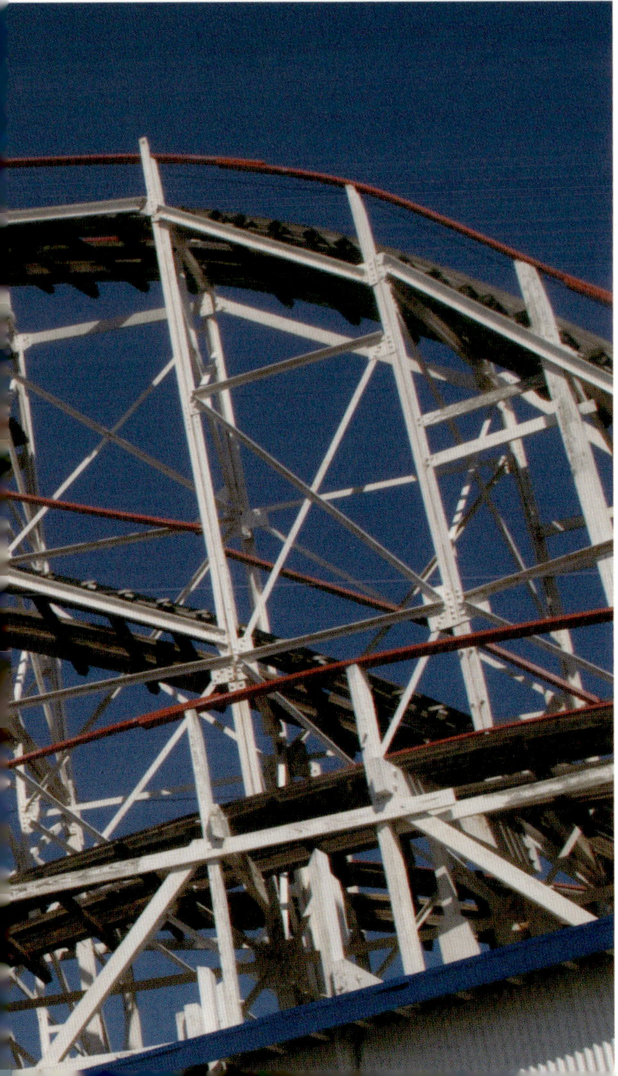

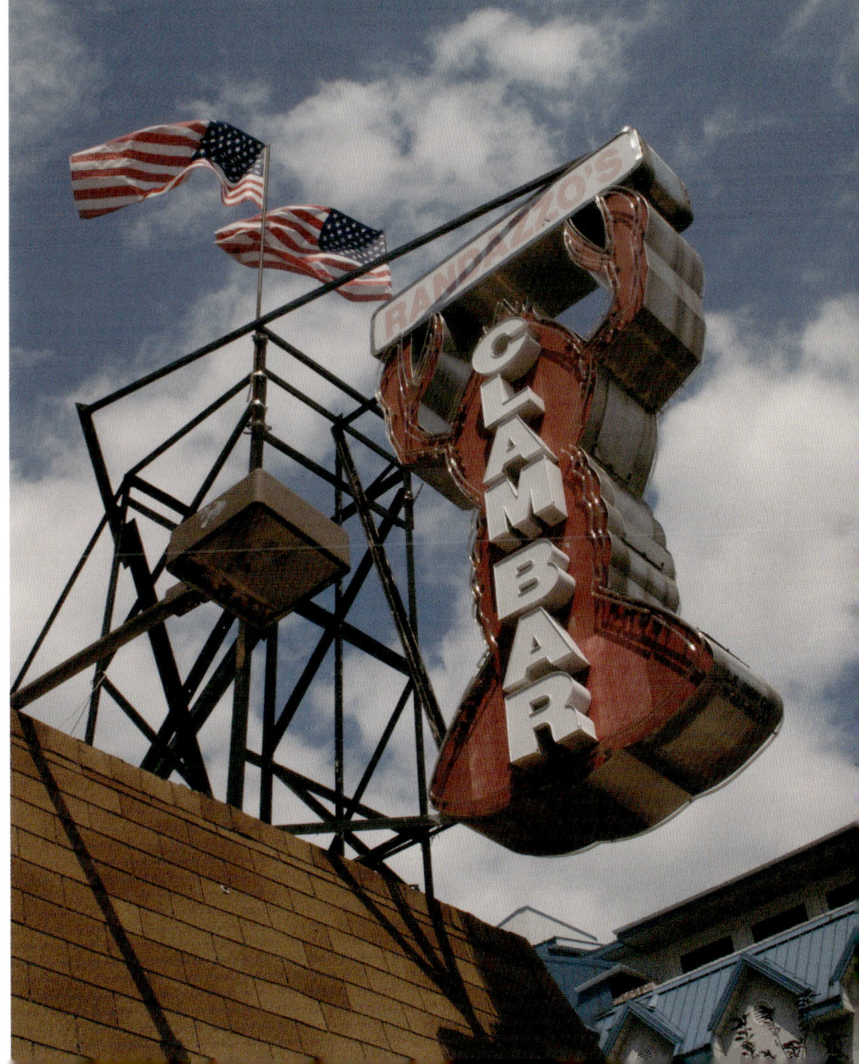
RANDAZZO'S
CLAMBAR

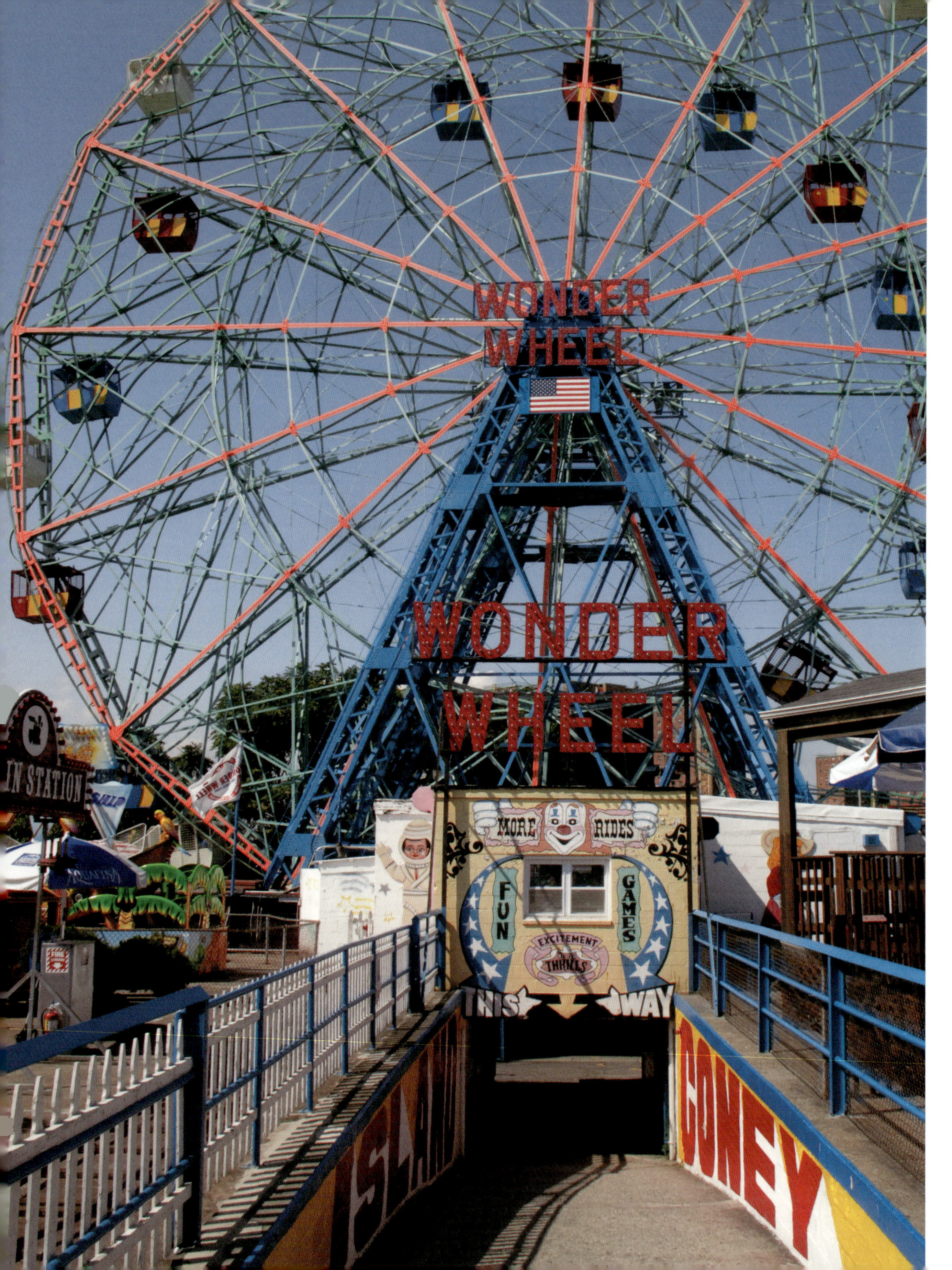

WONDER WHEEL
WONDER WHEEL
IN STATION
MORE RIDES
FUN
GAMES
EXCITEMENT
THRILLS
THIS WAY
CONEY

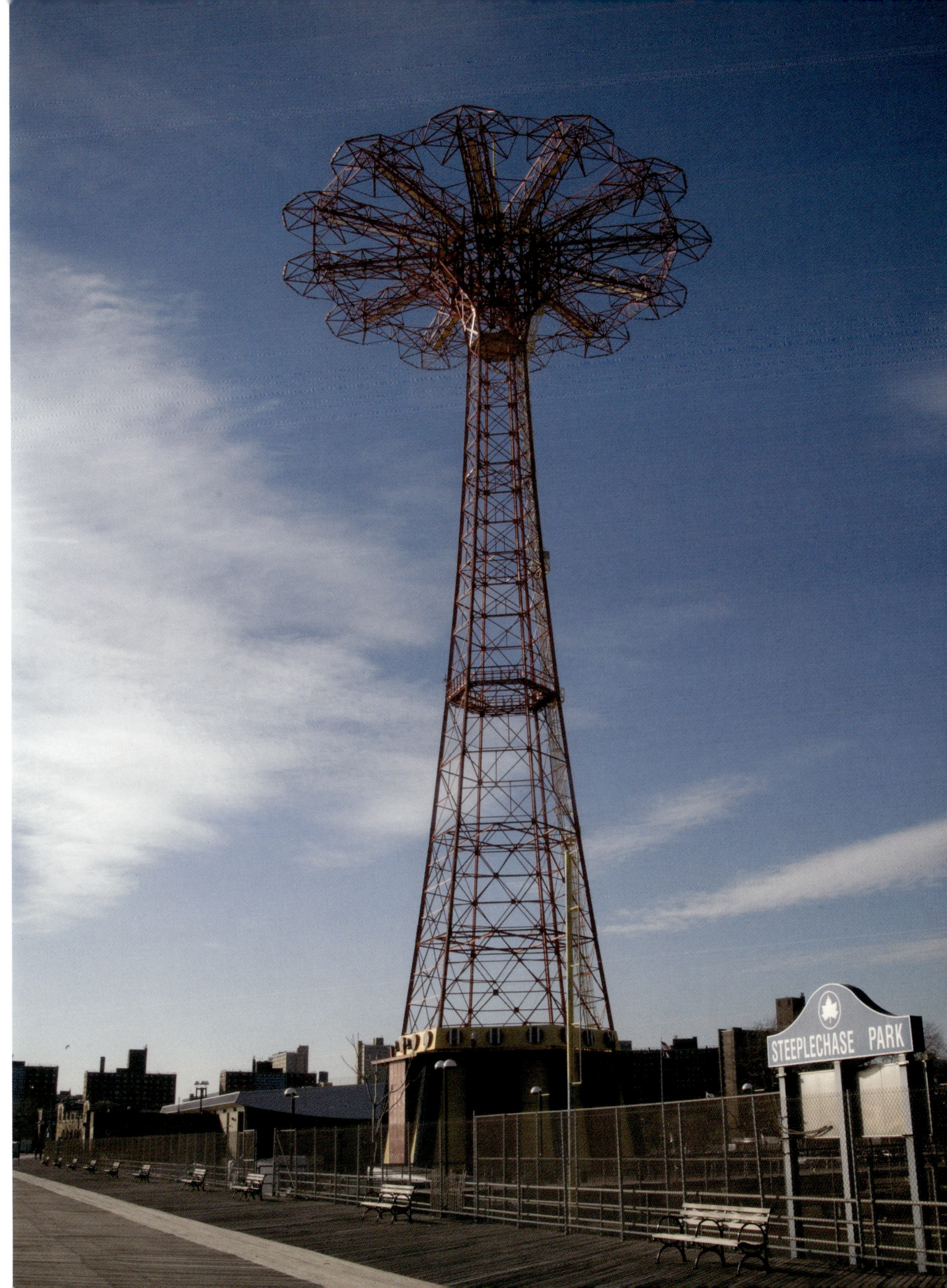
STEEPLECHASE PARK

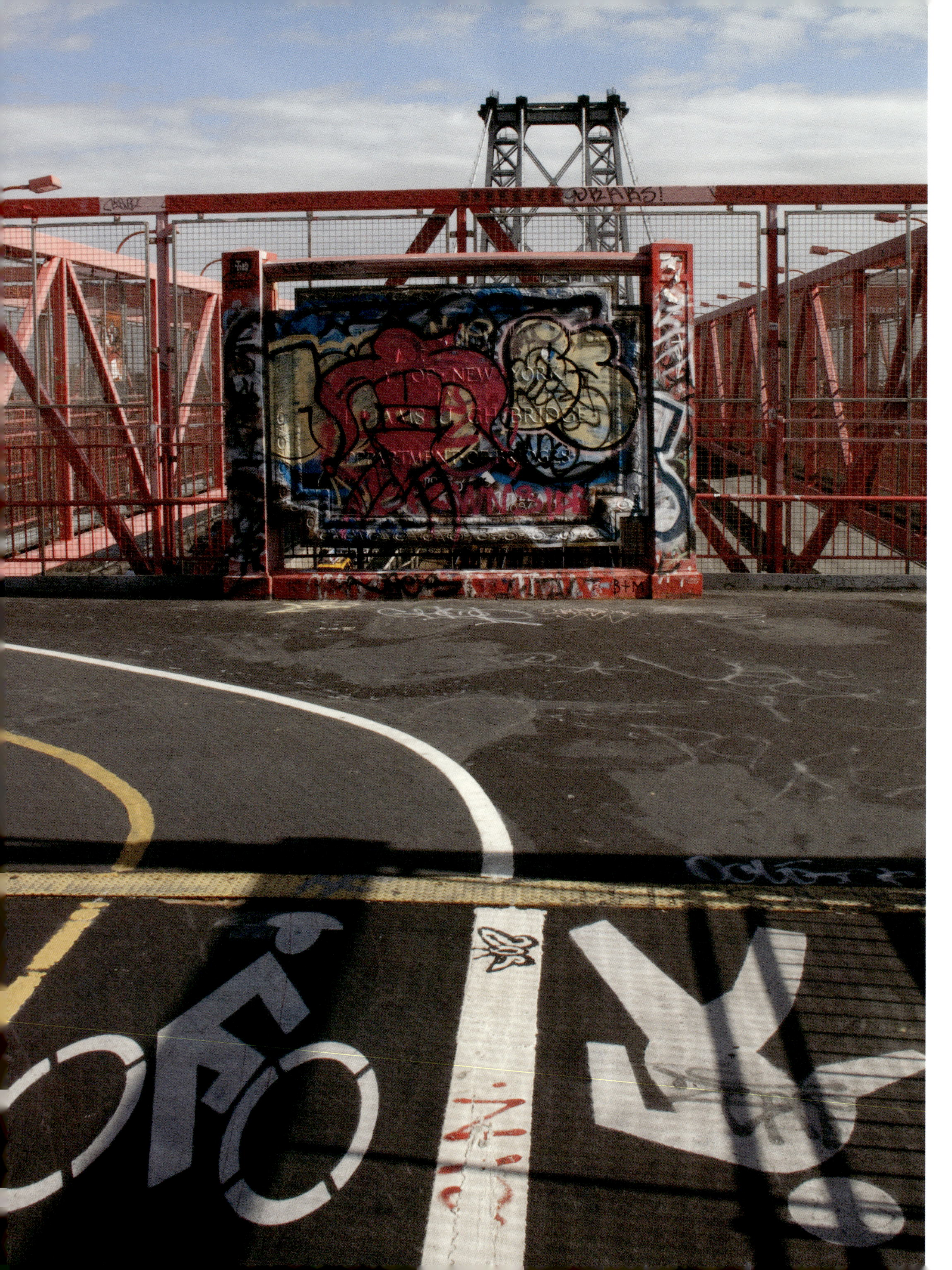

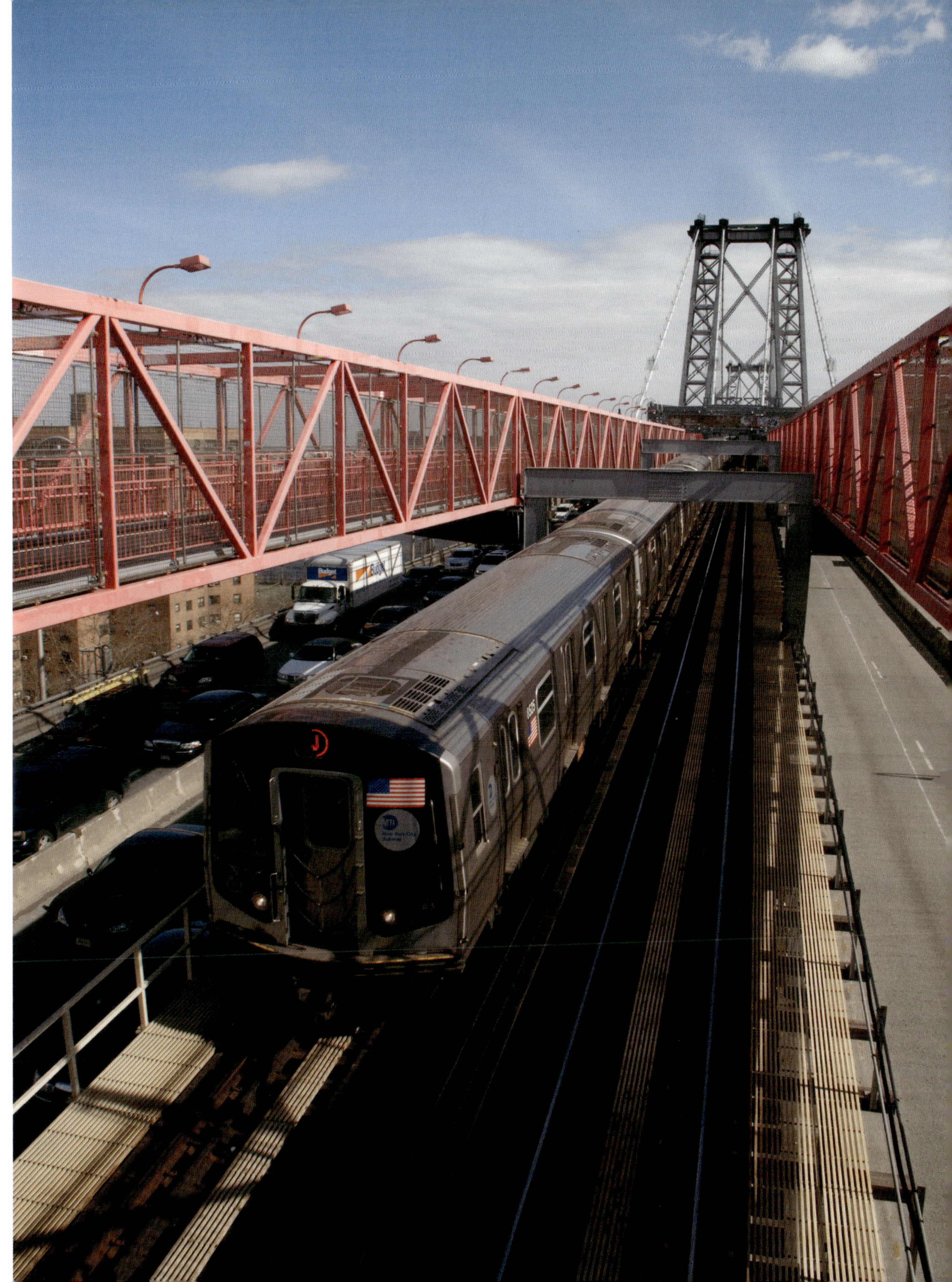
Budget
J

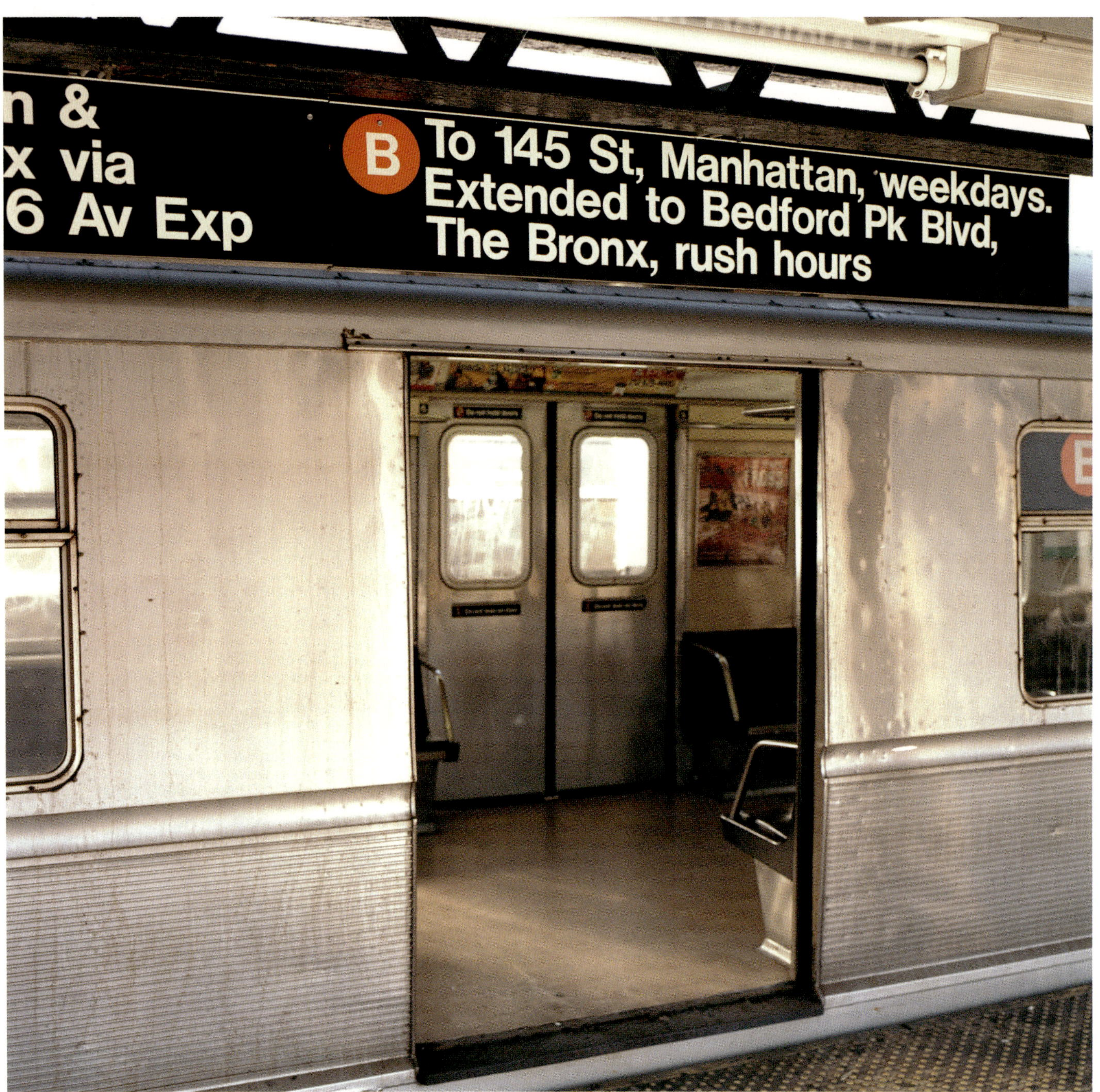

IN NEW YORK it's easy to forget that miles of sandy beaches are just a subway ride away. The B train takes you right to the shores of Brighton Beach. While you contemplate an ocean dip, savor some Russian street food—if you order too much you can always share your leftovers with the seagulls!

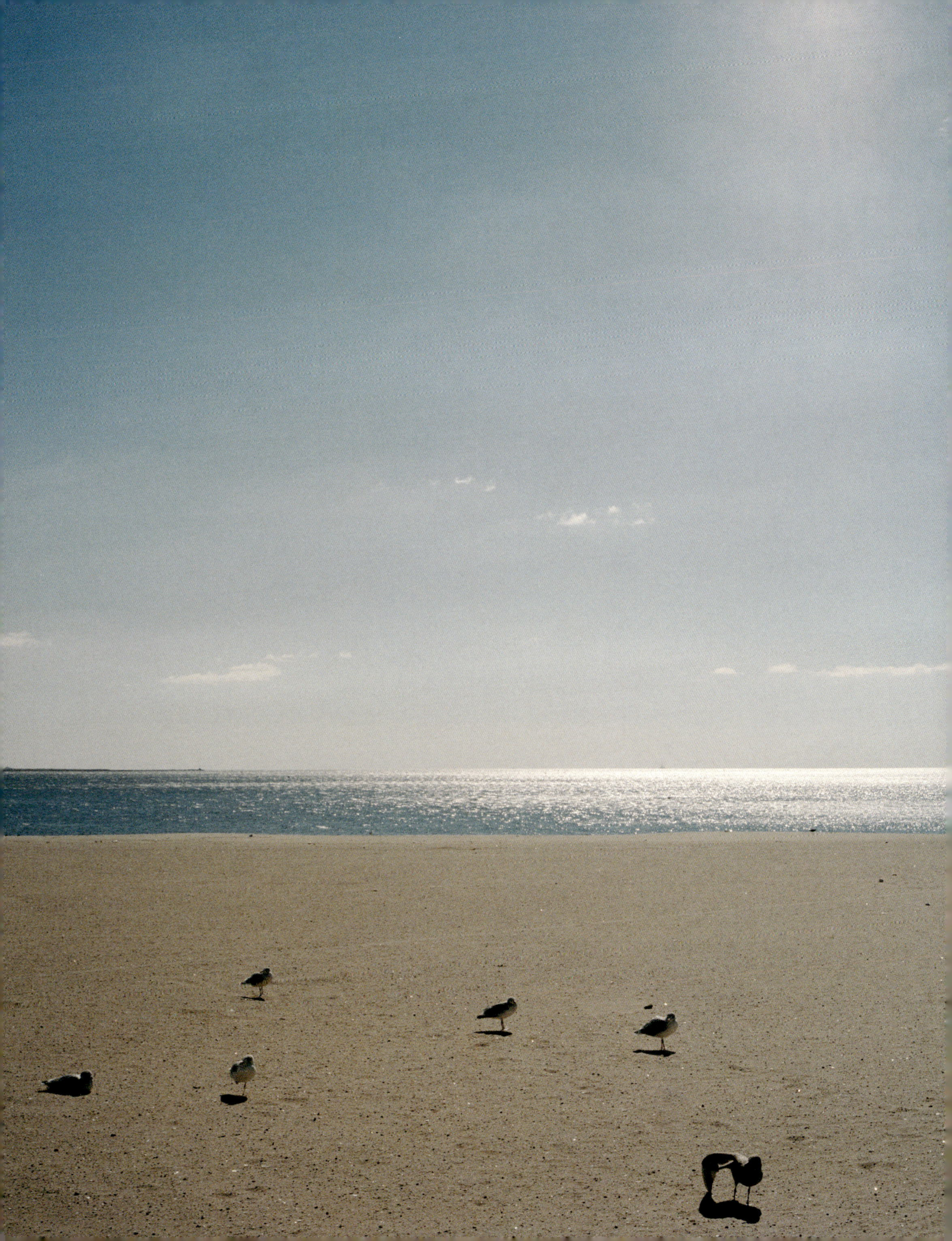

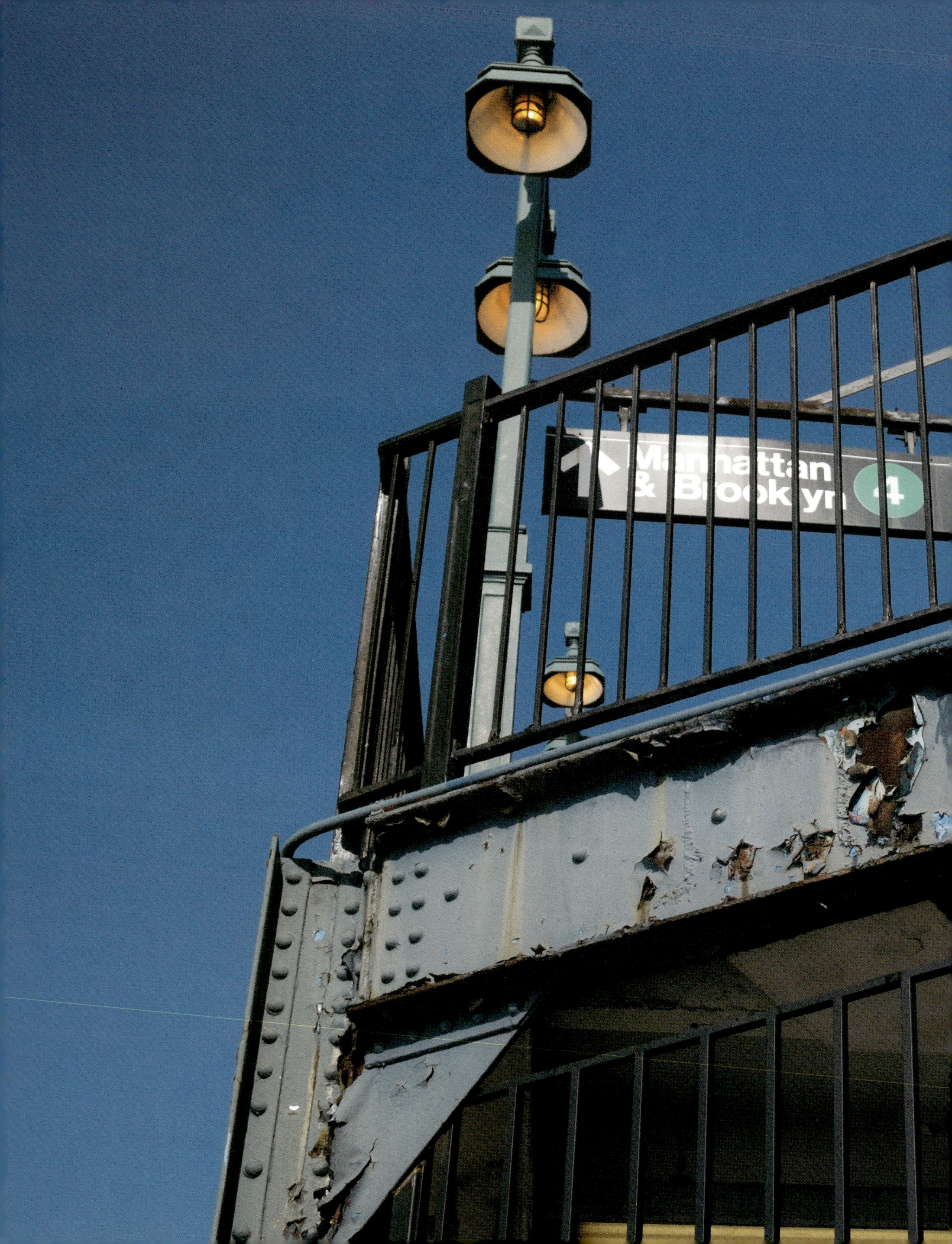
Manhattan
& Brooklyn
4

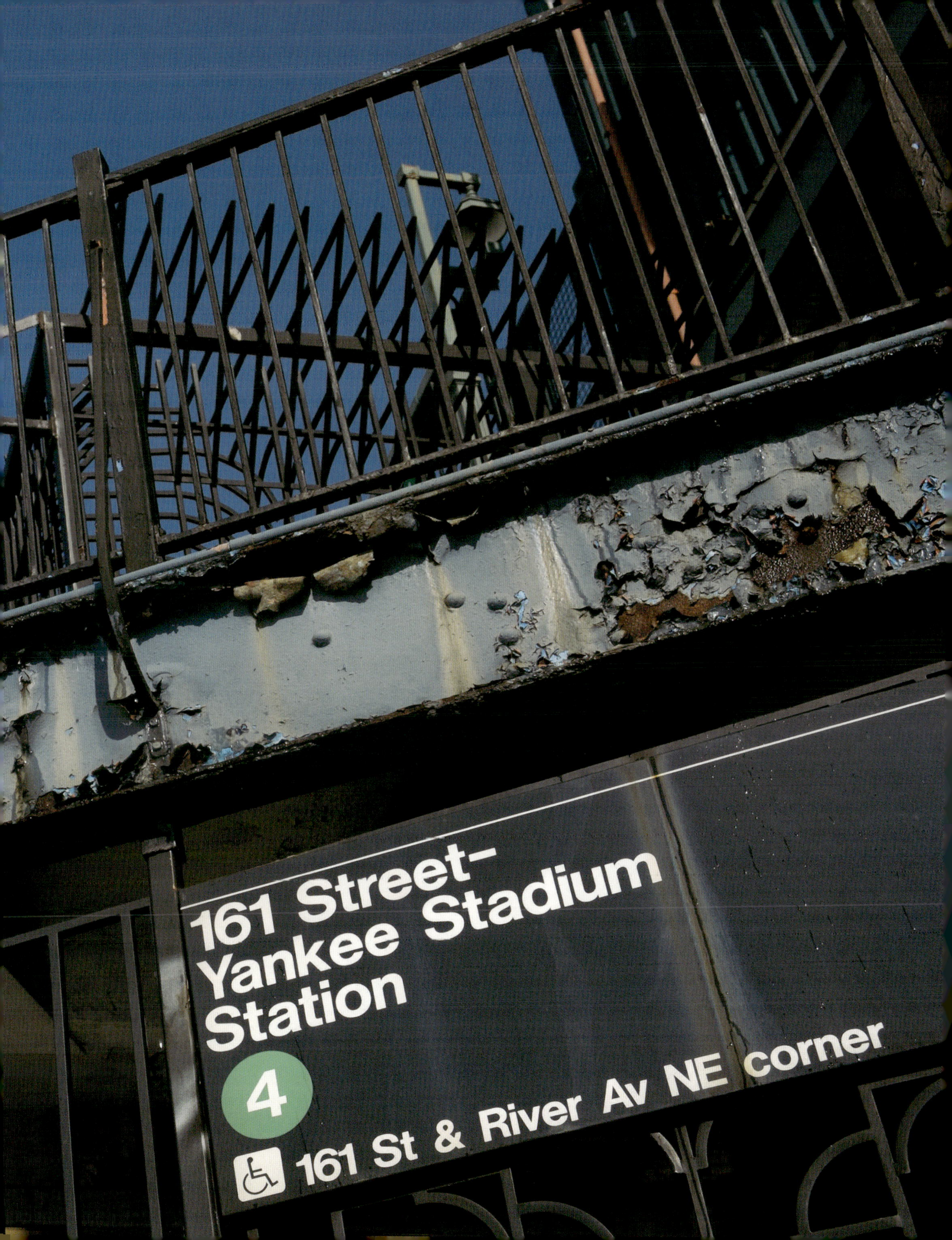
161 Street-
Yankee Stadium
Station
4
161 St & River Av NE corner

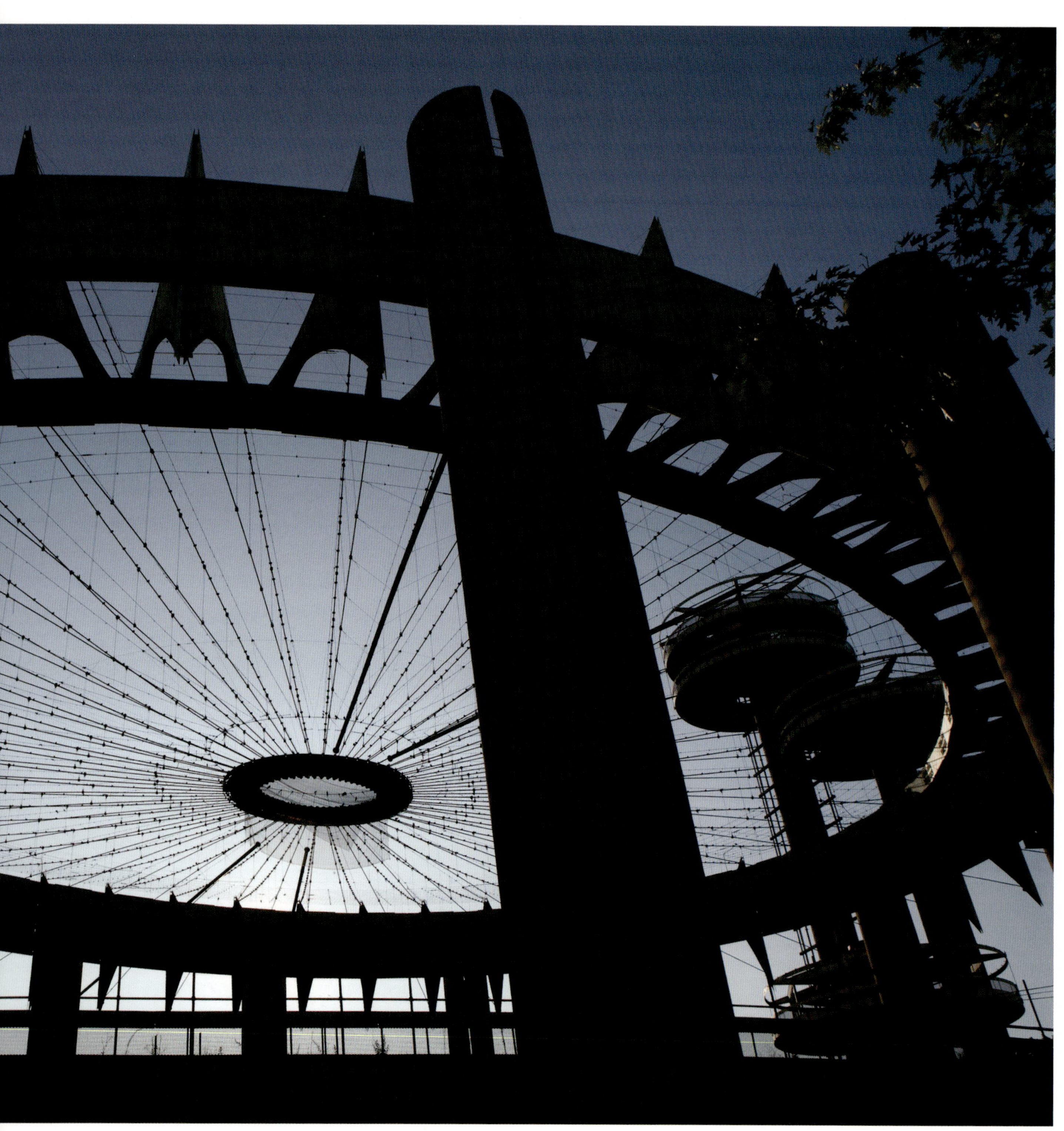

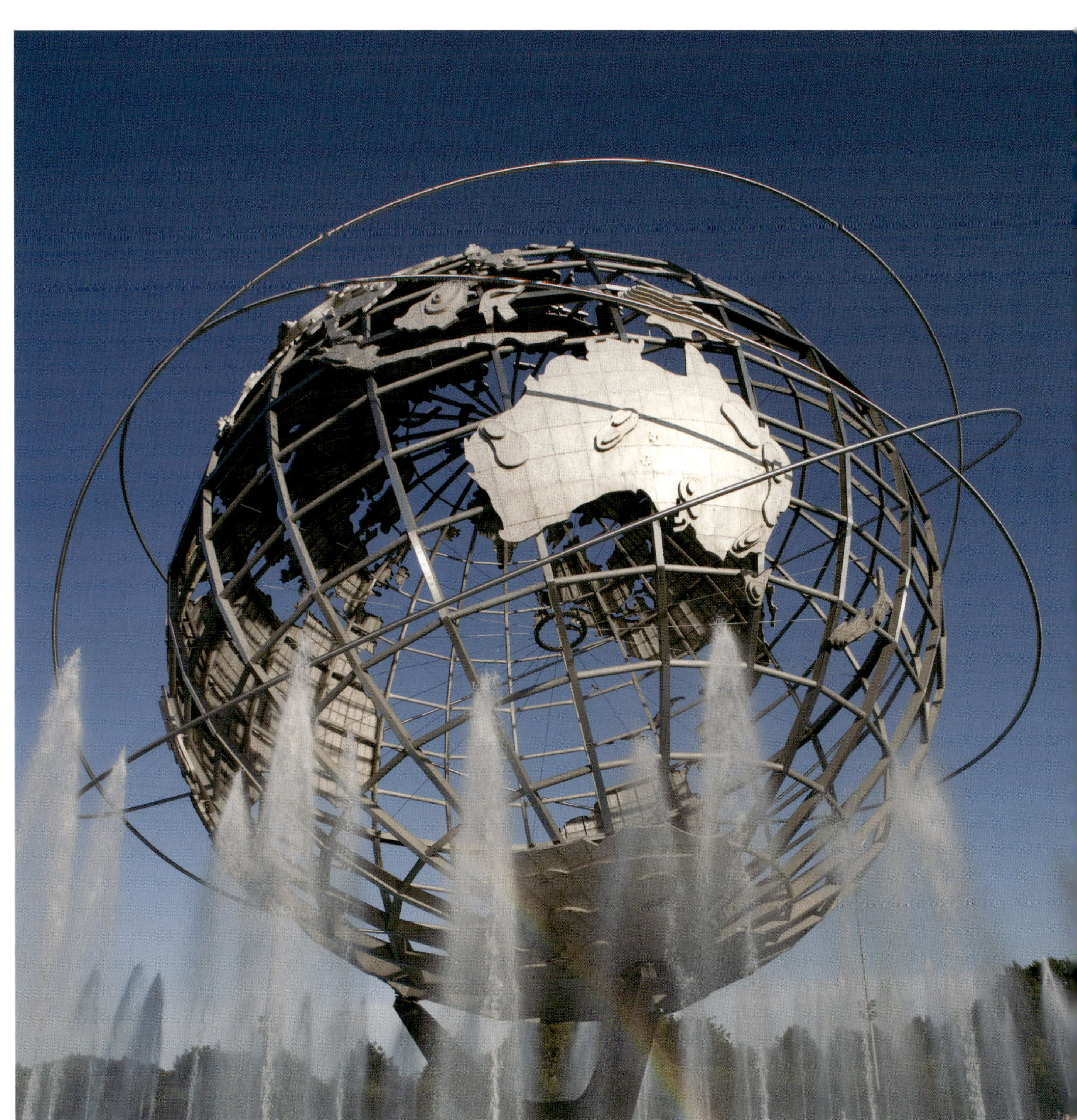

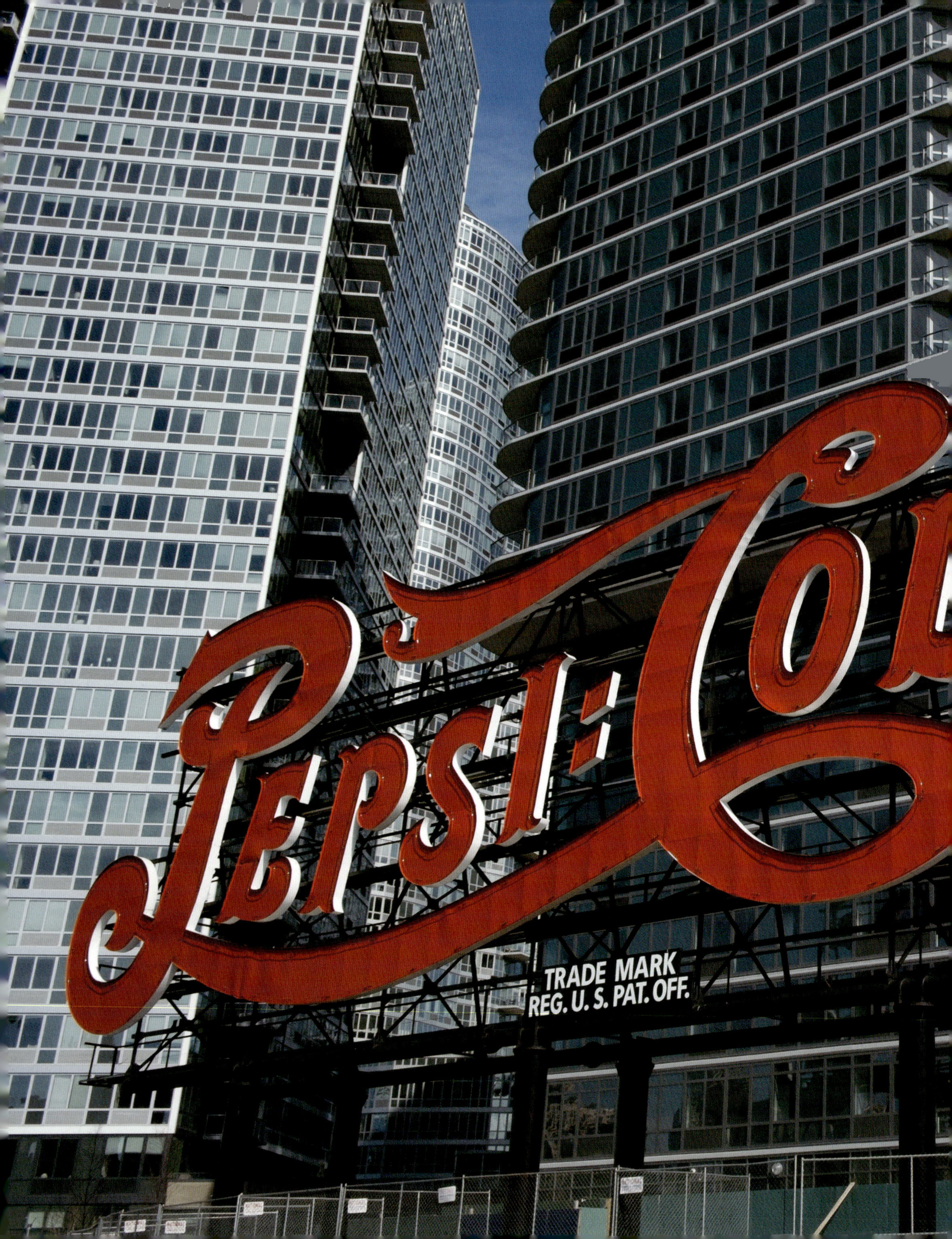
TRADE MARK
REG. U. S. PAT. OFF.

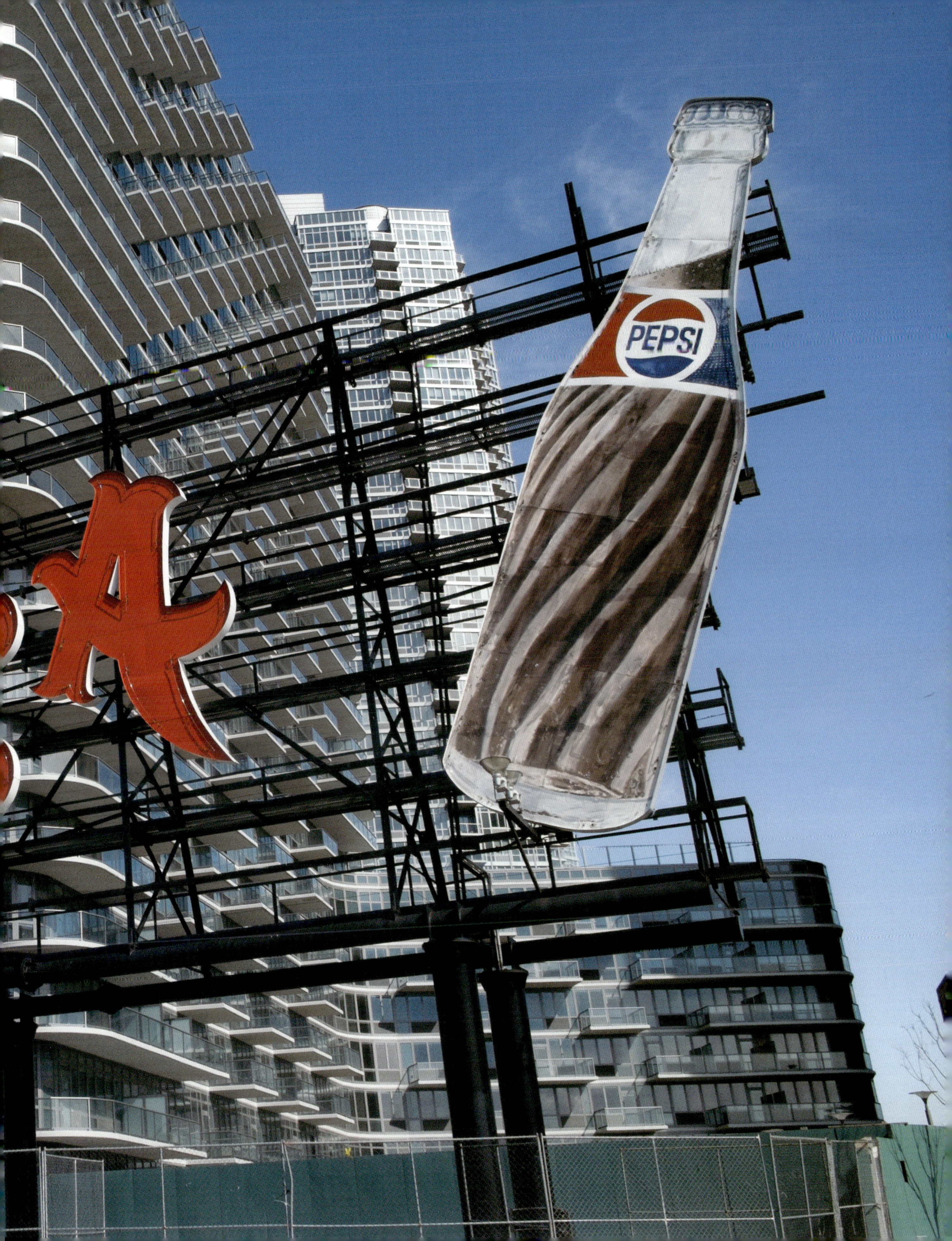
PEPSI

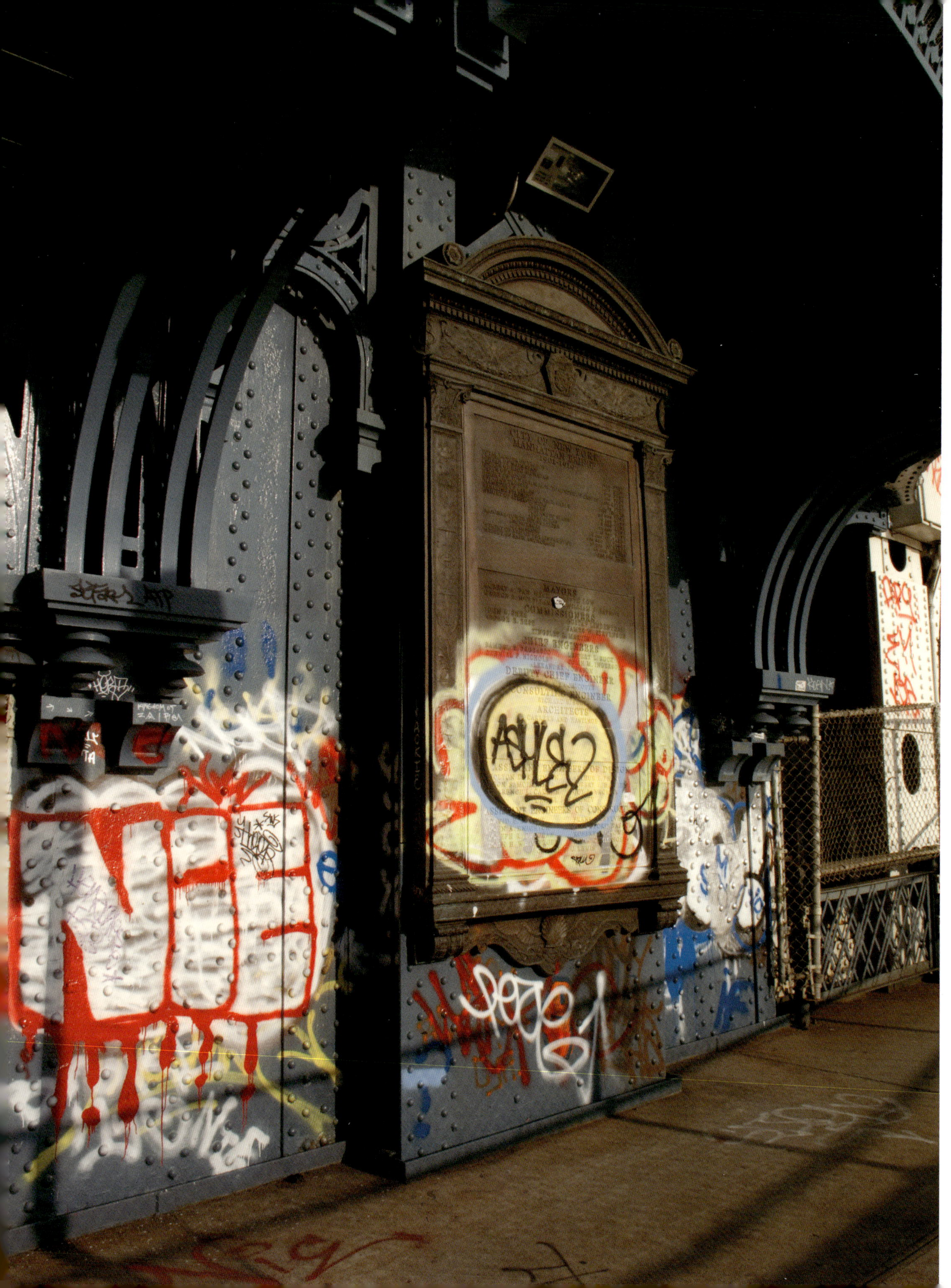
MAYORS
COMMISSIONERS
CHIEF ENGINEERS
DEPUTY CHIEF ENGINEER
CONSULTING ENGINEER
ARCHITECTS

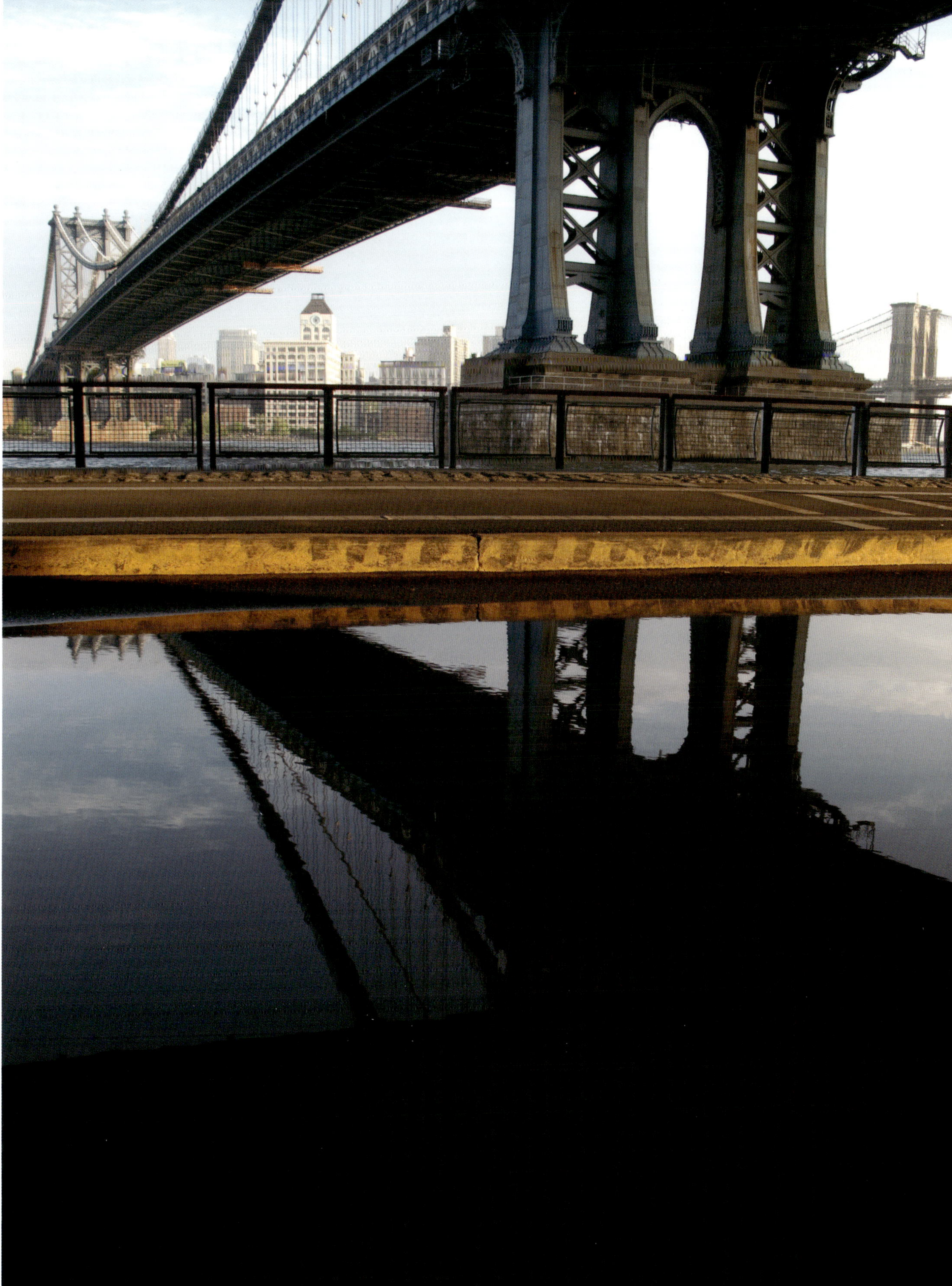

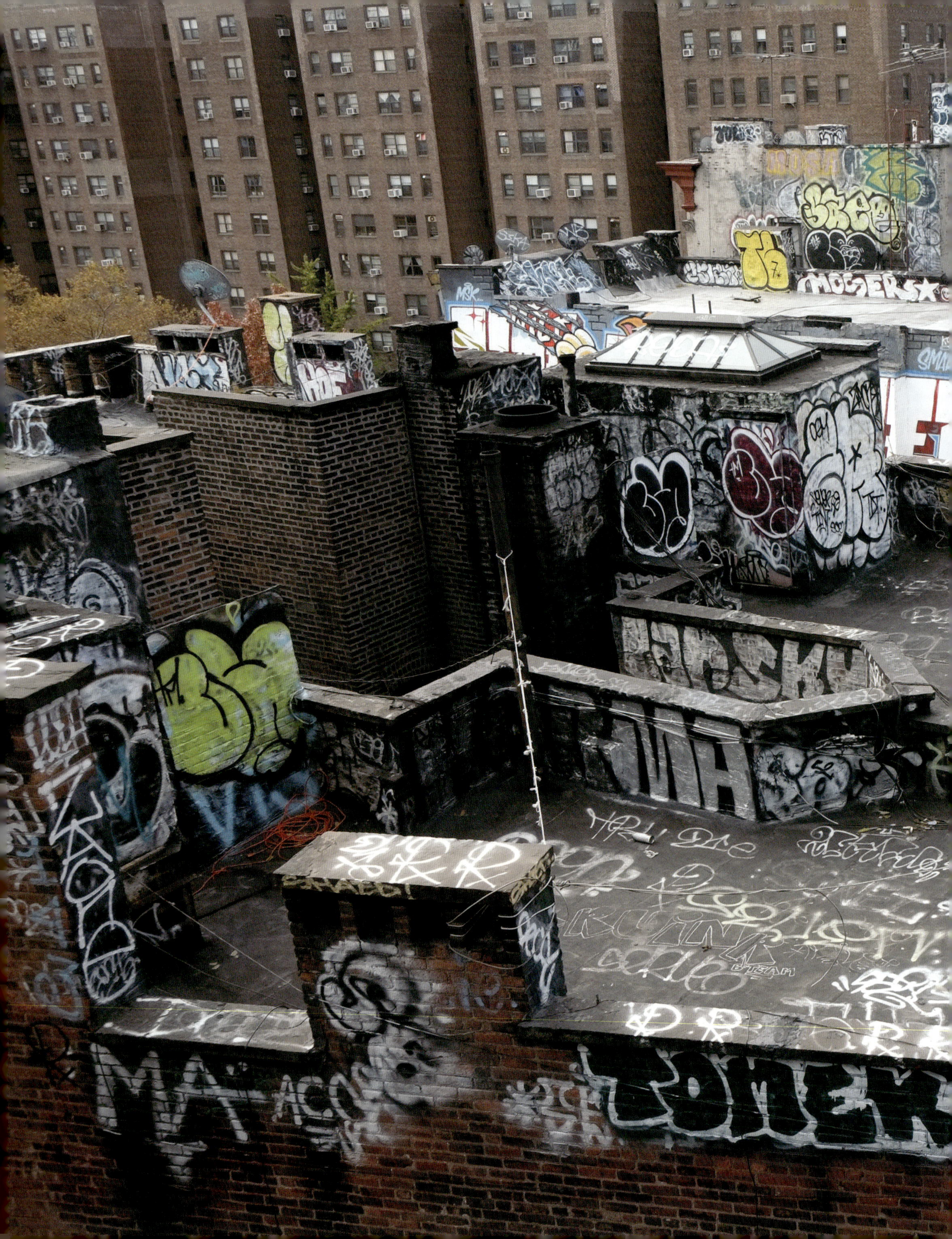

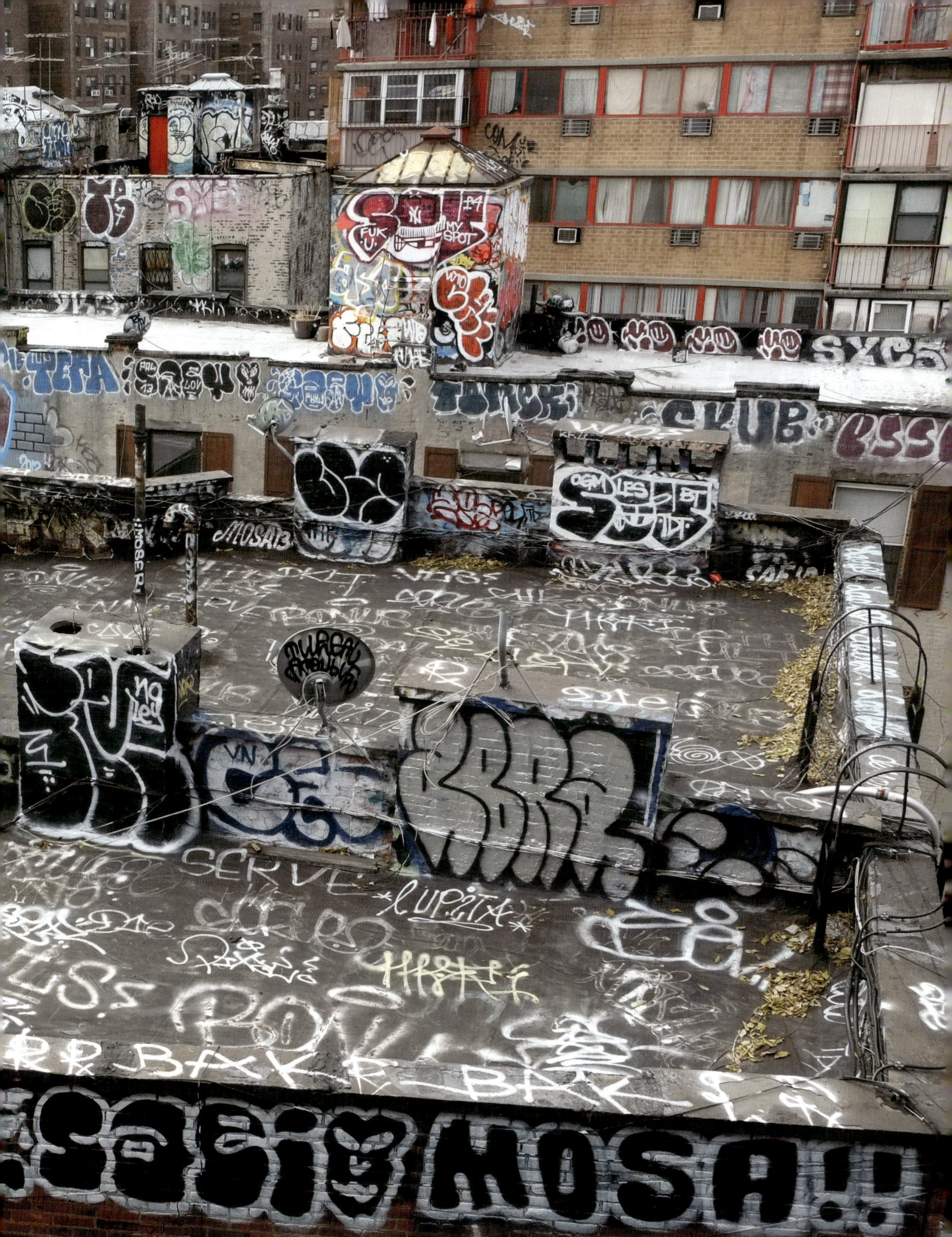
SXC5
SKUB
MOSA13
SERVE
LUPITA
MOSA!!

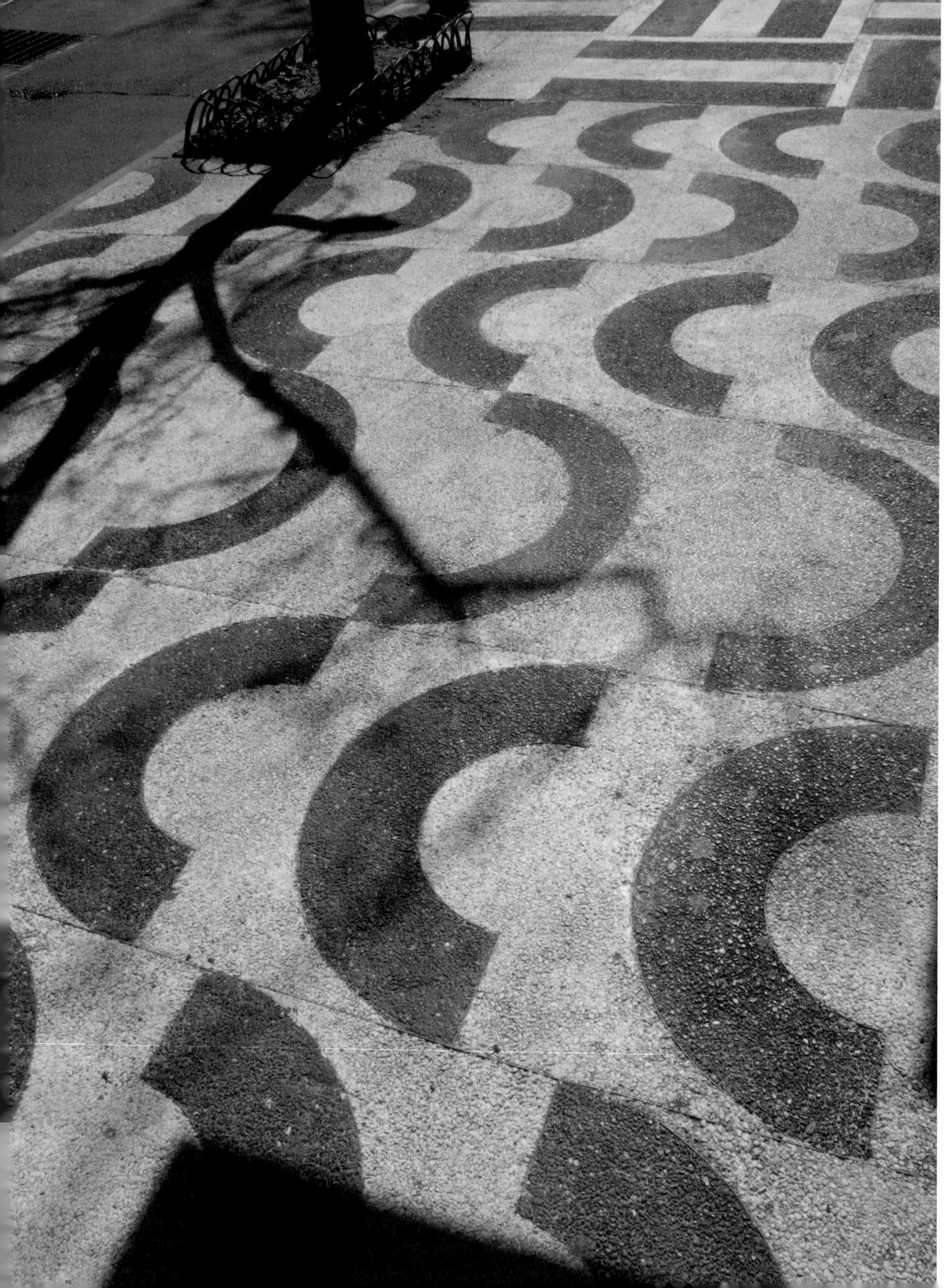

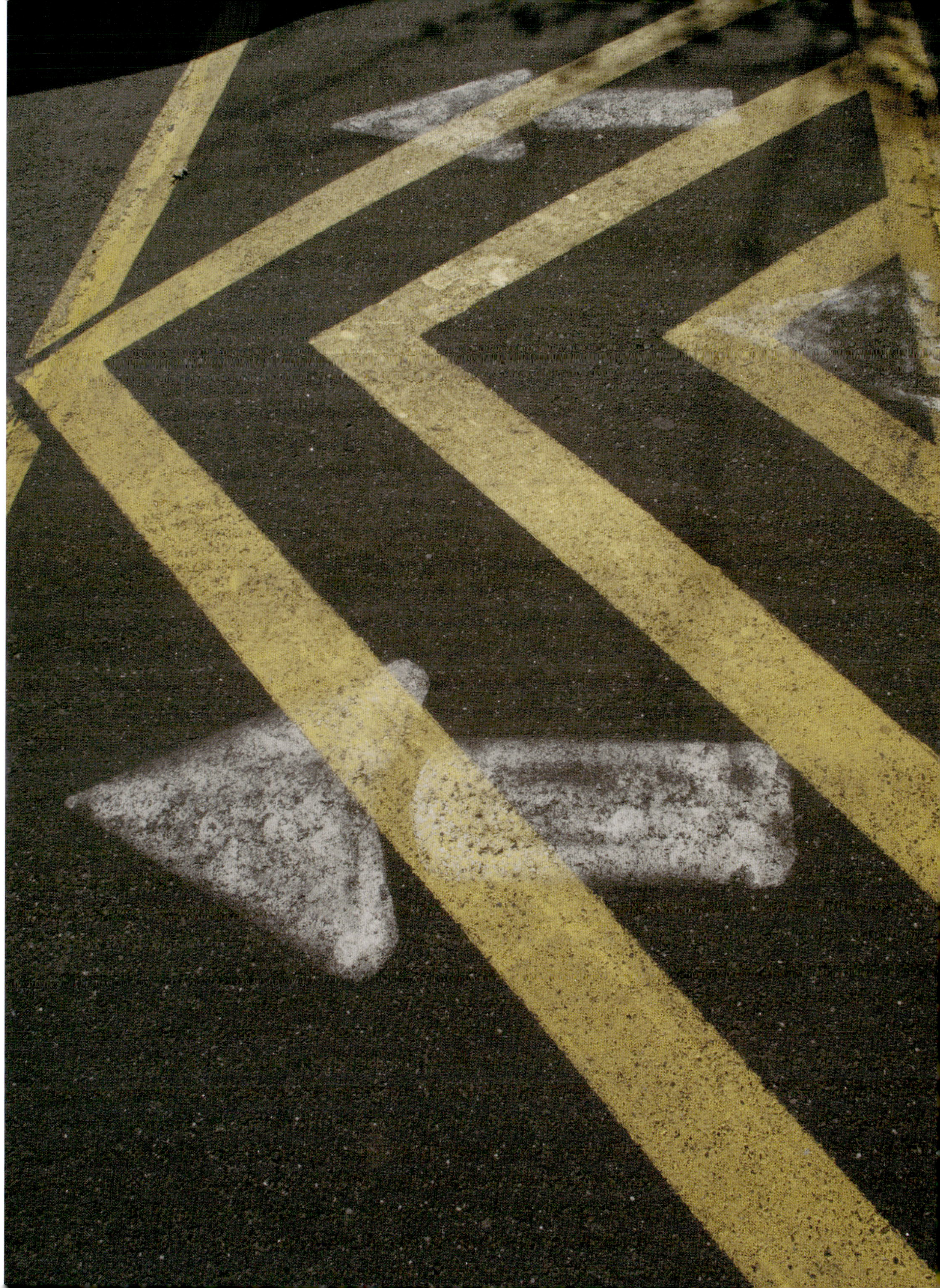

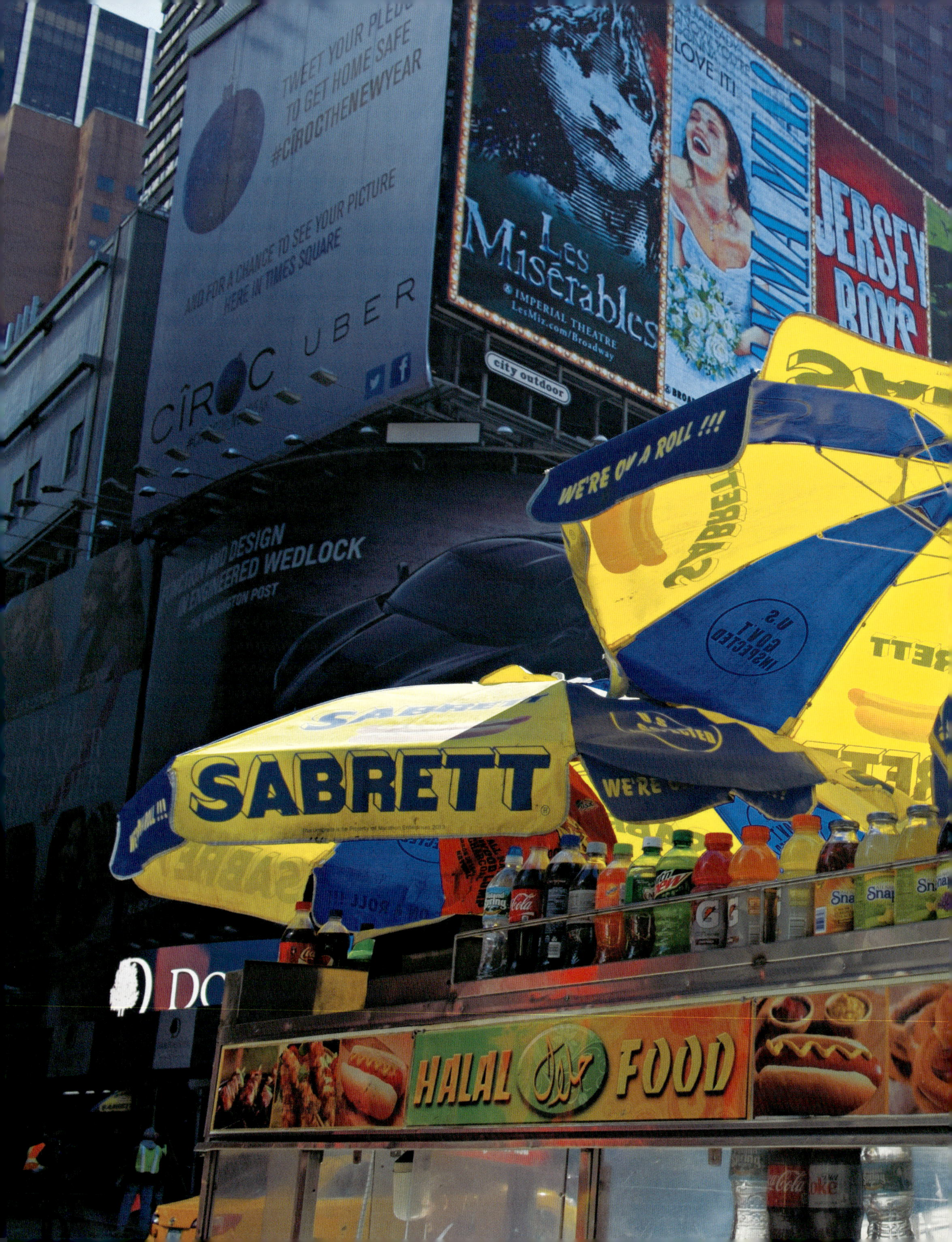

TO GET HOME SAFE
#CÎROCTHENEWYEAR
AND FOR A CHANCE TO SEE YOUR PICTURE
HERE IN TIMES SQUARE
CÎROC
UBER
Les Misérables
IMPERIAL THEATRE
LesMiz.com/Broadway
city outdoor
LOVE IT!
JERSEY BOYS
ENGINEERED WEDLOCK
WE'RE ON A ROLL !!!
SABRETT
HALAL FOOD

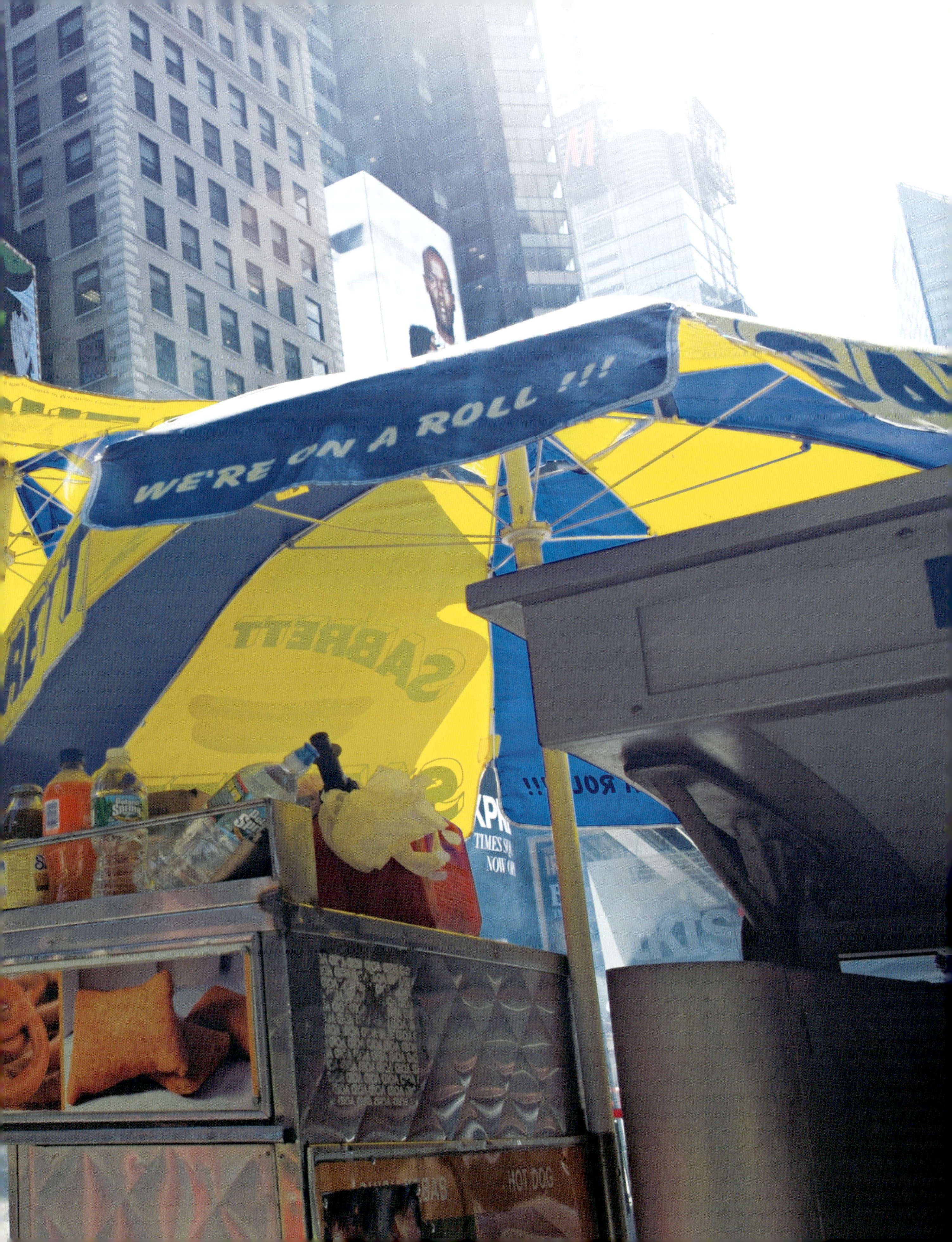
WE'RE ON A ROLL !!!
SABRETT
HOT DOG

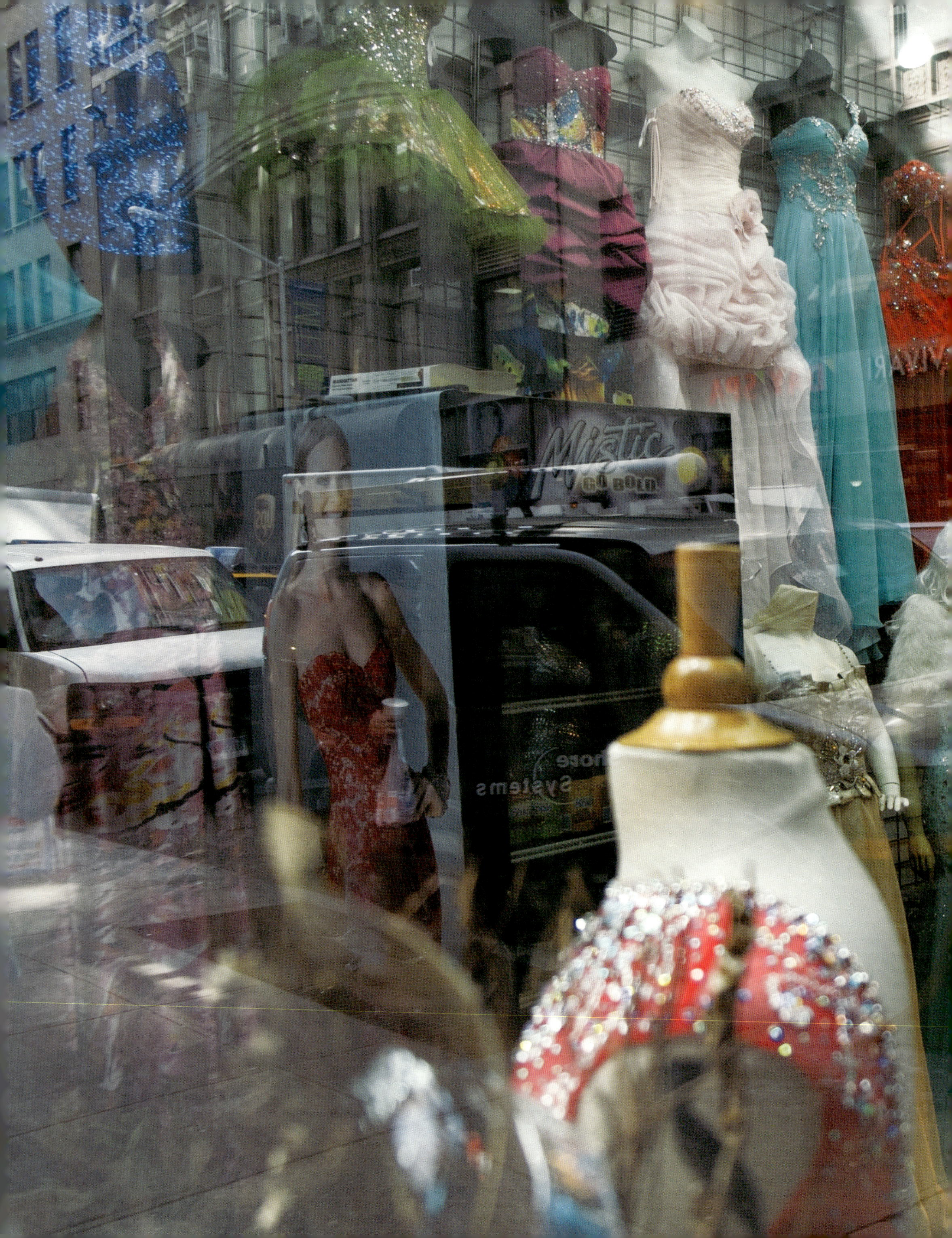
Mistic
GO BOLD
Systems

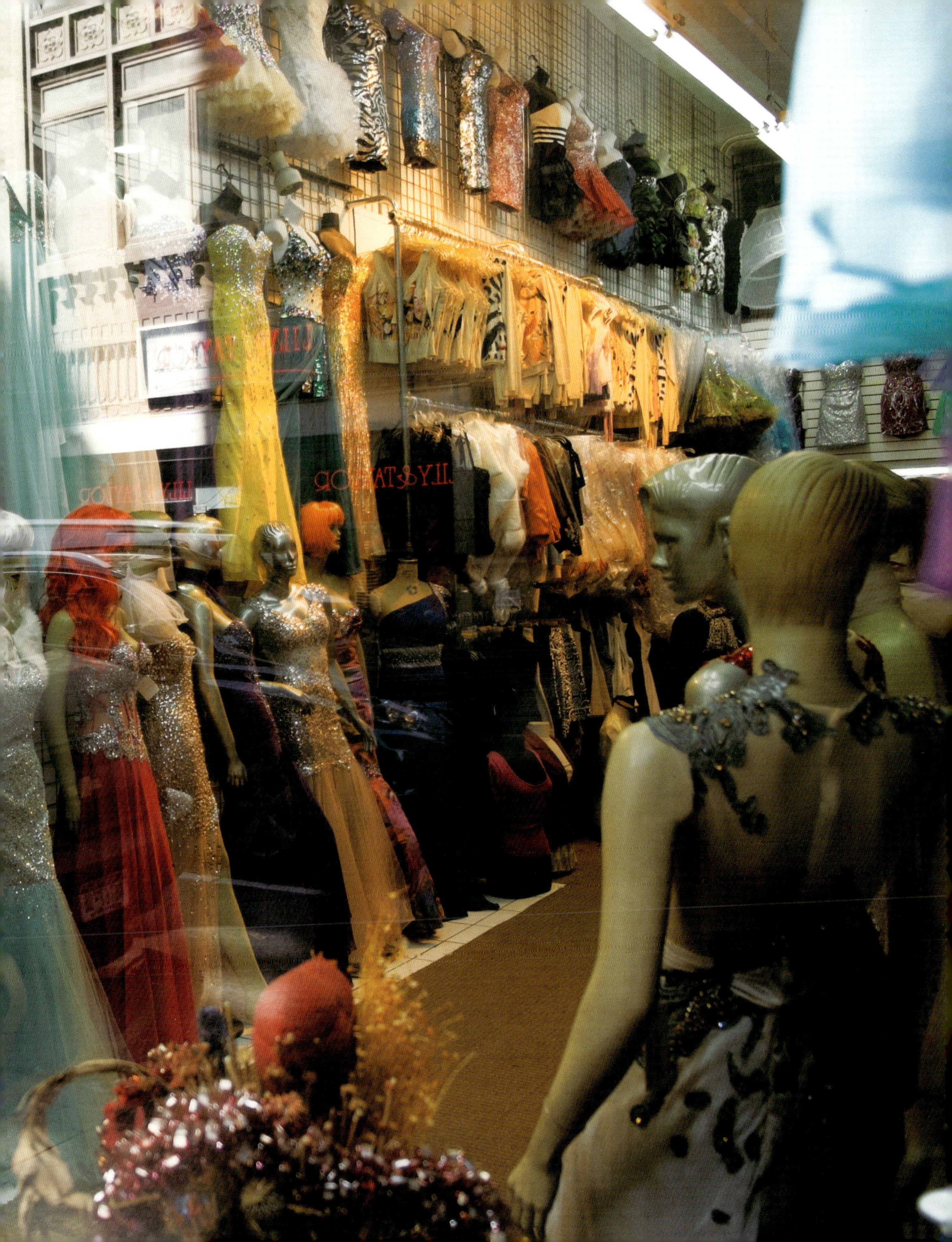

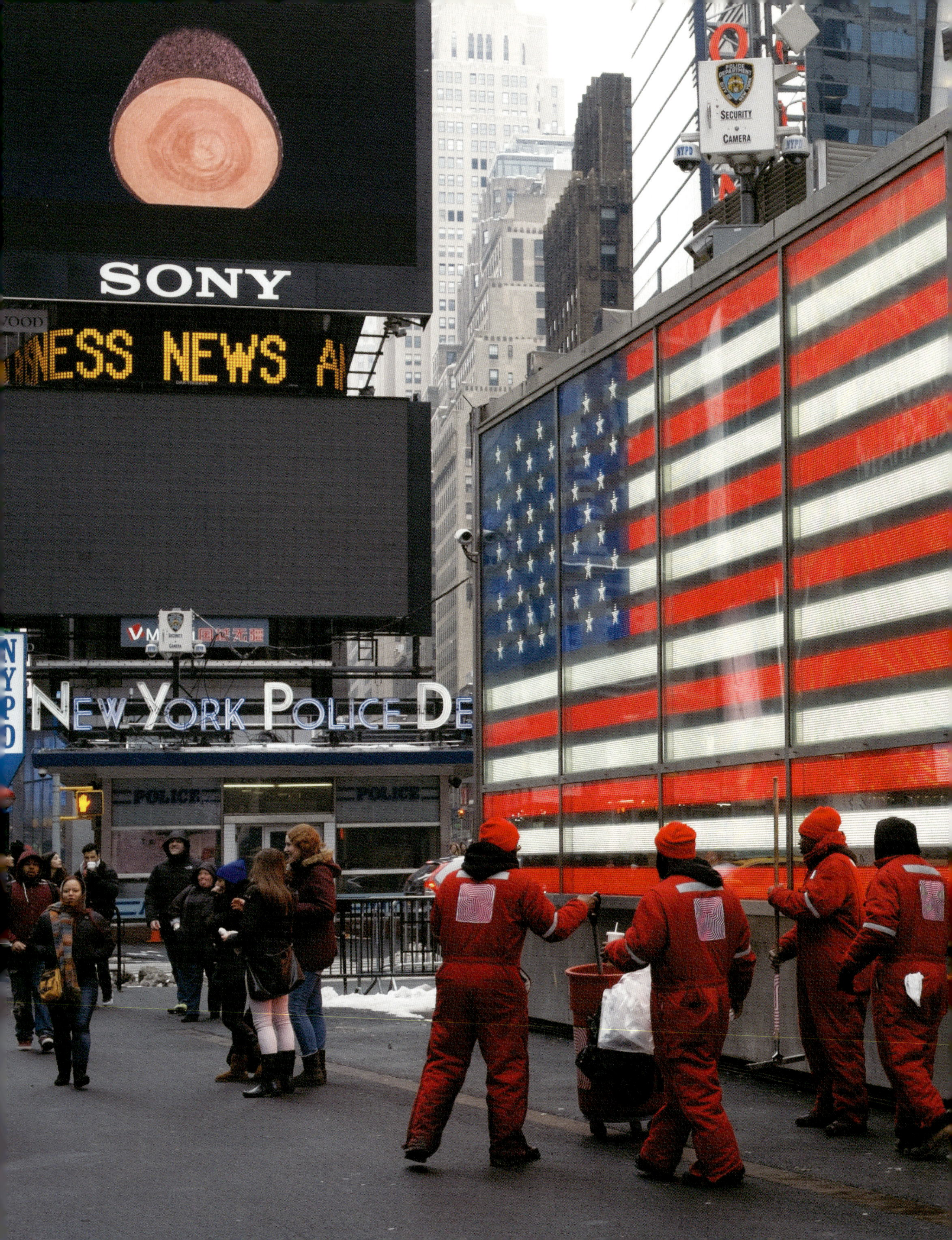
SONY
NEWS
NEW YORK POLICE
POLICE
POLICE
NYPD
SECURITY
CAMERA

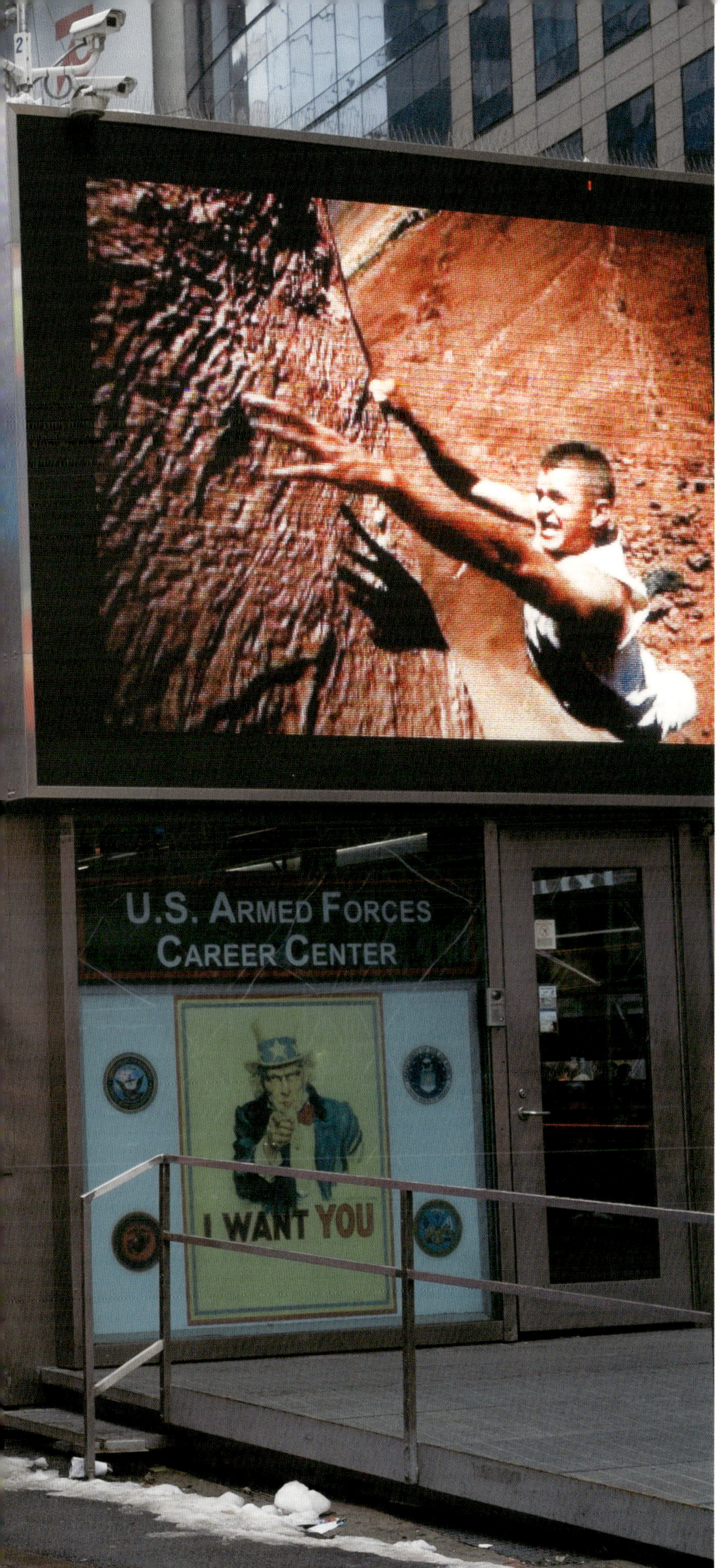
U.S. ARMED FORCES
CAREER CENTER
I WANT YOU

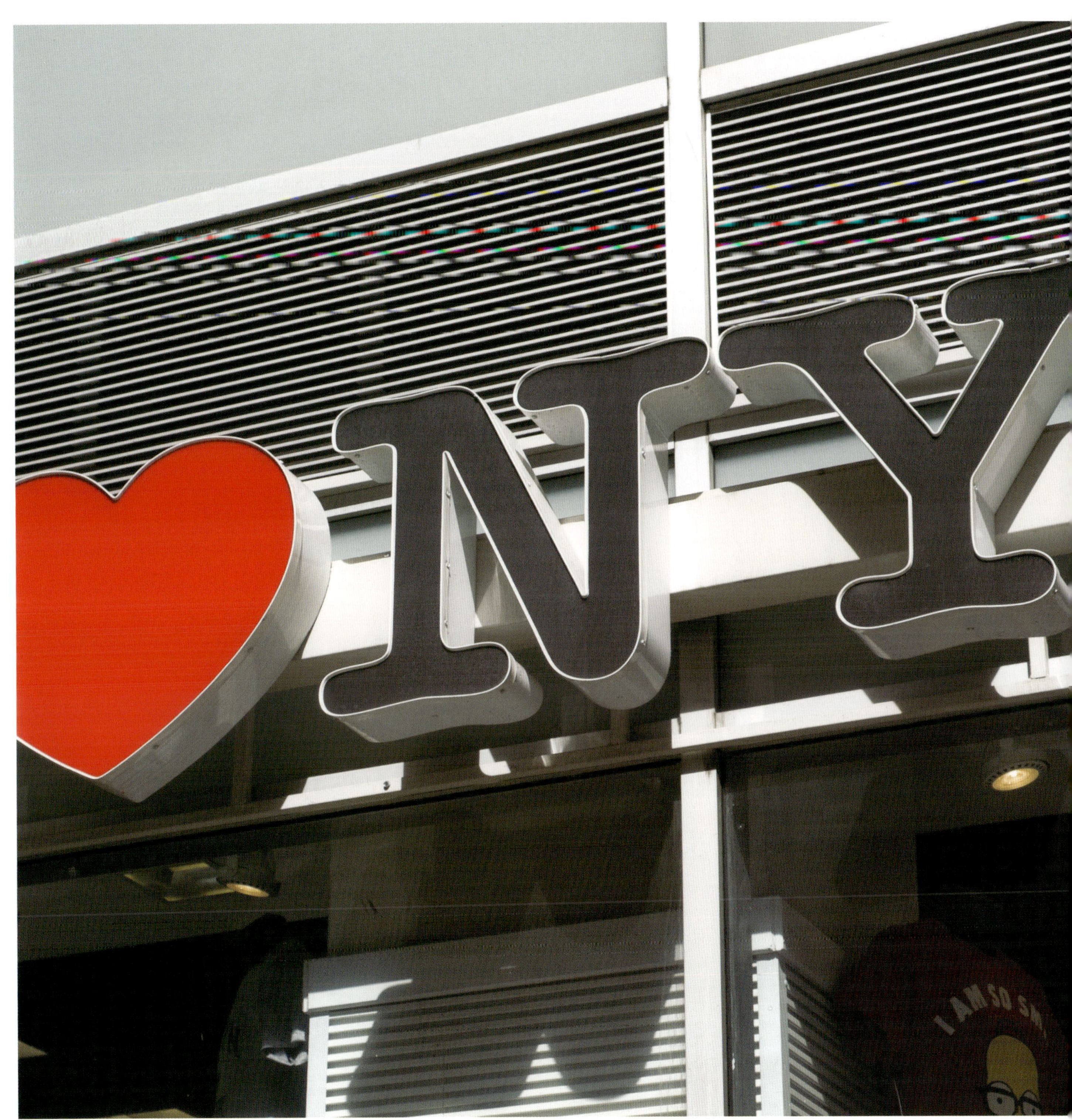
NY

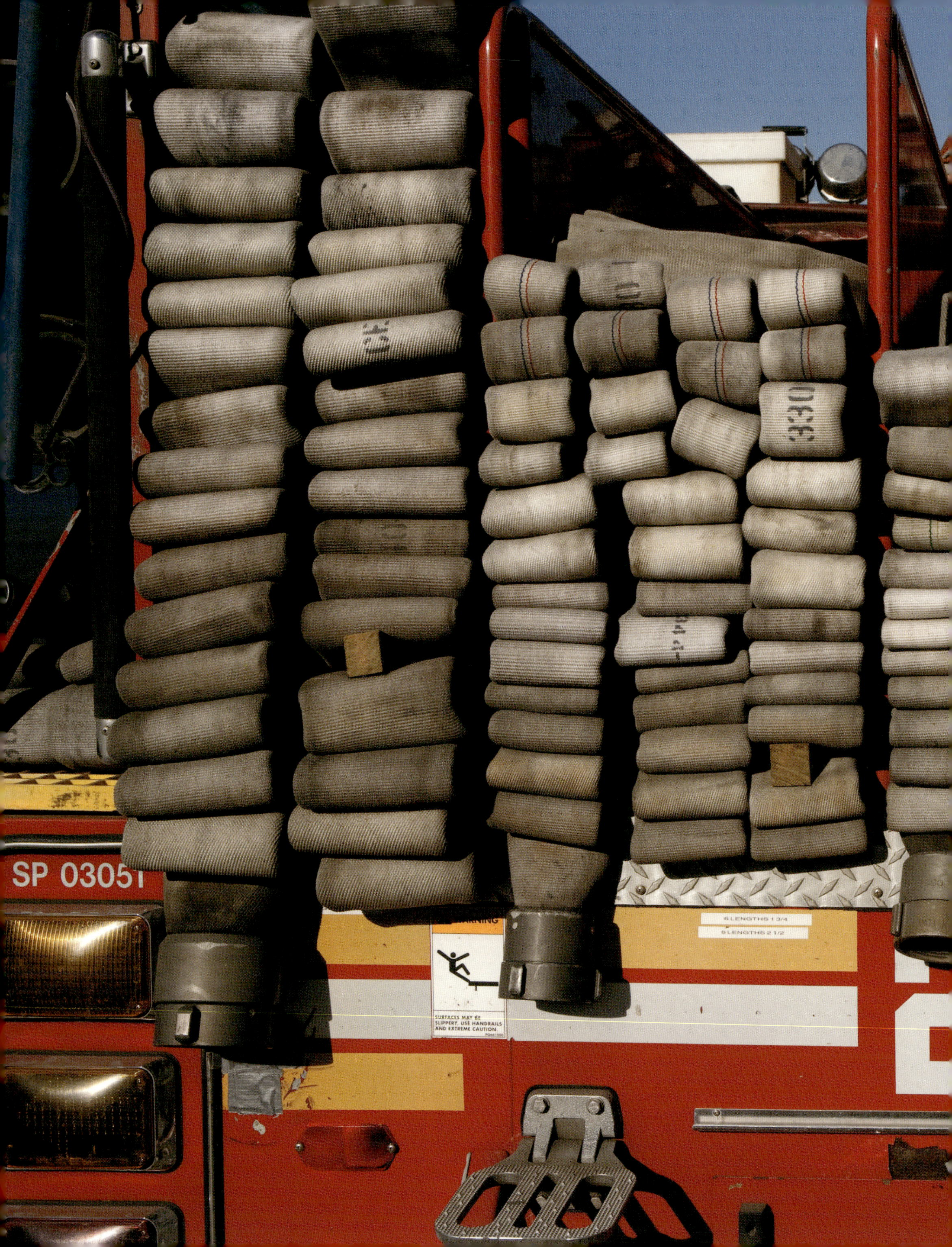
SP 03051
SURFACES MAY BE SLIPPERY. USE HANDRAILS AND EXTREME CAUTION.
6 LENGTHS 1 3/4

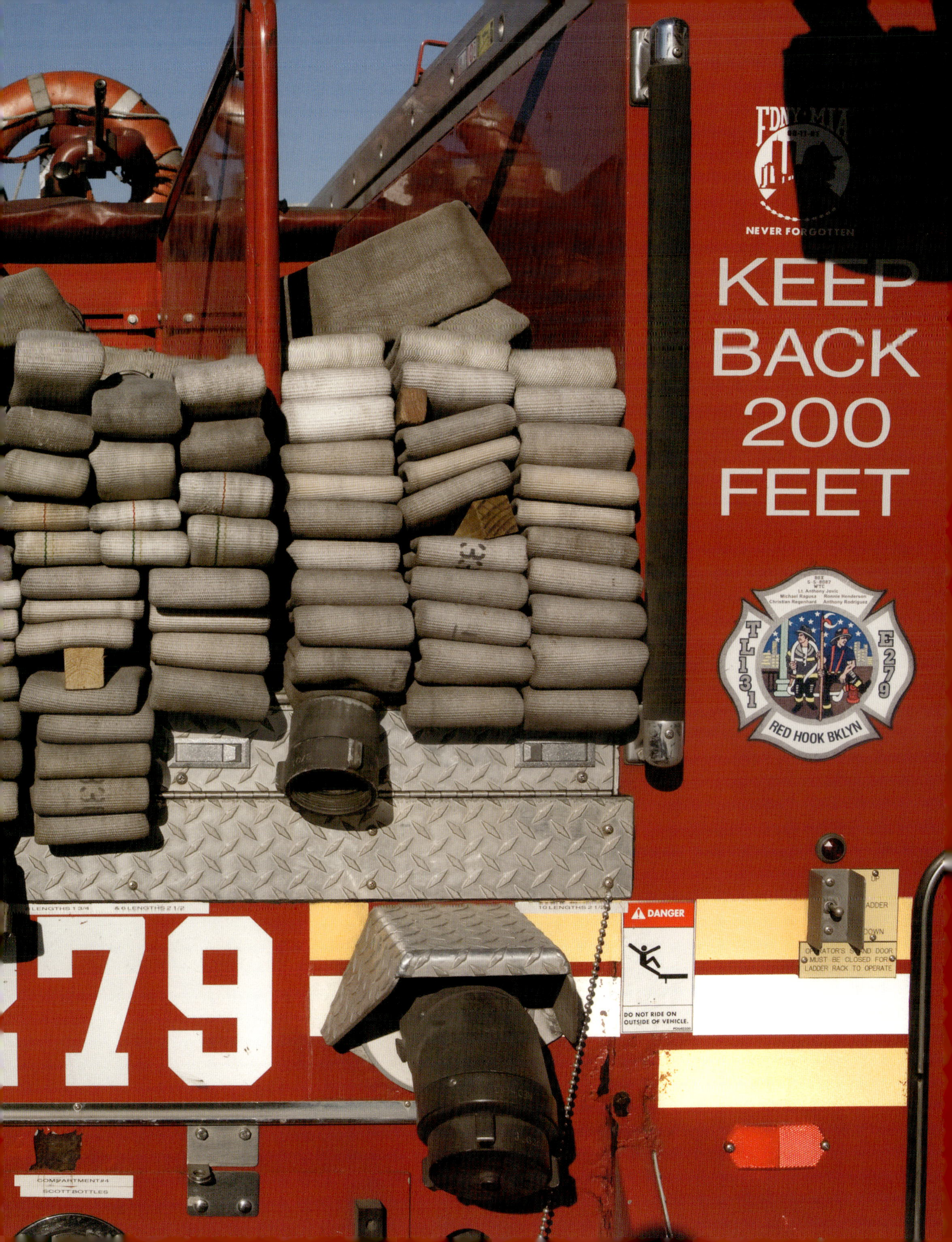

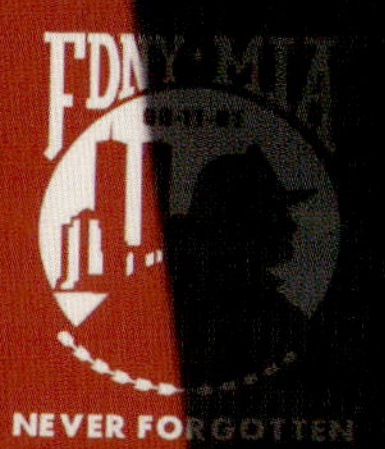
FDNY · MIA
NEVER FORGOTTEN
KEEP
BACK
200
FEET

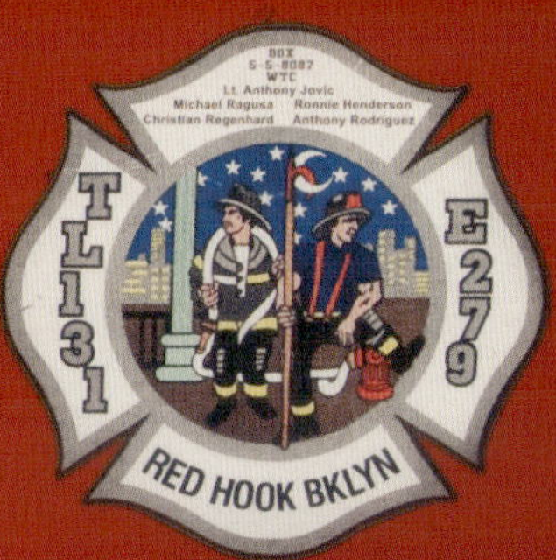
TL 131
E 279
RED HOOK BKLYN

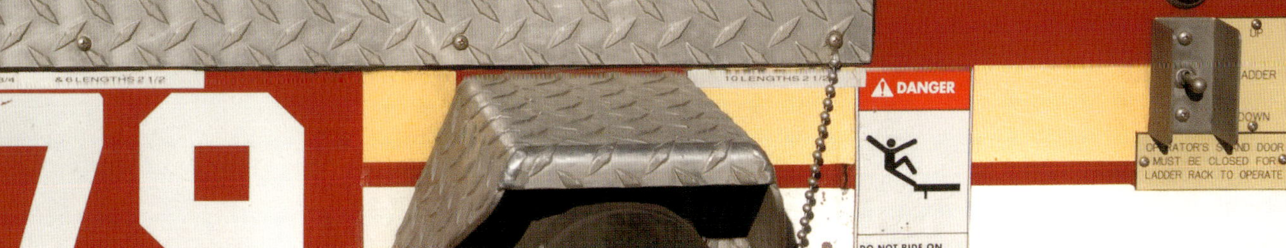
279
DANGER
DO NOT RIDE ON
OUTSIDE OF VEHICLE.
LADDER RACK TO OPERATE

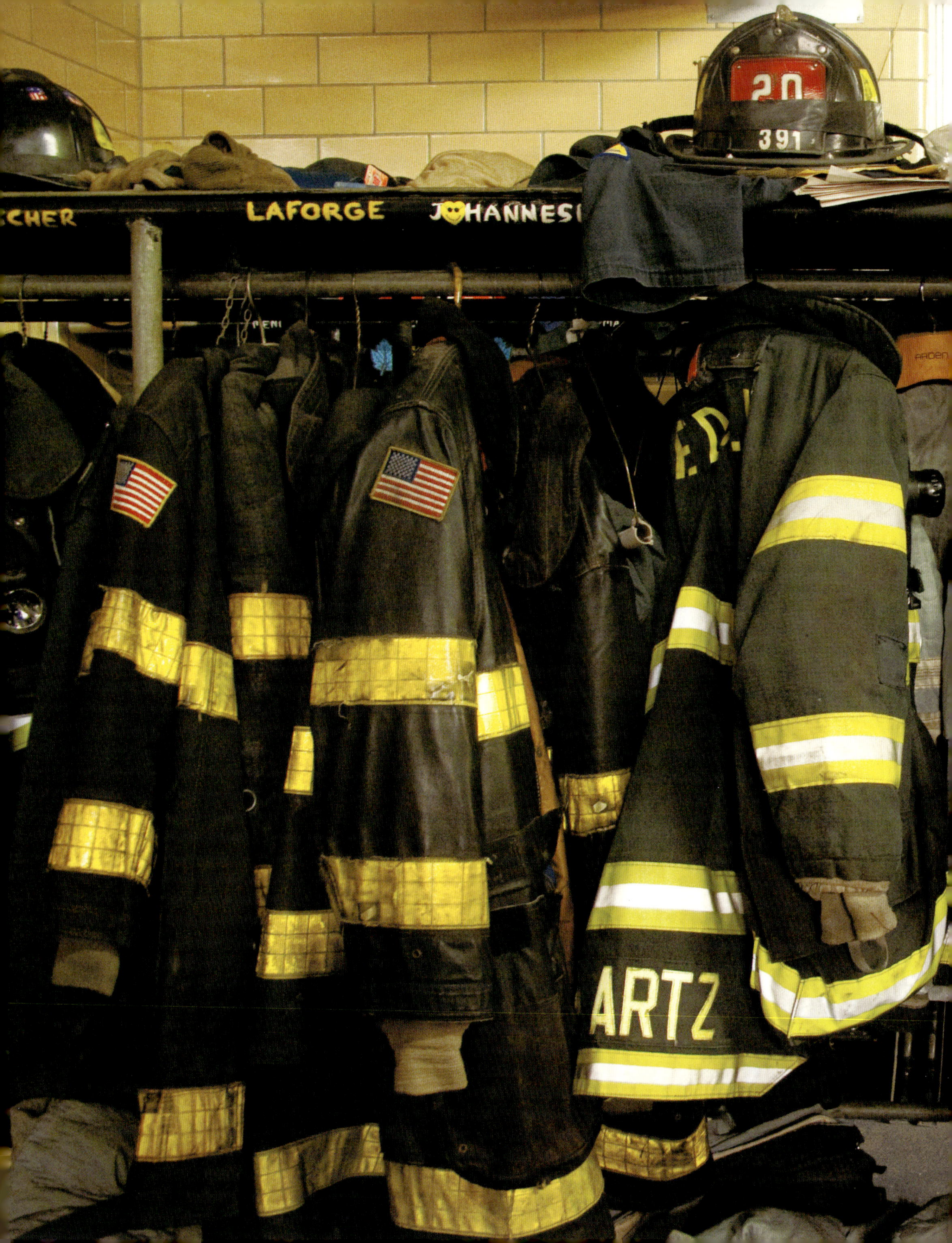
CHER
LAFORGE
J HANNES
20
391
ARTZ

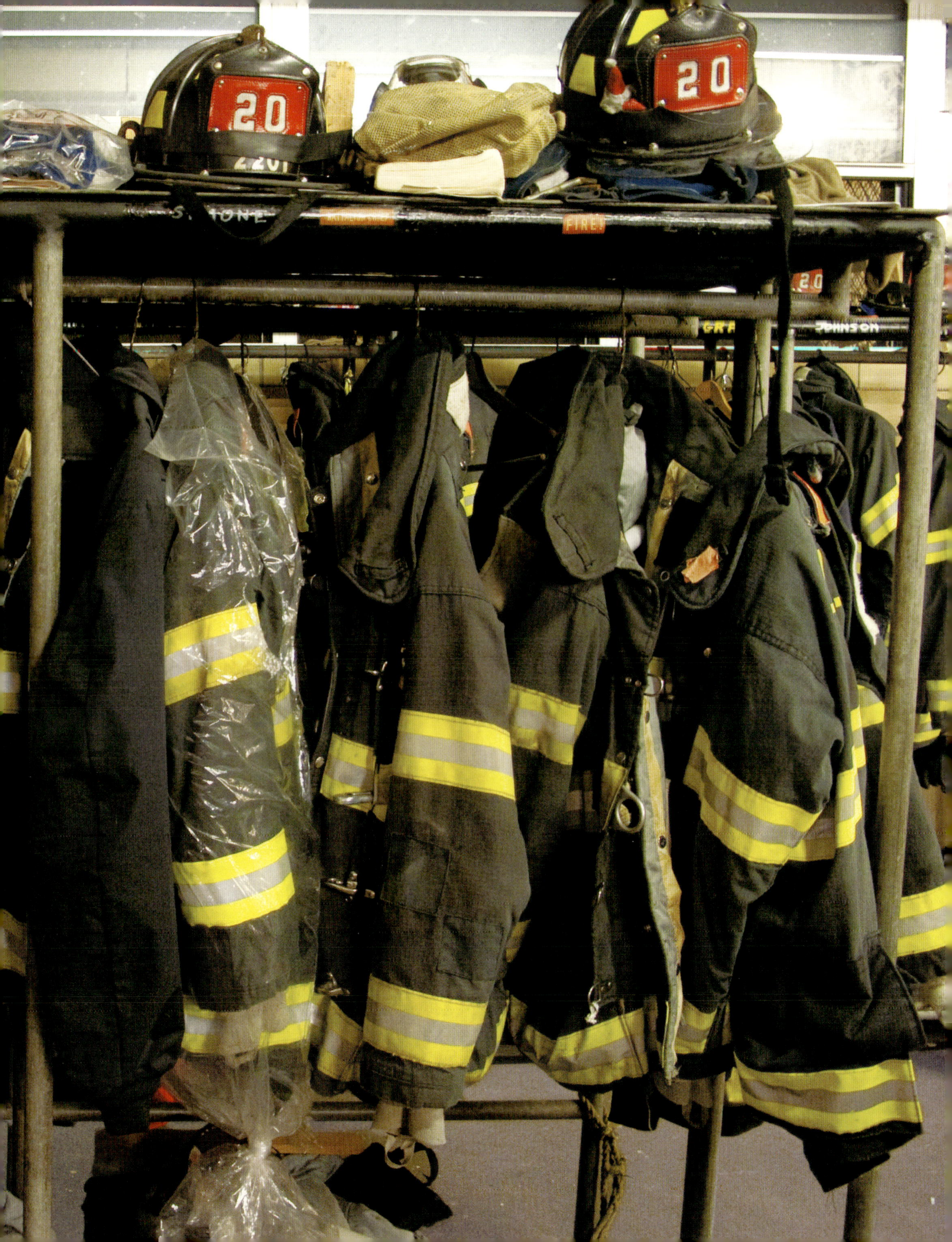

20
20
FIRE!

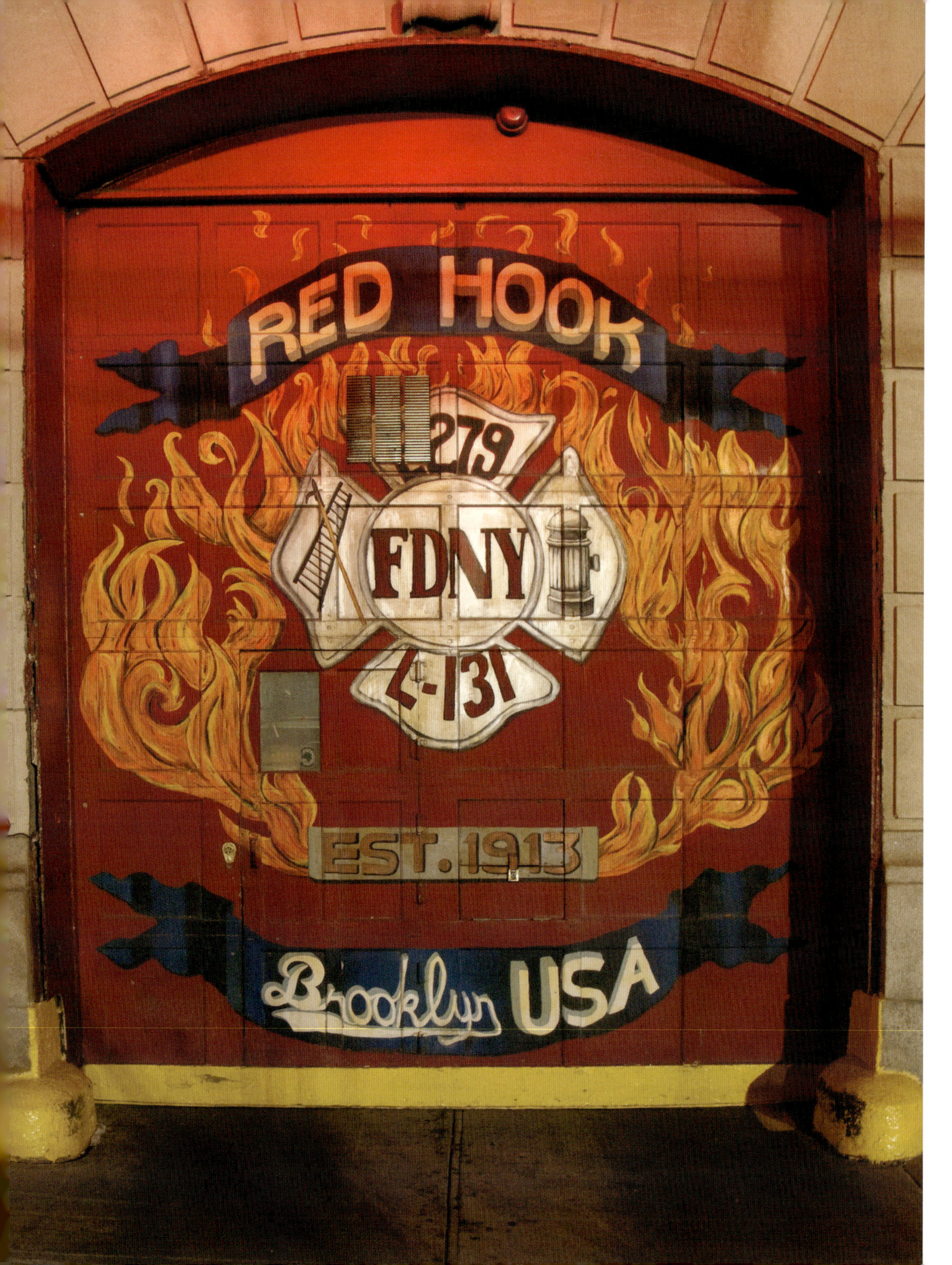
RED HOOK
279
FDNY
L-131
EST. 1913
Brooklyn USA

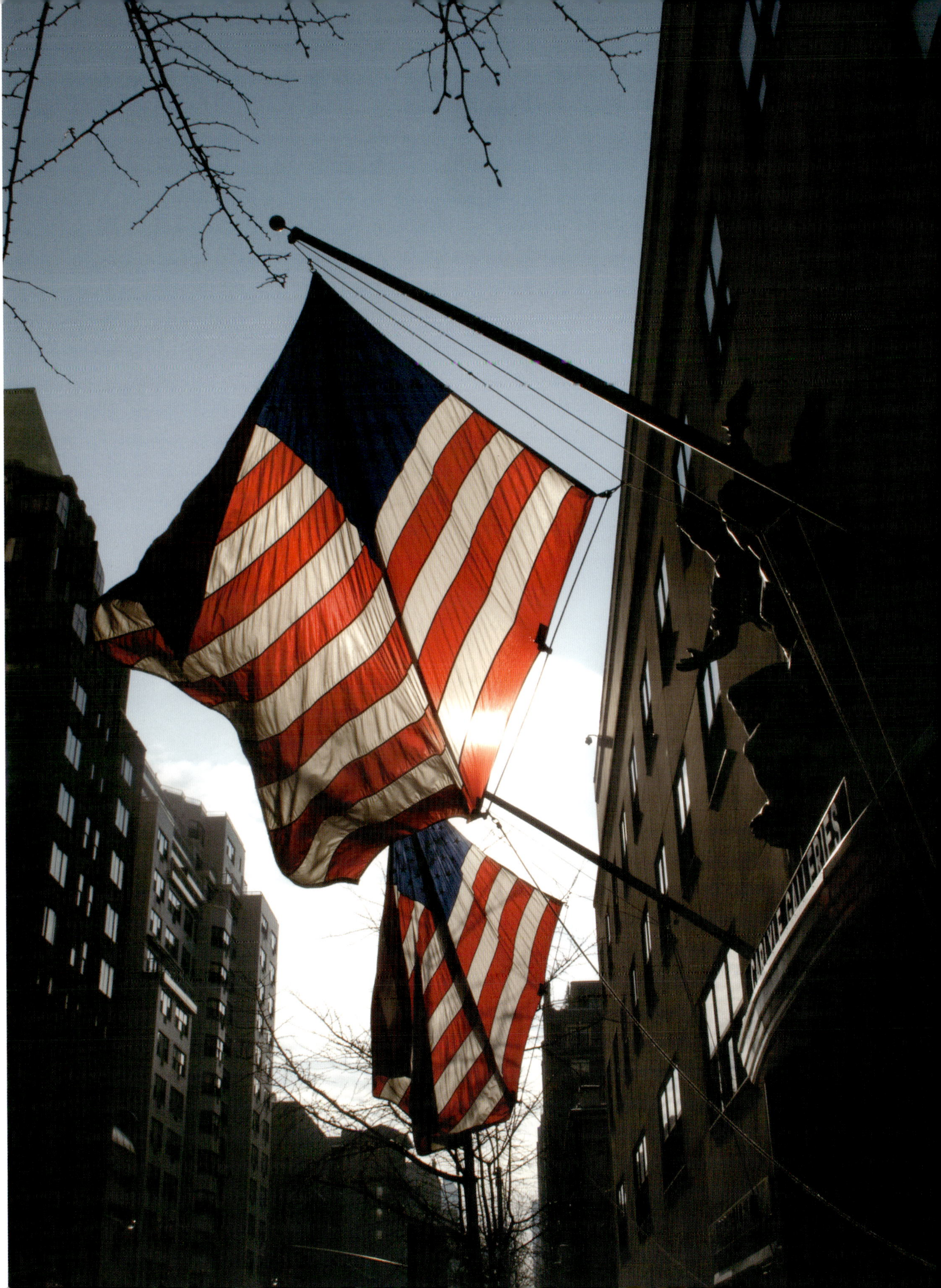
GALLERIES

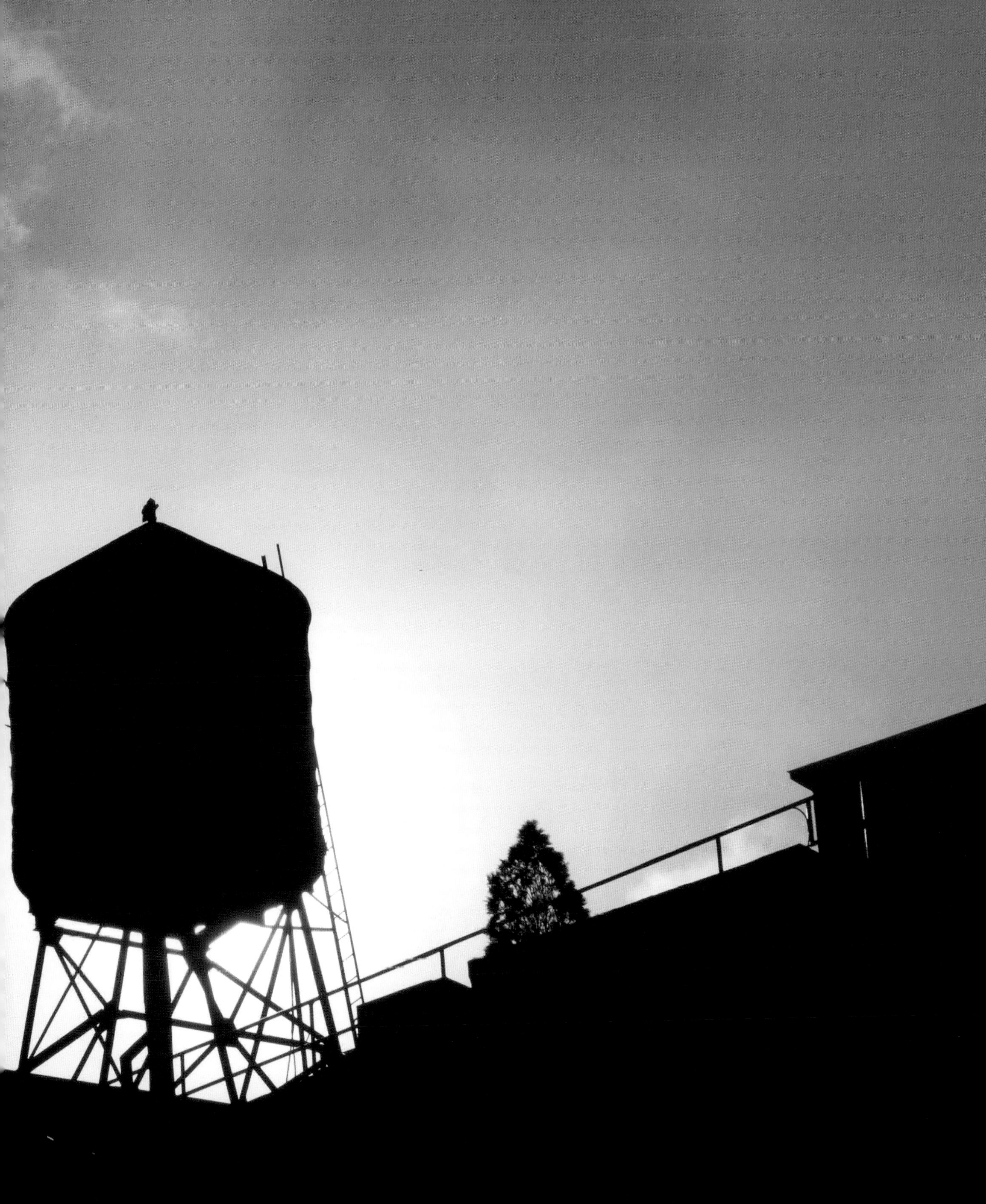

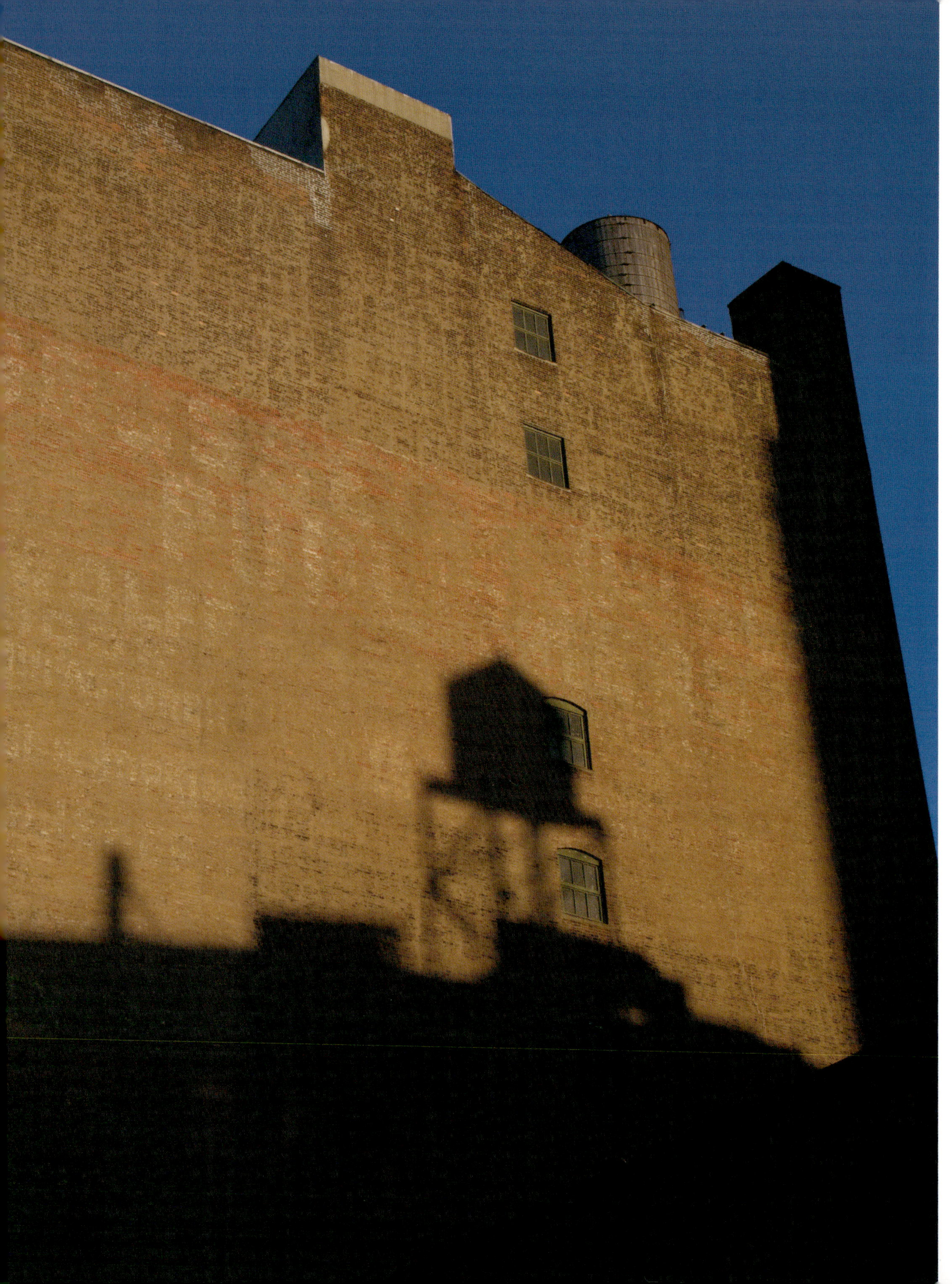

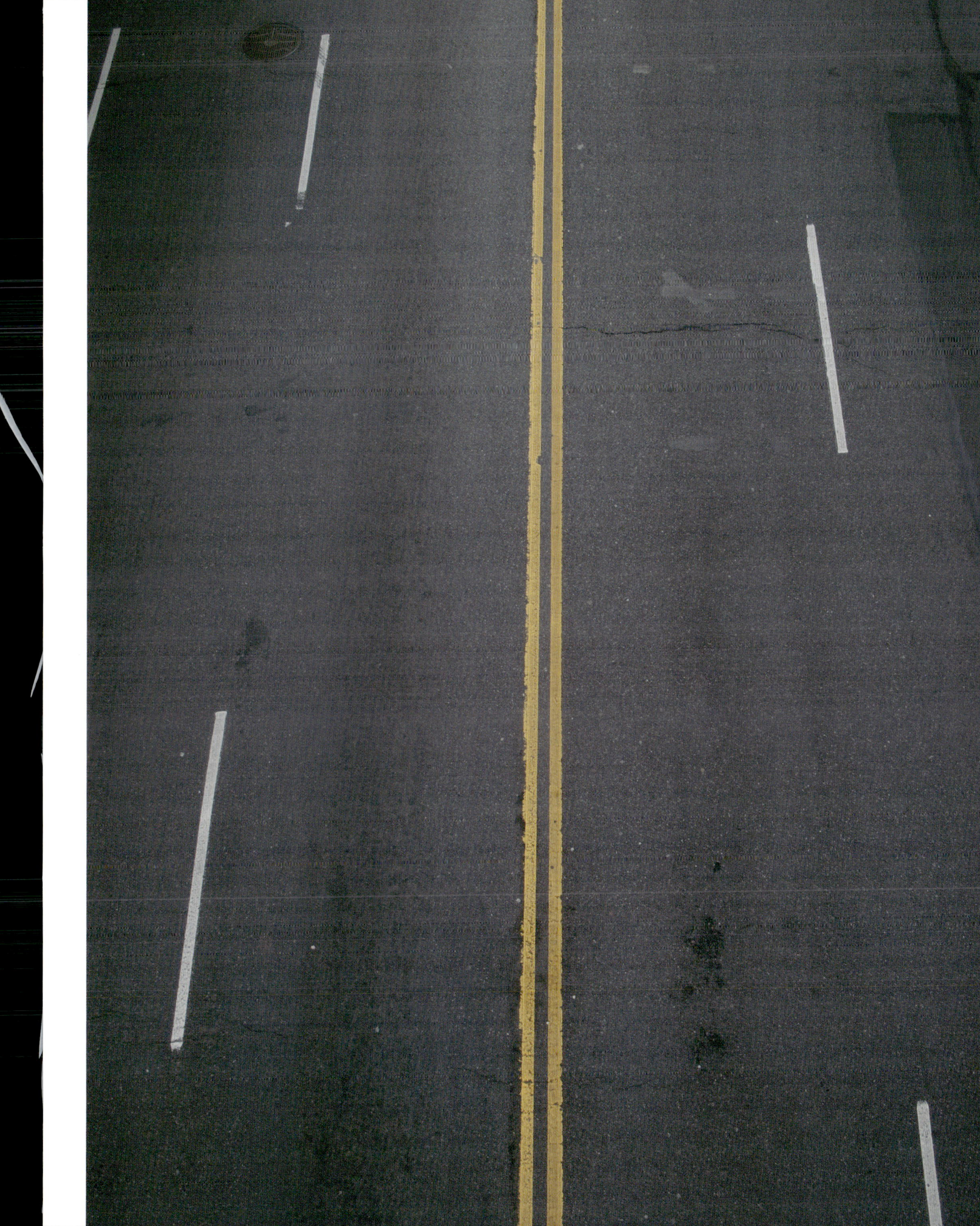

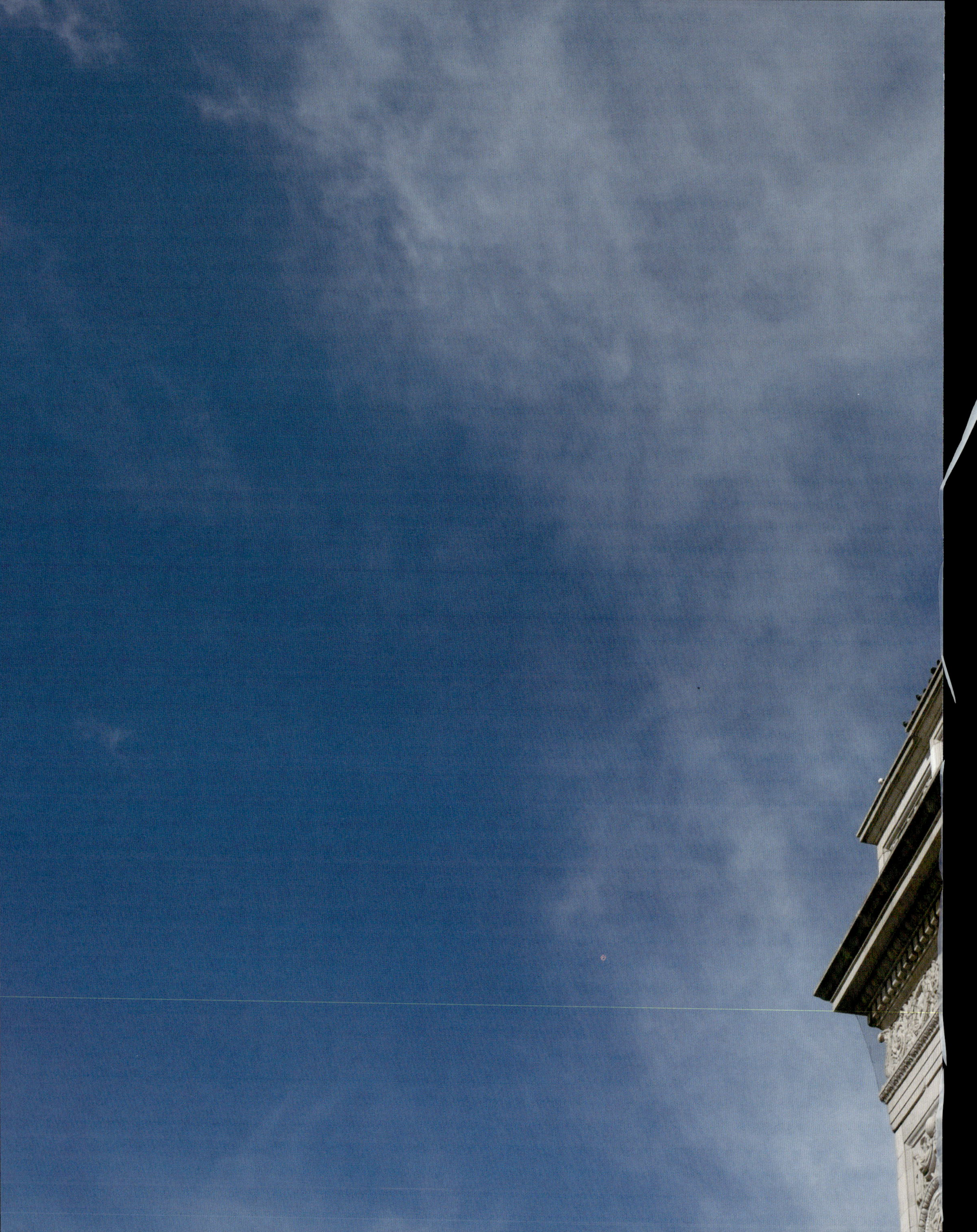

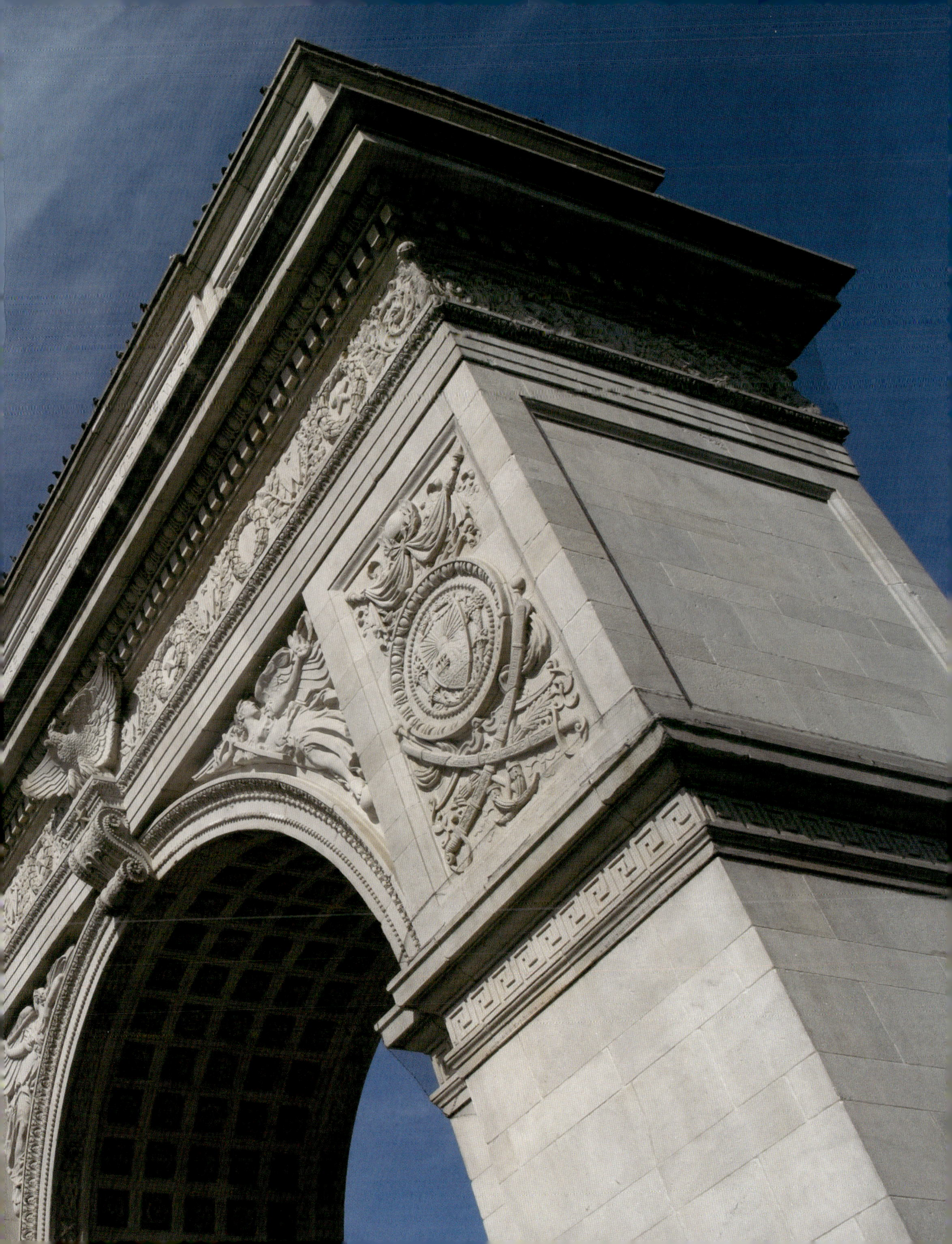

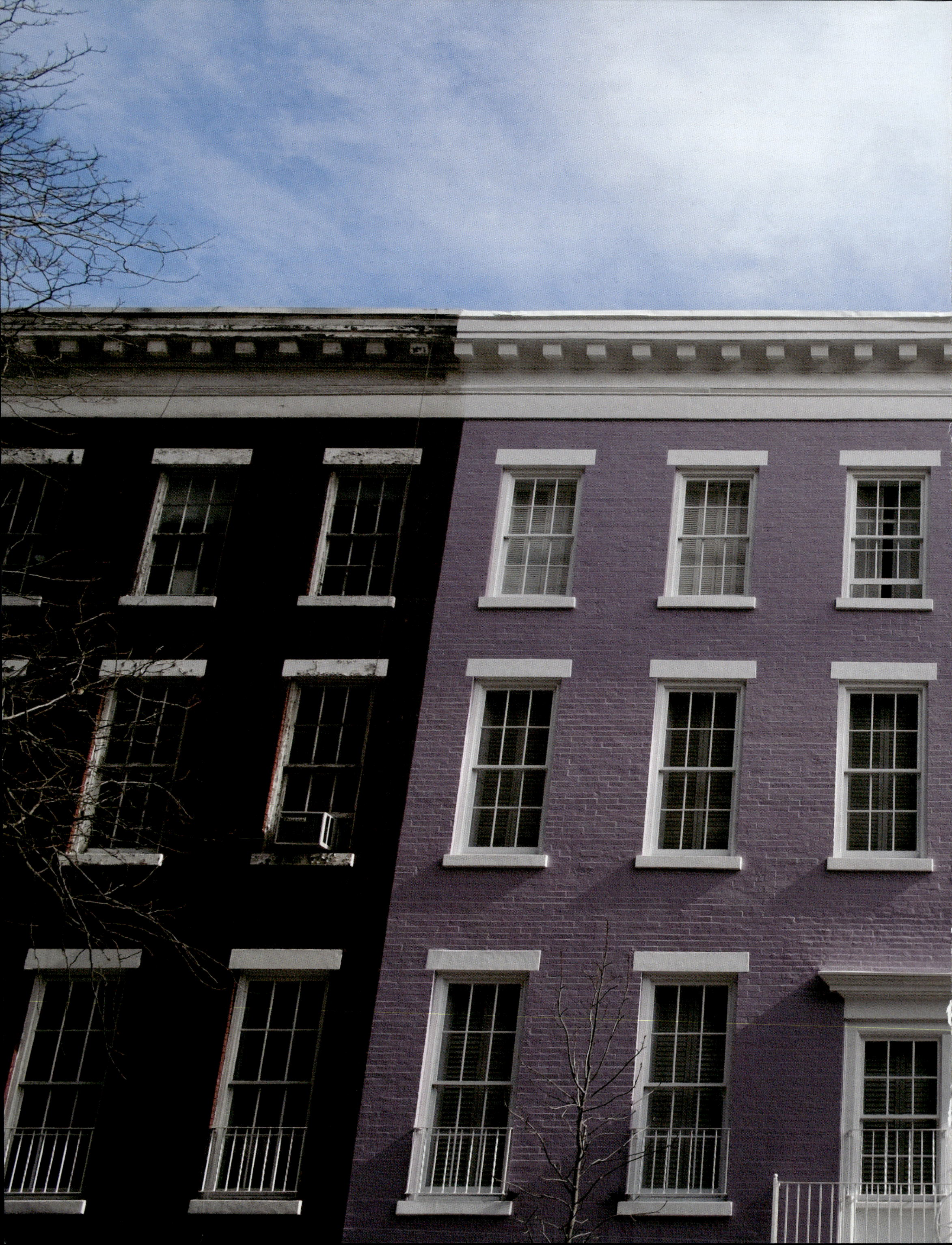

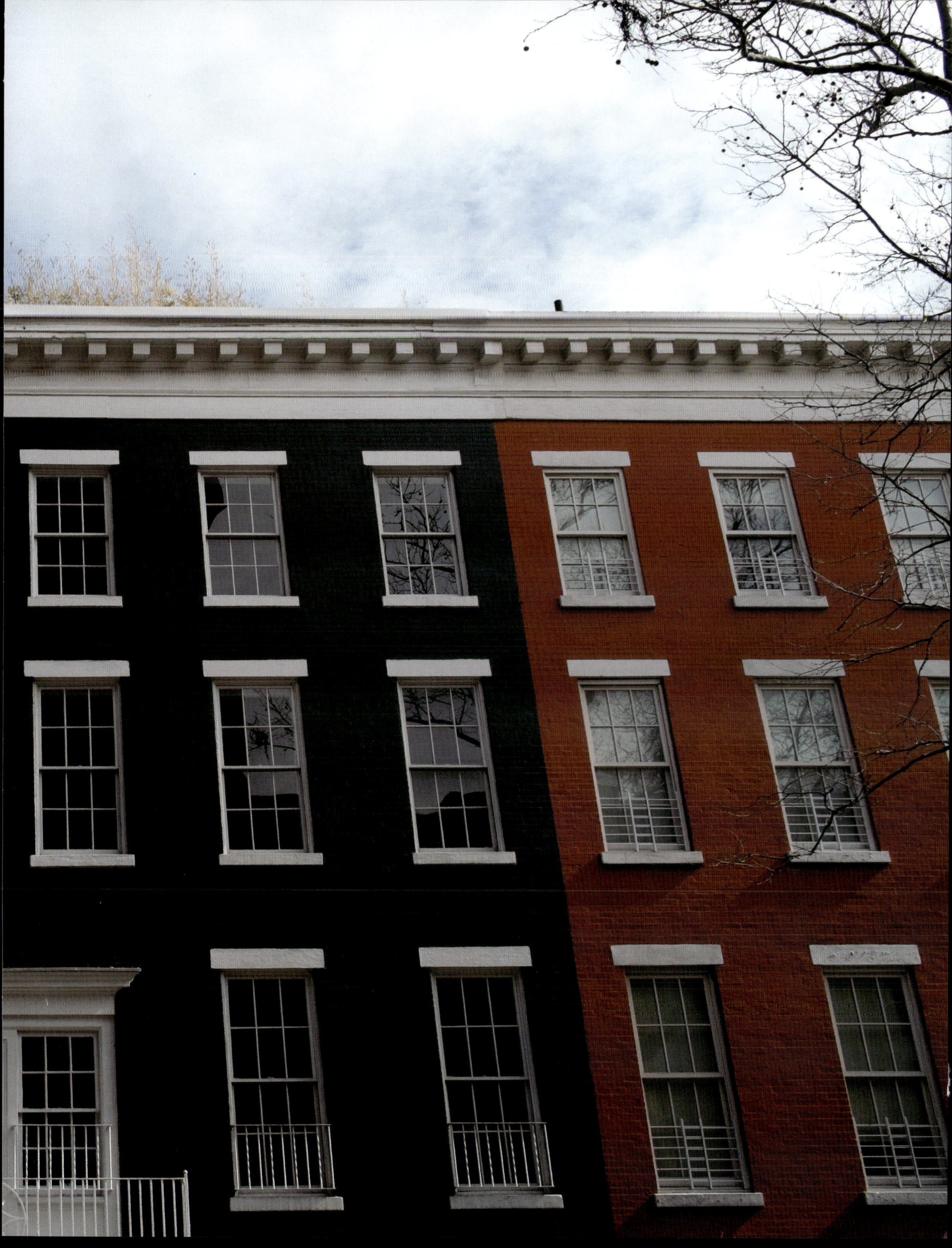

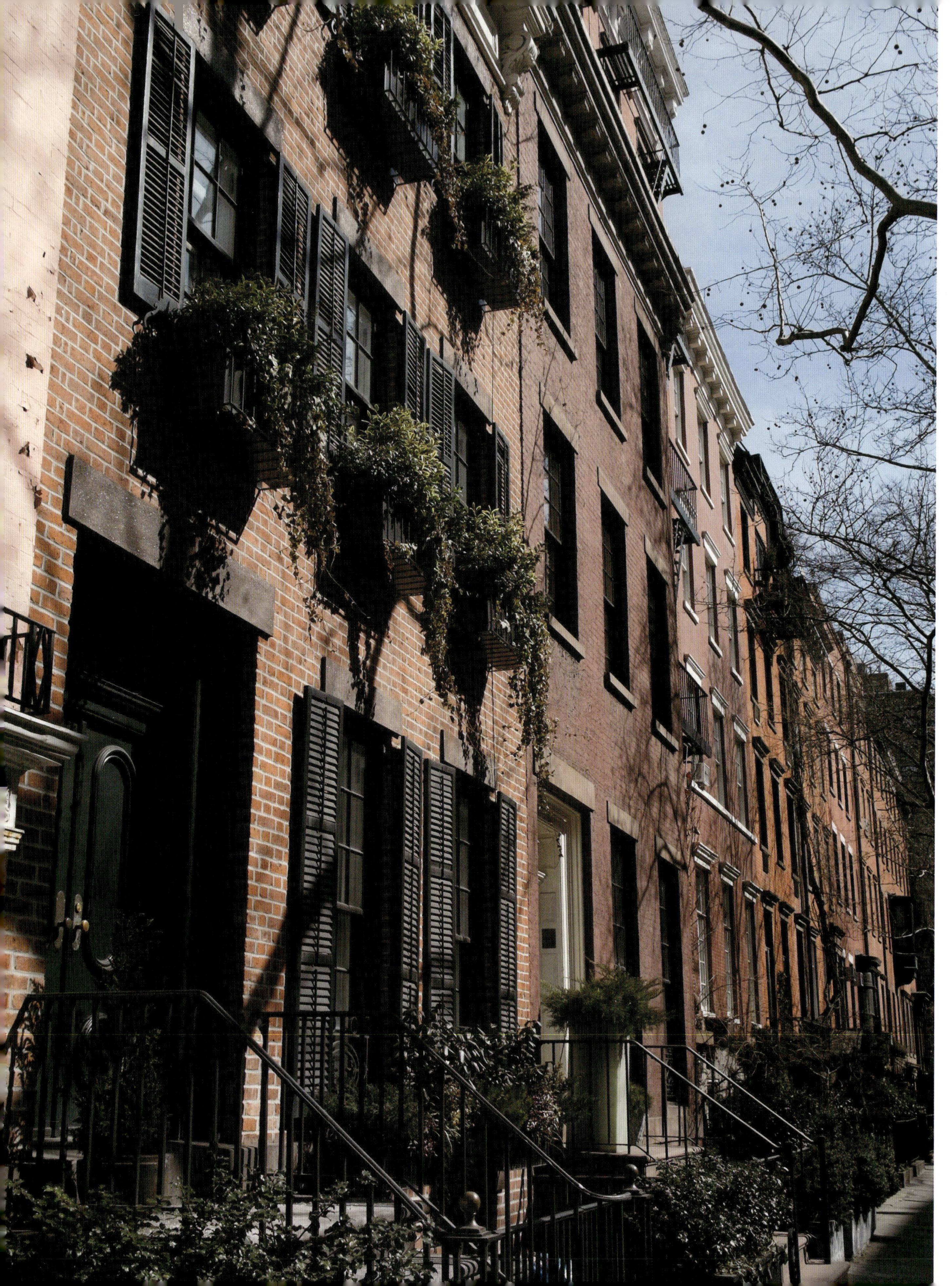

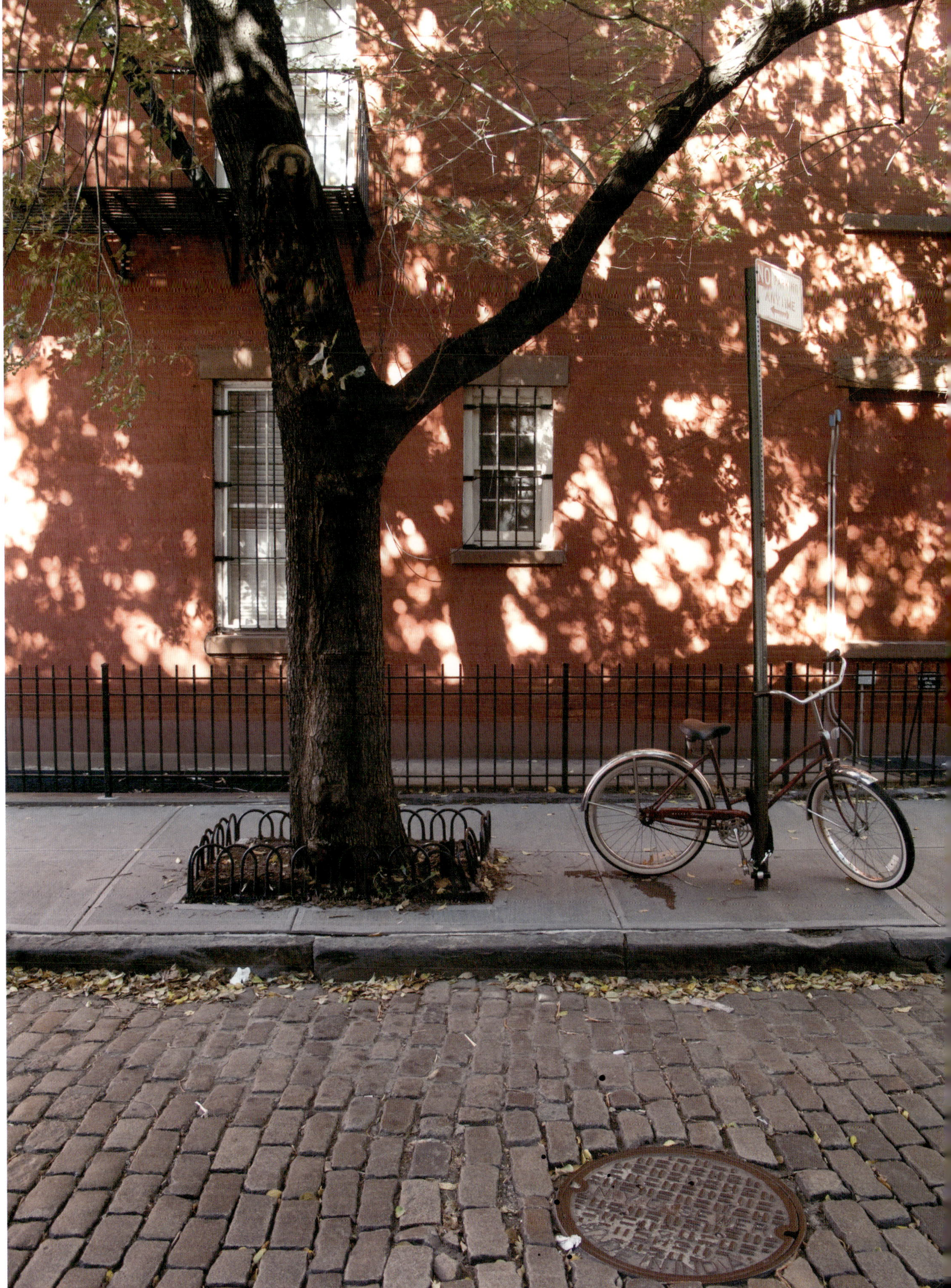
NO

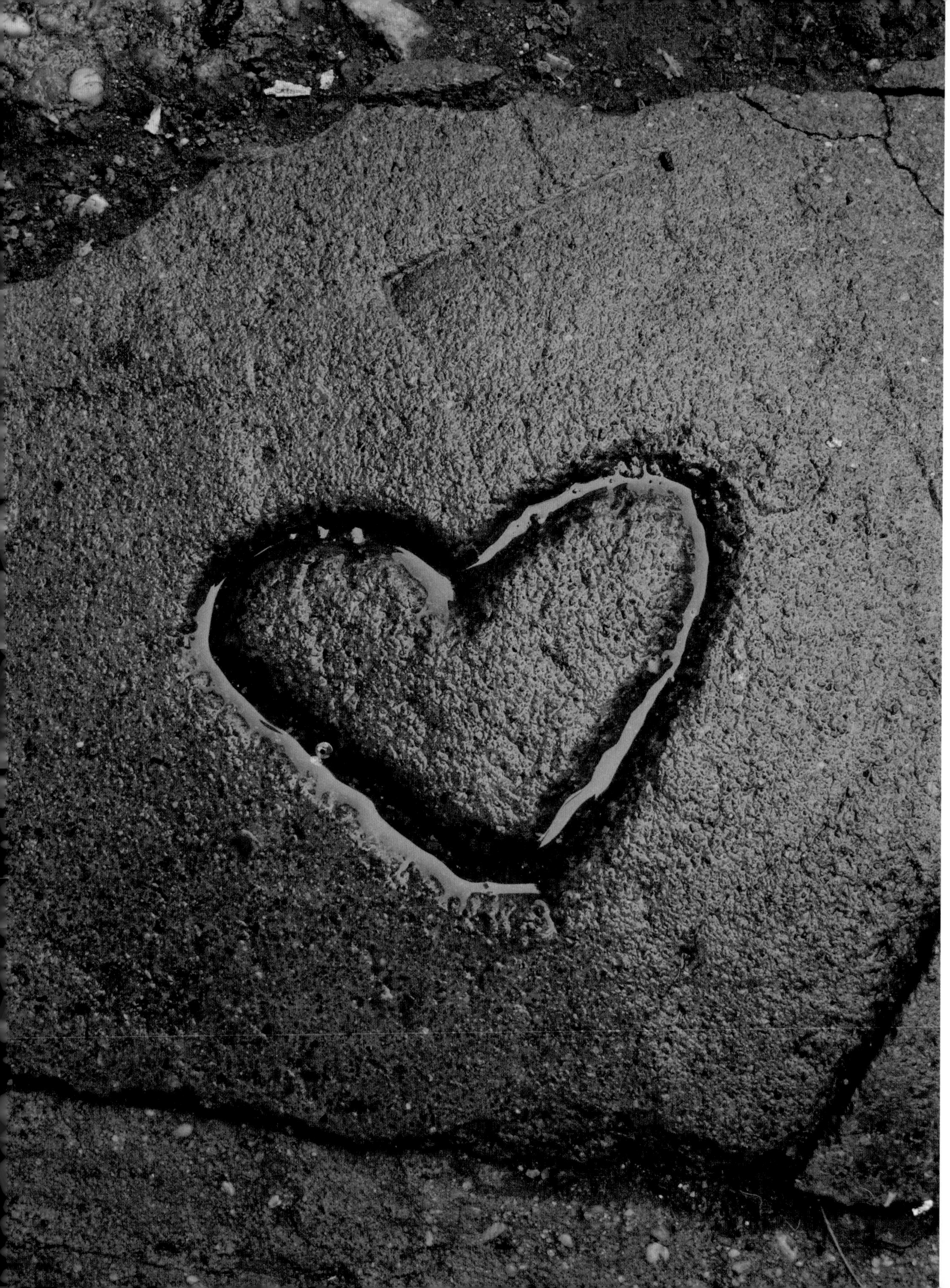

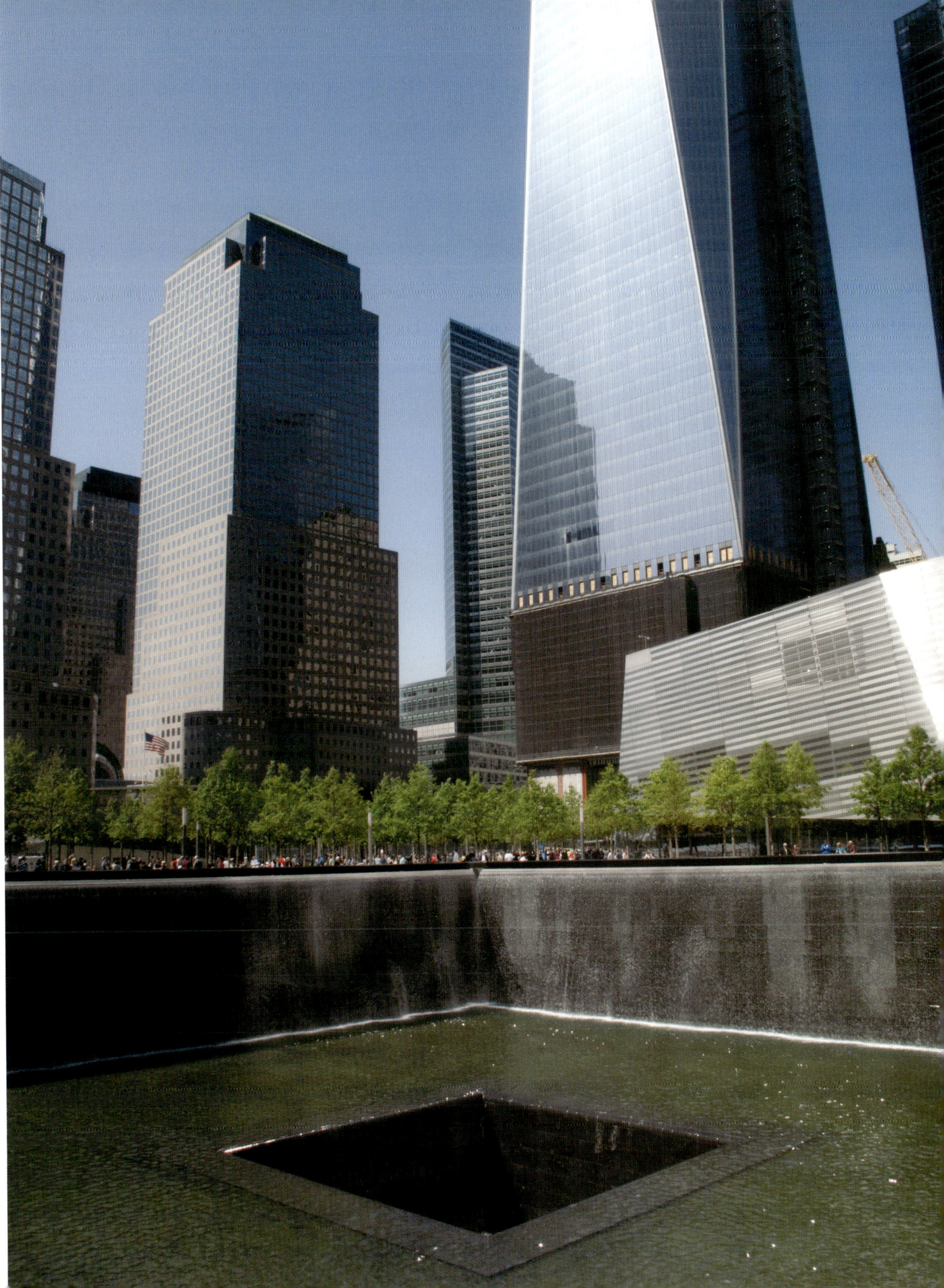

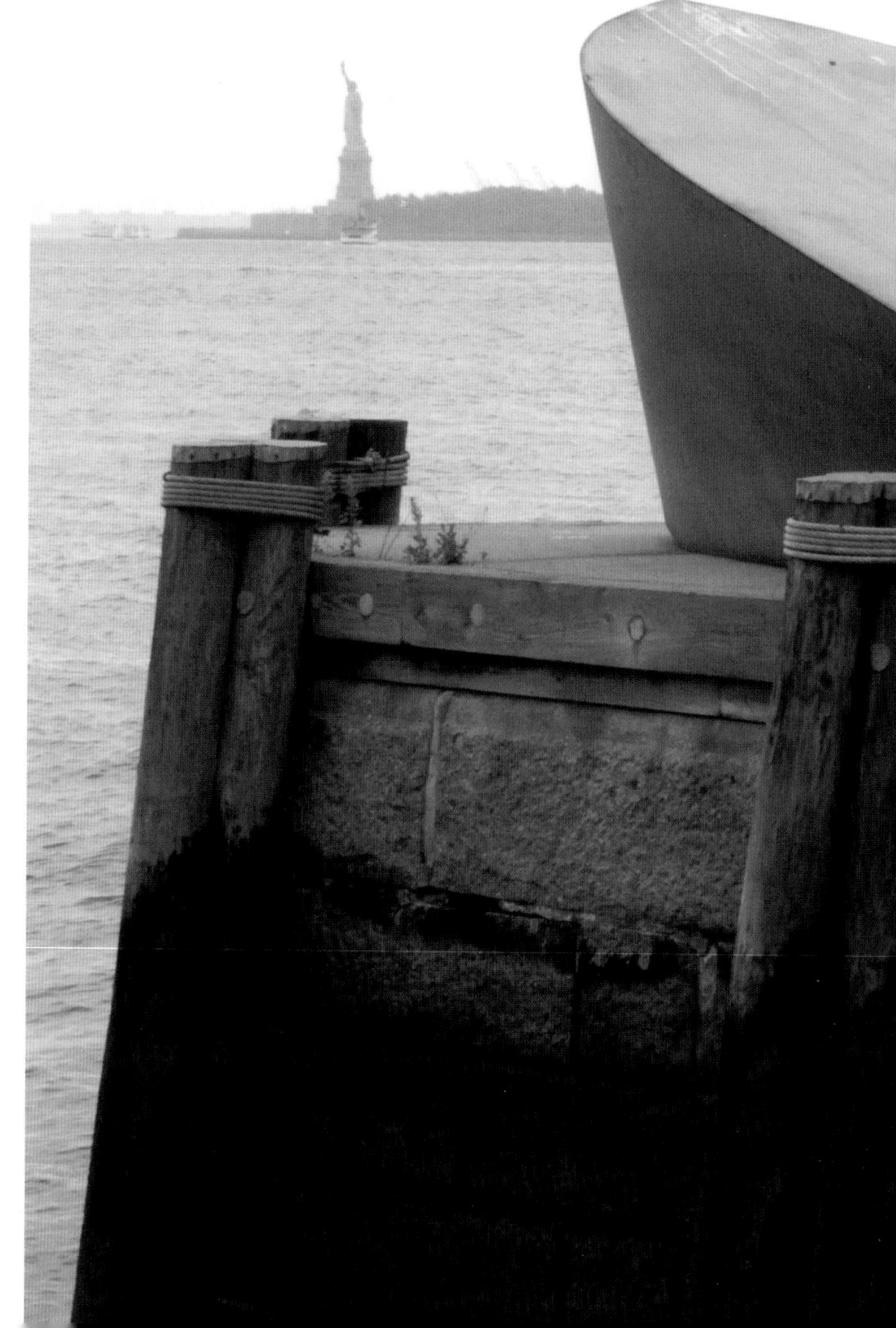

THE MODERN CITY OF NEW YORK owes its existence to its ample natural harbor and its position at the juncture of two major riverways. Throughout its history, the settlement has relied on merchant marines to supply its businesses and people with provisions and merchandise from across the globe. The monument shown here in the foreground is based on the sinking of a U.S. vessel by a German U-boat during World War II, but also pays tribute to the many brave individuals throughout the centuries who risked their lives coming to and from the city on the open seas. In the background you can glimpse both the Statue of Liberty and Ellis Island, both memorials to our long history as a destination for millions of immigrants and refugees.

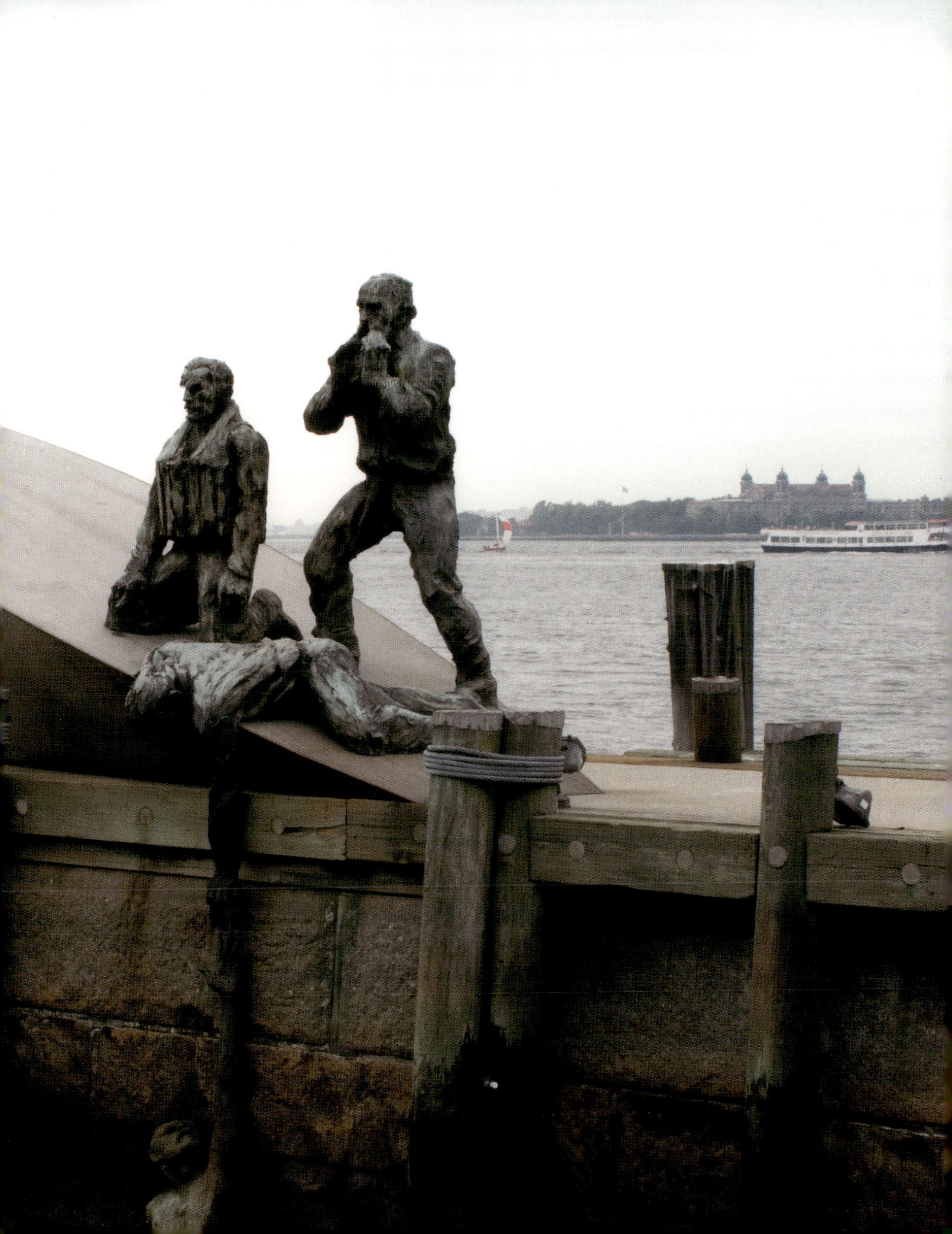

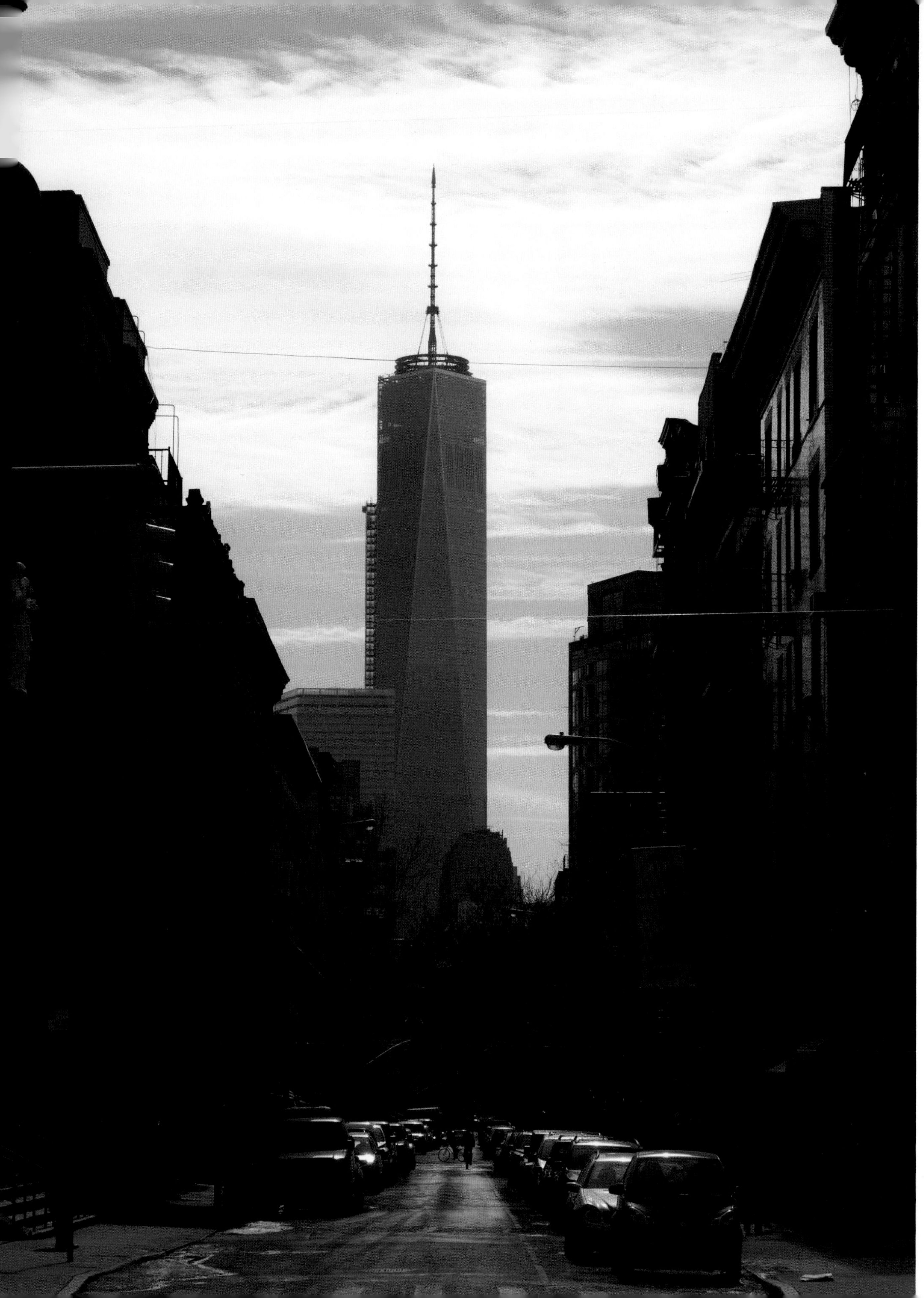

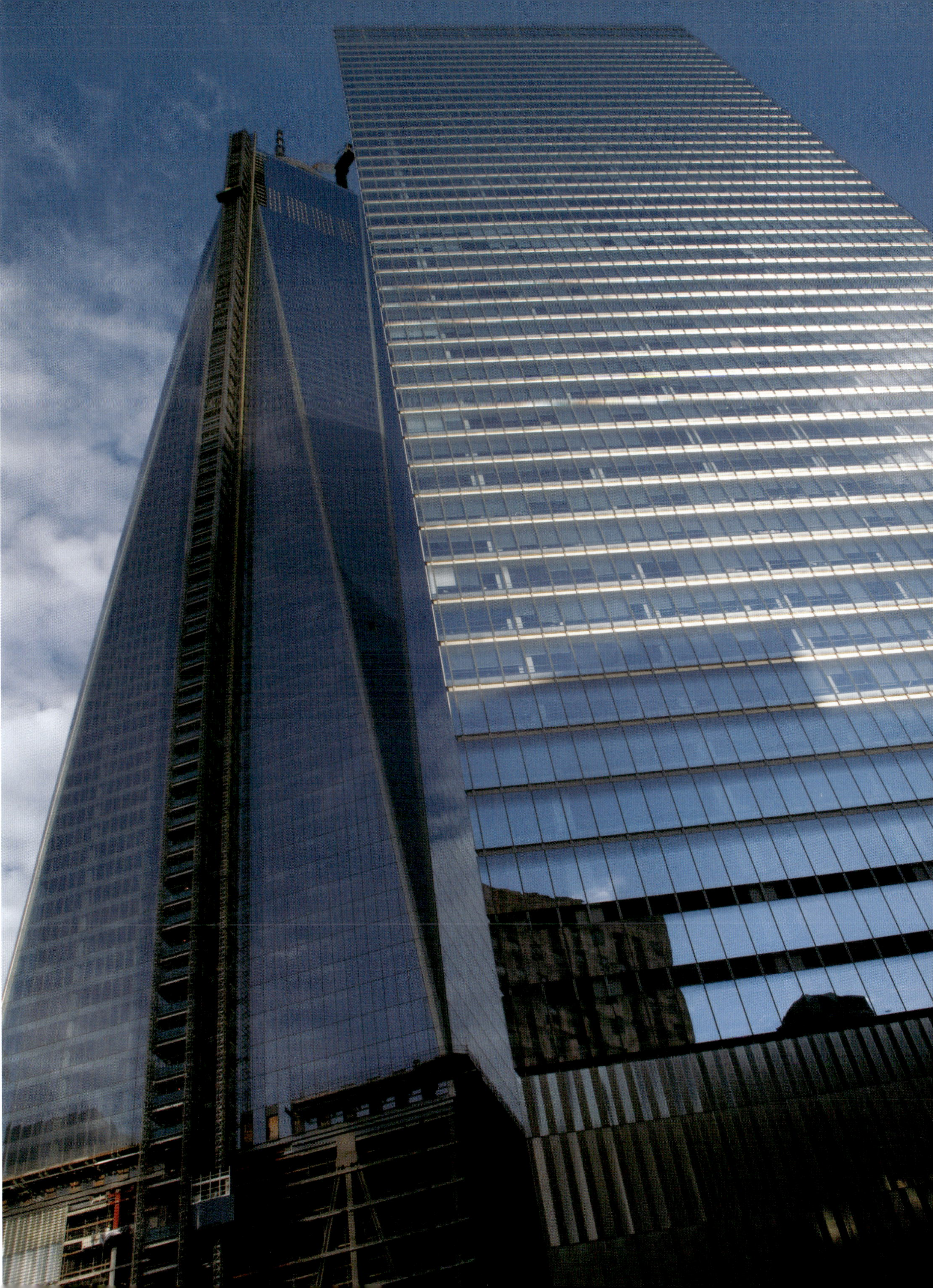

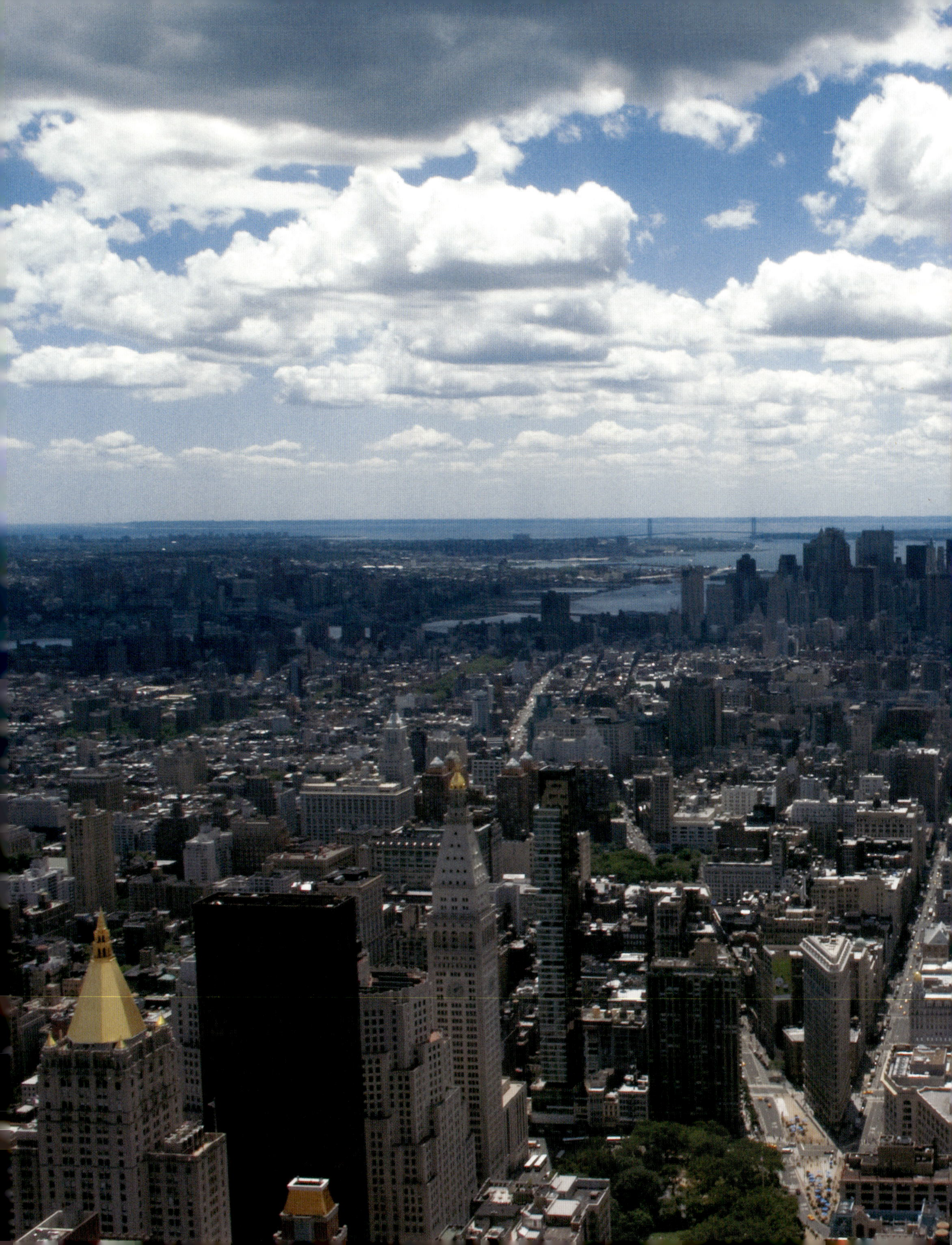

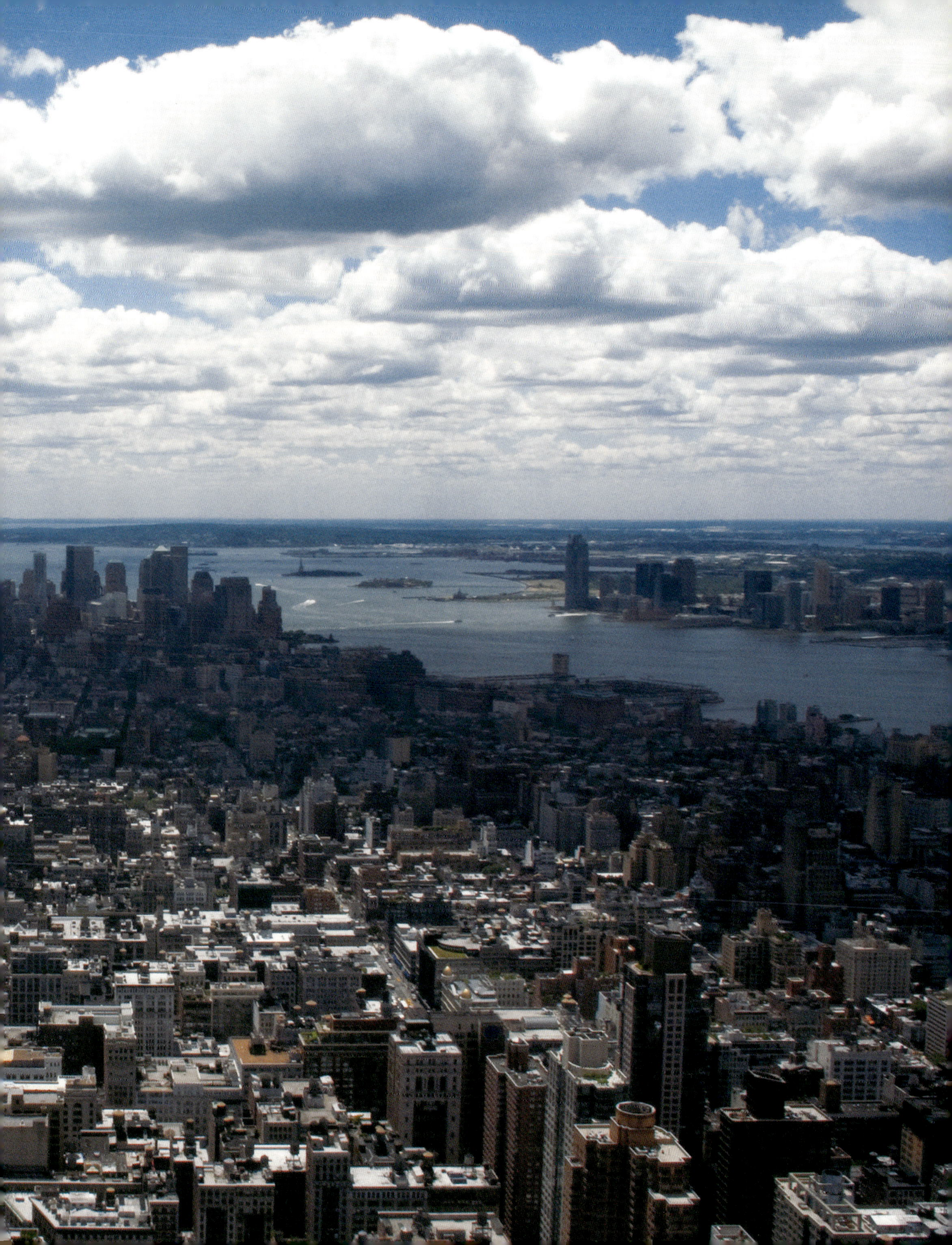

CARTER BERG was born and raised in New York City. The impulse to become a photographer began when he was still in college. During spring break of his senior year, he worked as a production assistant on a Bruce Weber shoot. "I watched Bruce and his gang and I thought, 'I want to do that."' This momentary inspiration became a full-fledged passion and he spent several years as a freelance photographer's assistant, eventually becoming first assistant to Oberto Gili, with whom he traveled the world before going out on his own. "I learned quickly that the really memorable images are the ones that can happen in between the pictures you're supposed to be taking." With that in mind, Berg carries his camera with him everywhere—just as he does his keys, always at the ready to "unlock" those special unexpected moments. Carter Berg's work has appeared internationally in numerous publications such as *Elle Décor*, *Madame Figaro*, *The Wall Street Journal*, and *Departures*. He has also shot advertising campaigns for Ralph Lauren, as well as photographed for several lifestyle books. He and his wife, Kasia, live in Manhattan, where they met.

ACKNOWLEDGMENTS: To my wife, Kasia, for sharing this journey and for being with me while many of these pictures were taken. For always being patient when, in the middle of a walk, I would suddenly go left instead of right to capture a moment. My Dad, for always being ready to get in the car to explore the outer boroughs of New York City. For teaching me how to navigate the streets, avenues, bridges, and tunnels that keep the city connected. And most importantly, for teaching me how to parallel park, perhaps the most important skill needed to live in the Big Apple. My brother, Sam, who shares with me a great love for the city where he, too, was born and is very proud to call home. My Mom, who brought photography into my life, and whose constant guidance and belief in my ability has given me a true passion I will always have. Ralph Lauren, who has given me the incredible opportunity to photograph the people, places, and things that make up his world. Seamus Mullarkey and Allison Stern, for steering the wheel of this book and pushing me to capture more snapshots of this city we all live in and love. And finally to Hendrik teNeues, for immediately deciding to publish my book when he saw my proposal. I am very honored to be a part of the teNeues family of iconic photography books.

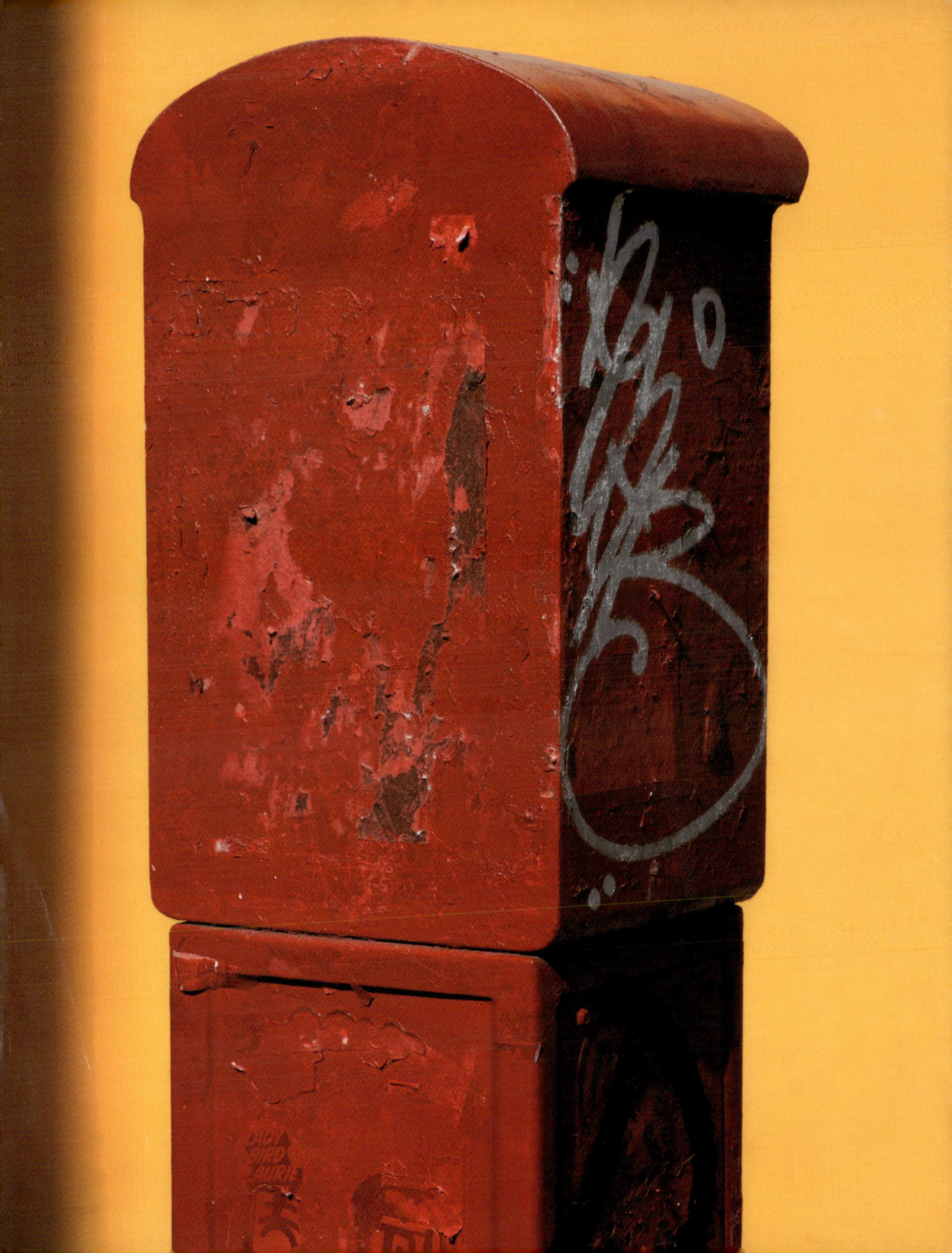

New York Snapshots

Photographs by Carter Berg
Editorial Coordination by Seamus Mullarkey
Design by Allison Stern

Published by teNeues Publishing Group

Artwork Credit: page 93 by Keith Haring.

teNeues Media GmbH + Co. KG
Am Selder 37, 47906 Kempen, Germany
Phone: 0049-(0)2152-916-0
Fax: 0049-(0)2152-916-111
E-mail: books@teneues.com

Press Department: Andrea Rehn
arehn@teneues.com
Phone: 0049-(0)2152-916-202

teNeues Digital Media GmbH
Kohlfurter Strasse 41-43, 10999 Berlin, Germany
Phone: 0049-(0)30-60-031102
e-mail: mail@tndm.com

teNeues Publishing Company
7 West 18th Street
New York, NY 10011, USA
Phone: 001-212-627-9090
Fax: 001-212-627-9511

teNeues Publishing UK Ltd.
12 Ferndene Road
SE24 0AQ, UK
Phone: 0044-20-8670-7522
Fax: 0044-20-8670-7523

teNeues France S.A.R.L.
39, rue des Billets
18250 Henrichemont, France
Phone: 0033-2-4826-9348
Fax: 0033-1-7072-3482

www.teneues.com

ISBN 978-3-8327-9817-8

Library of Congress Control Number: 2013957677

Printed in China.

Bibliographic information published by the Deutsche Nationalbibliothek. The Deutsche Nationalbibliothek lists this publication in the Deutsche Nationalbibliografie; detailed bibliographic data are available in the Internet at http://dnb.d-nb.de.

teNeues Publishing Group
Kempen
Berlin
London
Munich
New York
Paris

teNeues

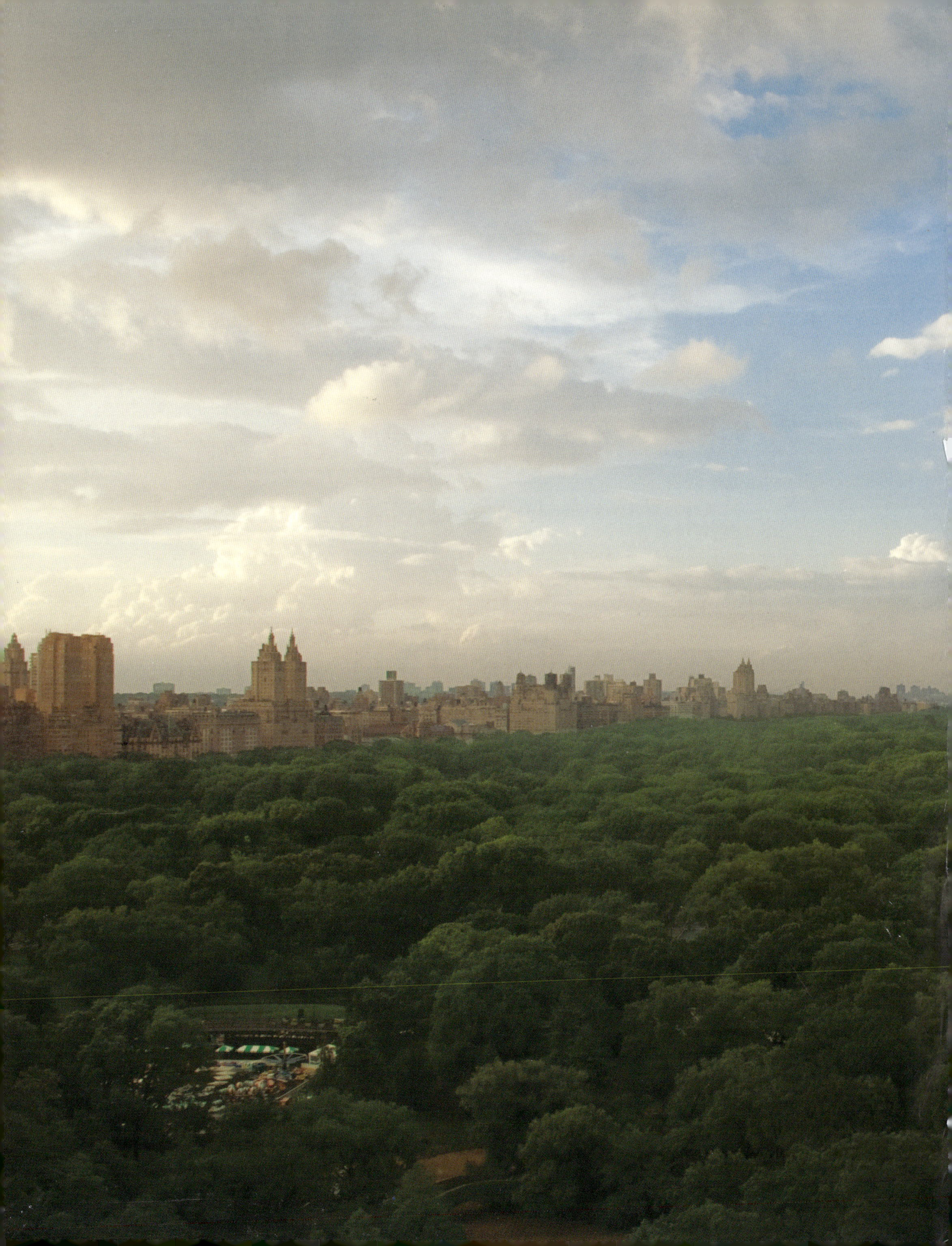